FEMINIST BIBLICAL INTERPRETATION IN THEOLOGICAL CONTEXT

This book presents a new model for biblical interpretation, exploring the intersecting perspectives of feminism, postmodern philosophies and Christian theology. Feminist biblical interpretation, like other areas of feminist scholarship, has increasingly moved beyond aggregating information about women in patriarchy and developed complex and nuanced hermeneutic theories.

Answering a need to bring together feminist approaches to the bible with a theological framework for interpretation, the book is structured in two parts. Part one considers two major paradigms of biblical interpretation, the historical and the literary, through analysis of Elisabeth Schüssler Fiorenza and Phyllis Trible. Part Two draws on these various overlapping approaches to develop an innovative model of biblical interpretation which is rooted not only in feminism and postmodern worldviews, but also in Christian theology. Students and scholars of feminism, postmodernism, interpretation theory and Christian theology will find this book offers a particularly valuable contribution to the debate.

ASHGATE NEW CRITICAL THINKING IN THEOLOGY & BIBLICAL STUDIES

Ashgate New Critical Thinking in Theology & Biblical Studies presents an open-ended series of quality research drawn from an international field of scholarship. The series aims to bring monograph publishing back into focus for authors, the international library market, and student, academic and research readers. Headed by an international editorial advisory board of acclaimed scholars, this series presents cutting-edge research from established as well as exciting new authors in the field. With specialist focus, yet clear contextual presentation, books in the series aim to take theological and biblical research into new directions; opening the field to new critical debate within the traditions, into areas of related study, and into important topics for contemporary society.

Series Editorial Board:

David Jasper, University of Glasgow, UK
James Beckford, University of Warwick, UK
Raymond B. Williams, Wabash College, USA
Geoffrey Samuel, University of Newcastle, Australia
Richard Hutch, University of Queensland, Australia
Paul Fiddes, University of Oxford, UK
Anthony C. Thiselton, The University of Nottingham, UK
Tim Gorringe, University of Exeter, UK
Adrian Thatcher, College of St Mark and St John, Plymouth, UK
Mary Grey, Sarum College, Salisbury, UK
Alan Torrance, University of St Andrews, UK
Judith Lieu, King's College London, UK
Terrance Tilley, University of Dayton, USA
Miroslav Volf, Yale Divinity School, USA
Stanley J. Grenz, Carey Theological College, Canada
Vincent Brummer, University of Utrecht, The Netherlands
Gerhard Sauter, University of Bonn, Germany

Other Titles in the Series:

Charismatic Glossolalia
Mark J. Cartledge
God in the Act of Reference
Erica Appelros
A Poetics of Jesus
Jeffrey F. Keuss
The Rhetorical Word
Theo Hobson

Feminist Biblical Interpretation in Theological Context
Restless readings

J'ANNINE JOBLING
Liverpool Hope University College, UK

LONDON AND NEW YORK

First published 2002 by Ashgate Publishing

Reissued 2018 by Routledge
2 Park Square, Milton Park, Abingdon, Oxon OX14 4RN
711 Third Avenue, New York, NY 10017, USA

Routledge is an imprint of the Taylor & Francis Group, an informa business

Copyright © J'annine Jobling 2002

The author has asserted her moral right under the Copyright, Designs and Patents Act, 1988, to be identified as the author of this work.

All rights reserved. No part of this book may be reprinted or reproduced or utilised in any form or by any electronic, mechanical, or other means, now known or hereafter invented, including photocopying and recording, or in any information storage or retrieval system, without permission in writing from the publishers.

Notice:
Product or corporate names may be trademarks or registered trademarks, and are used only for identification and explanation without intent to infringe.

Publisher's Note
The publisher has gone to great lengths to ensure the quality of this reprint but points out that some imperfections in the original copies may be apparent.

Disclaimer
The publisher has made every effort to trace copyright holders and welcomes correspondence from those they have been unable to contact.

A Library of Congress record exists under LC control number: 2002100761

ISBN 13: 978-1-138-73389-3 (hbk)
ISBN 13: 978-1-138-73379-4 (pbk)
ISBN 13: 978-1-315-18753-2 (ebk)

Contents

Acknowledgements   vi

1   Introduction   1

2   The Historical Paradigm   5

3   Biblical Interpretation and the *Ekklesia*   32

4   Redeeming the Text   60

5   The Terrors of the Text   87

6   Towards an Eschatological Hermeneutic   99

7   Truth, God and Interpretation   116

8   The *Ekklesia*   142

9   Conclusions   163

Selected Bibliography   165

Index   179

Acknowledgements

The support of Liverpool Hope and Canterbury Christ Church University College during the undertaking of this project is gratefully acknowledged. I would like to thank Professor Simon Lee, Rector and Chief Executive of Liverpool Hope, for his encouragement and assistance. I should also like to make mention of St. Deiniol's Library, in which congenial surroundings much of the text here took shape.

For academic and personal support during its completion, I would like to give particular thanks to Professor Ian Markham. Other individuals whose warmth and supportiveness have assisted in the completion of this book are too numerous to name, but include all my friends from Canterbury, Cambridge and Liverpool. However, I must include a special thank you to Ursula Leahy, whose inestimable cat-sitting services facilitated enormously the practicalities of my research, and who also compiled the index.

Some of the material in Chapters 5 and 6 may be found in different form within my chapters in: Robert Hannaford and J'annine Jobling (eds.), *Theology and the Body* (Gracewing: Leominster, 1999) and J'annine Jobling and Ian Markham (eds.), *Theological Liberalism* (London: SPCK 2000).

This book is dedicated to my mother.

Chapter 1

Introduction

> The rules break like a thermometer,
> quicksilver spills cross the charted systems,
> we're out in a country that has no language
> no laws, we're chasing the raven and the wren
> through gorges unexplored since dawn
> whatever we do together is pure invention
> the maps they gave us were out of date by years ...[1]

This poetic fragment by Adrienne Rich embodies a central problematic for feminist thought, and by extension, for this book. Feminist philosophies are attempts at *thinking otherwise*. To think *otherwise* on the basis of existing prevailing categories and models of truth, reason and knowledge would lock feminism into the system which it strives to dismantle.[2] To articulate a feminist philosophical perspective requires a comprehensive restructuring of epistemology, ontology and subjectivity. However, feminists cannot simply take a leap into pure alterity and set sail for new and uncharted lands; thinking *otherwise* requires a renegotiation of the landscapes in which feminists already are. In this territory, nothing can be taken for granted.

The impact of feminism, then, radiates out in shockwaves which leave no area undisturbed. This book is positioned at one particular nexus of feminist disturbance, namely, the area of biblical hermeneutics within Christian theological context. A recurring theme is the interaction of feminist biblical hermeneutics with postmodern philosophies. It is an exercise, proceeding from these intersecting perspectives, which seeks to put forward constructive proposals for a paradigm of feminist and theological interpretation.

The premise of the book is that there is a continuing need for biblical hermeneutic proposals and frameworks which emerge from the fields of both feminism and Christian theology. This is not, naturally, virgin territory. A considerable number of writers have made significant contributions to such an

---

[1] Rich, *The Dream of a Common Language*, 31.
[2] The classic expression of this comes from Audre Lorde: '[F]or the master's tools will never dismantle the master's house. They may allow us temporarily to beat him at his own game, but they will never enable us to bring about genuine change'. ('The Master's Tools Will Never Dismantle The Master's House', in Moraga, Cherrie and Anzaldua, Gloria [eds.], *This Bridge Called My Back: Writings by Radical Women of Colour* [Watertown, MA: Persephone Press, 1981], 99.)

endeavour.³ Nevertheless, this book seeks to make a distinctive contribution. It certainly does not claim (or desire) to replace or supersede the rich and valuable body of literature already in existence, but, more modestly, to add another feminist voice to the dialogue. In its outworking, it does not strive to develop a new 'method' for interpretation, but rather to articulate a meta-framework hospitable to the presuppositions and emphases of feminist theological scholarship.⁴ The distinctiveness of the argument lies, then, not its goals, but in the particularity of the pathways which it follows and opens up.

Feminism demands not only the plotting of new routes but, as already intimated, the restructuring of entire landscapes. As such this project, since it seeks to develop a feminist theological frame for meaning, impinges on and is impacted by innumerable interrelating questions. In consequence, the scope of the book is necessarily both broad and interdisciplinary, and it is sited in feminist, philosophical, theological, historiographical, literary, ecclesiological, sociological, psychoanalytical and biblical domains which are even broader. Methodologically, this has required a ruthless restriction of discussion to the purposes for which it is undertaken; it is, in this respect, 'led from the front'. Supporting literature is, of course, cited – but a comprehensive survey of relevant secondary material was not possible within the parameters of space. Thus one might say that full coverage of material has been sacrificed to the production of a multidirectional constructive paradigm which weaves with threads from many angles.

For these pragmatic reasons, but also by preference, the dominant methodology is Socratic. It interacts critically and creatively with particulars, in a dialogic process which both advances and shapes the discussion. This is by preference because I consider it an especially appropriate mode of proceeding for a feminist piece of work. Feminism stresses contextual thinking, and the importance of dialogic reasoning. For the purposes of this book, I interrogate particular texts and articulate my own positions in response to them. In this way the embodied practice of thinking-in-relation is mirrored in the text I have produced. This has determined the macro-structure of the thesis, which is based on analysis of two feminist biblical scholars: Elisabeth Schüssler Fiorenza (Chapters 2 and 3) and Phyllis Trible (Chapters 4 and 5). It can also be discerned in each of the component elements of the argument.

These authors were selected for three primary reasons: they are both seminal thinkers important to the development of feminist biblical hermeneutics; they work within contrasting methodological paradigms, namely the socio-

---

³ Indeed, the field of feminist biblical hermeneutics more generally is now so large and heterogeneous that surveying it would be a major undertaking in itself. The relationship of this thesis to some of the more significant works will be mapped as its contours take shape and its relative positioning will become gradually apparent.

⁴ What these presuppositions and emphases might be is, at the outset, underdetermined: they emerge from the dialogue and discussion, since they are dialectically related to the kind of framework and principles eventually advocated. However, minimally, by 'feminist' I refer to a worldview and practice committed to the emancipation of women from structures of socio-economics and politics, religions and ideologies, which explicitly or implicitly privilege men.

historical and the literary; and, taken together but not separately, they enable both the New Testament and the Hebrew Bible to enter into the debates. In other respects, the significance of their work to this thesis is not symmetrical. Schüssler Fiorenza has written much more substantively in the theoretical arena than has Trible, and it is theory with which this book is primarily concerned. Furthermore, she continues to exert a dominant and formative influence on New Testament feminist scholarship in ways which Trible, whilst still a significant figure in the parallel domain of the Hebrew Bible, does not. Nevertheless, the aspects of Trible's work on which I draw are appropriate to the movement of the argument, as shall be seen: however, the impact of Schüssler Fiorenza on my constructive proposals is rather more obvious and far-reaching. This imbalance in their respective contribution to the book is reflected in the relative weighting of discussion in terms of space.

From analysis of Schüssler Fiorenza and Trible, I identify two primary principles for interpretation: remembrance and destabilization (Chapter 6). This is a strategy which enables both materialist and post-structuralist perspectives to be set into play, each of which has vital contributions to make to feminist enterprises. The former grounds theory and praxis in specificities, the concrete actualities of women's lives. The latter dismantles stable categories, and sets interpretation free to roam in realms where subjectivity is constructed and unstable and truth is dissolved into signification.

The 'Bible' is understood as matrix, as a set of discourses which are permeable to and intersect with other cultural discourses. The task of feminist interpretation is then to reconstitute the fluid and heterogeneous biblical matrix in feminist horizons. This activity in my account is undertaken through the hermeneutics of remembrance and destabilization sited within a feminist emancipatory framework inspired by utopic impulses and a theology of hope – a context in which the polymorphous nature of interpretative strategies is stressed and the question of the ethical constitution of interpretation is paramount.

From remembrance to hope and back again, treading bridges which are not rooted in certainties but thrown across voids: the eschatological imagination, I argue, captures this movement between remembrance and hope in a context where meaning is neither present nor fixed but differed and deferred. Thus, I begin to articulate an eschatological hermeneutic. This offers not only an obvious theological context, but allows for the double movement of feminism between materialism and deconstruction.

It is also a fundamental tenet of this book that hermeneutics inhabits particular metaphysical constructs. Therefore, the argument ripples outwards in ever-increasing circles: from interpretation of the Bible to an epistemological framework in which an eschatological hermeneutic is recommended, to a metaphysical framework which likewise takes eschatology as its structuring principle. The discussion at that point (Chapter 7) is inevitably indicative only. Yet, a hermeneutic which claims to be theological cannot well proceed without reference to the kind of theological ontology which underlies it. Here, I begin to sketch in an alternative to the so-called onto-theological tradition, in which God is inevitably complicit with a metaphysics of presence, and seek to delineate a metaphysics better suited to my interpretative framework. As indicated, it is eschatology which, I argue, can provide the resources for an ontological model radically disruptive of a metaphysics of presence, and in which it is possible to discern the traces of God.

From this outermost limit of my hermeneutic investigations, I return to its centre: the feminist discursive community (Chapter 8). This is demanded by the epistemological model I adopt, which prioritizes the location of interpretation. I develop at this point a construct which emerged from the dialogue with Schüssler Fiorenza: the *ekklesia*, as a feminist deliberative space set oppositionally to structures, worldviews and ideologies which operate on patriarchal logics. I consider the relationship of this 'imagined community' to the Christian Church and to scripture, to ethics and to gendered identity within a logic of equity. This provides the discursive feminist location from which the eschatological hermeneutic I put forward can be deployed.

And now, let us turn to the first of my dialogue partners: Elisabeth Schüssler Fiorenza.

Chapter 2

The Historical Paradigm

Elisabeth Schüssler Fiorenza is without doubt a major figure in the field of feminist biblical hermeneutics. With Judith Plaskow, she is co-founder and co-editor of the *Journal of Feminist Studies in Religion*; she has also written a number of books revolving around questions of feminist approaches to biblical interpretation. What makes her work particularly of note and interest for my current purposes is the great weight of theoretical discussion in her writings, although she has also formulated specific historicial hypotheses. Perhaps the most well-known of these is her postulation of a so-called 'discipleship of equals', an emancipatory egalitarian movement among the early followers of Jesus.

My aims in the coming chapter are precisely focused. I should make it clear at the outset that no exegetical evaluation of Schüssler Fiorenza's work will be provided; the discussion here moves entirely in the realm of hermeneutic and feminist theory. In this chapter, I outline Schüssler Fiorenza's historiographical perspectives and methods, isolating and analysing its defining moments. I describe Schüssler Fiorenza's paradigm for historical reconstruction with a view to investigating fruitful shapes for feminist historiographical theory to take. Particular attention is given to the positioning of Schüssler Fiorenza's hermeneutics with respect to current historiographical debates over epistemologies, which focus especially on issues surrounding objectivity, the relationship between historical texts and historical realities, and the extent to which histories are constructed or discovered. From these explorations, the discussion moves into the relationship between Schüssler Fiorenza's historiography and politics.[1]

Having established Schüssler Fiorenza's stance with respect to these aspects of her historical-critical method, I then go on to indicate how her feminist historiography actually differs from so-called 'traditional' historical-critical method. The relationship between Schüssler Fiorenza's feminist historical-critical method and historical-critical method more generally is complex. Indeed, historical criticism itself has been somewhat beleaguered in recent years as the rise of postmodern historiographical critique and new literary paradigms have problematized what seemed to be founding assumptions of historical research. Debates over textuality, truth and objectivity have appeared to undercut – some

---

[1] I use 'politics' in a broad sense throughout, to indicate distributions of power in a materialist context.

think fatally – the guiding principles of historical-criticism.[2] The discussion here takes its cues from Schüssler Fiorenza's own writings on this. Finally, I extract from the explorations as a whole some general conclusions for method in feminist biblical interpretation.

Schüssler Fiorenza's hermeneutic framework revolves around the concept of the *ekklesia gynaikon* (women-church) as the centre of and deliberative space for interpretation. Investigating this is the topic of the next chapter. Here I am only concerned with the historiographical paradigm in which she locates her historical-critical methods. These she utilizes in pursuit of her goal to reconstruct Christian origins in feminist and theological key. I shall initially locate the discussion within the context of feminist historiography and then go on to detail more thoroughly Schüssler Fiorenza's methodological theories.

Feminist Historiography: The Telling of 'Her-Story'

Schüssler Fiorenza's classic historical work on the New Testament is *In Memory of Her* (1983). This is, as its subtitle indicates, 'a feminist theological reconstruction of Christian Origins'. The goals of the book are twofold: it represents an 'attempt to reconstruct early Christian history as women's history in order not only to restore women's stories to early Christian history but also to reclaim this history as the history of women and men'.[3] In other words, she aims to restore women to history and history to women.[4]

Historiography, she argues, is by nature selective in operation and arises from contemporary contexts and interests. Historiographers writing from a feminist perspective insist that this particularity has operated with a pronounced gender bias and that the writing of history has neglected women; as it is ironically suggested, 'history' is indeed 'his-story'. Schüssler Fiorenza is one of many contemporary feminists who seek to write 'her-story' as well.

A principal base of this movement is that historical silence should not be confused with historical absence; the production of history and culture both can and should be conceptualized as a human rather than male enterprise. Connotations of authoritarianism and of silen*cing* are often found in feminist critiques of patriarchal history; this non-absent silence demands that erasure be resisted. Silence is not, indeed, absence. This is central to Schüssler Fiorenza's argument, the crux of which is that the biblical texts have been codified and interpreted in an androcentric, patriarchal culture. Thus, to feminist scholarship has fallen the task of constructing new ways of seeing, of making visible the historical reality of women's agency and oppression in Christian origins.

---

[2] For this position, see The Bible and Culture Collective's *The Postmodern Bible*; Francis Watson, *Text, Church and World*; for a defence, see John Barton's 'Historical-critical approaches'.
[3] Schüssler Fiorenza, *In Memory of Her*, xiv.
[4] Kelly, *Women, History and Theory*, xii-xiii.

The interconnections between Schüssler Fiorenza's work and the women's history movement are obvious.[5] Yet, as the noted feminist historian Joan Scott points out, it is important to be aware of the diversity and complexity encompassed by the term 'women's history'. In the absence of a definable historiographic tradition, 'woman as subject has been grafted on to other traditions or studied in isolation from any of them';[6] the common focus is to make women a subject of the story and an agent of the narrative. The result has frequently been a women's history which substitutes women for men in historiography but does not lead to any fundamentally different way of doing history. Moreover, it risks an atomization of the study of women and fosters separatism by its topical approach to 'woman'. In contrast to this is the social history approach, which Scott believes is too integrationist: it subsumes women into the received categories of (primarily economic) analysis.[7] 'Finding women' in history is not sufficient: what is missing, Scott argues, is a crucial political dimension. It is the politics of gender which enables a genuinely new historical analysis.[8] She suggests that:

> The realization of a radical potential of women's history comes in the writing of narratives that focus on women's experience *and* analyse the ways in which politics construct gender and gender constructs politics.[9]

Schüssler Fiorenza's brand of feminist historiography clearly moves beyond cataloguing the activities of women in the early Church and fulfills Scott's call for a radicalization of women's history. Schüssler Fiorenza insists upon the use of gender as a vital heuristic tool. At the same time, analytical categories based on essential gender differences are rejected. Such a gender dimorphism, as we shall explore in some detail in Chapter 3, is itself understood to be a product of

---

[5] One possible location for the 'women's history' movement is within an an overall historiographical shift in the subject-matter of history, associated with the so-called 'New History'. Social historians have shown us how little we know about everyday lives. New History hence emphasizes 'history from below'; it is what has been termed 'total history'. It undertakes to write the history of those previously excluded: that is, nearly all women and non-elite men. It regards the lives and experiences of ordinary people as a central subject for historical enquiry. The phrase 'New History' has its origins in France, where it is associated with the journal *Annales* (and Marc Bloch and Lucien Febvre), especially from the 1930s on. It also is a reaction against so-called Rankean history (which will be discussed in some length later with relation to Schüssler Fiorenza's work), particularly in its insistence on history as the history of the state. However, the origins of interest in 'women's history' predate the emergence of the *Annales* school, most notably in the ninteenth-century 'first wave' feminist movement. I think here particularly of writers such as Elizabeth Cady Stanton and Alice Clark. What is more, feminist historians have generally moved beyond an aggregative view of historiography to more sophisticated models.
[6] Scott, 'Women in History: The Modern Period', 142.
[7] Ibid., 145, 149ff.
[8] Ibid., 153.
[9] Ibid., 157.

patriarchy.[10] Rather, gender as a category should be understood in terms of historical and social specificities, in the context of patriarchal relationships of inequality.[11] The unity of women as a social group is perceived to rest in 'their common historical experience as an oppressed group struggling to become full historical subjects'.[12] Such a common experience as an oppressed group need not be consciously perceived as struggle, although the groundswell of feminist identity is based on just this awareness.[13] Feminist heuristic models must 'explore women's participation in social-public development and their efforts to comprehend and transform social structures'.[14] This is all very consistent with Schüssler Fiorenza's broader feminist framework as shall become apparent.

Moreover, this use of gender as a category should not result in 'women's history' being relegated to its own personal ghetto.[15] Writing in a similar vein to Joan Scott, Schüssler Fiorenza rightly notes that too narrow a focus on the topic 'women' must be avoided.[16] Such a narrow focus is actually self-defeating from a feminist perspective, for once more 'woman' is posited as 'other', an addendum to (male) humanity. Rather, feminist consciousness of gender should be used to formulate new conceptual models – models that do not elide women in mainstream history. On the contrary, the complexities of women's power and women's oppression should be placed firmly at the centre (as opposed to the margins) of human history. In this way history earns the adjective 'human' rather than simply 'male'.

Schüssler Fiorenza's Feminist Model of Interpretation

The important insights of feminist historiography have led to the demand for heuristic models that leave this theoretical space for women's power and influence in patriarchal culture as well as for women's subjugation. Necessarily such a

---

[10] Schüssler Fiorenza, 'Remembering the Past in Creating the Future', 57f.
[11] Schüssler Fiorenza, *In Memory of Her*, 86. Since much of the material I use here is drawn from *In Memory of Her*, the language of 'patriarchy' rather than her later term 'kyriarchy' will frequently be found. However, even in her early work, Schüssler Fiorenza clearly understood patriarchy in the pyramidical terms articulated more thoroughly in her later projects, as a system of 'graded subordinations and exploitations' (*Bread not Stone*, xiv).
[12] Schüssler Fiorenza, *In Memory of Her*, 86; see also 31.
[13] Ibid., 31.
[14] Schüssler Fiorenza, 'Remembering the Past in Creating the Future', 58; Schüssler Fiorenza, *In Memory of Her*, 86.
[15] Perrot articulates this possibility particularly nicely: 'Our goal is not to create a new territory called women's history, a quiet concession where women could work in peace, protected from contradiction, but rather to change the direction of historical attention by posing the question of the relationship between the sexes as central' (Introduction to *Writing Women's History*, 8).
[16] Schüssler Fiorenza, *In Memory of Her*, 42, 84.

theoretical framework must maintain a dialectical tension between women as historical subjects and women as historical objects under patriarchal oppression.[17]

Schüssler Fiorenza is aiming to formulate a model which fulfills these criteria: that is to say, which allows for recognition of both the oppression of women and of their contribution to Christian origins as historical agents. She maintains that traditional biblical scholarship is not capable of discerning the reality of women's roles in the earliest church because it is captive to an antithetical paradigm which is implicitly (or even explicitly) androcentric-patriarchal. Historical-critical method situates texts within their socio-cultural context; it is hence apparent that how that context is understood will rebound on textual interpretation. Historical data is interpreted within a framework. Schüssler Fiorenza employs the analogy of a quilt, of historical information being 'stitched' into a coherent design or model. 'Just as other sources, so androcentric biblical texts are part of an overall puzzle and design that have to be "fitted" together in creative critical historical interpretation.'[18] What characterizes feminist interpreters is the claim that classical models of understanding are androcentric-patriarchal and make it impossible to identify the true contribution of women and the roles they played.[19]

She cites the example of Gerd Theissen's model for the social structures of the early church, which he terms 'love-patriarchalism'.[20] According to this model, the Christian missionary movement cohered well with the social structures of Graeco-Roman cities because it maintained the familiar patriarchal structures but softened them with Christian love. The congregations met in the households of the wealthy and prospered because of their patronage, but ultimately this resulted in the concentration of authority with the rich and perpetuated the existing patriarchal system. If it is supposed that the position of women also cohered with Graeco-Roman patriarchal structures, it would evidently act as a 'filter' for interpreting available information about women.

Schüssler Fiorenza, conversely, aims to demonstrate that Christianity was not patriarchally determined from the very first and, *contra* Theissen, was not integrated into the dominant patriarchal Jewish or Graeco-Roman societies. Rather, there existed egalitarian tendencies both within Christianity and in its surrounding culture. She believes it is significant that the New Testament does not attribute misogynist sayings to Jesus and that those New Testament texts apparently most hostile to women, such as 1 Corinthians 14:34-35 and 1 Timothy 2:9-15, do not appeal to the Jesus tradition but rather to cultural custom or to Genesis 2-3.

---

[17] Ibid., 85f. This, then, navigates a more nuanced path than writing either the history of oppression (Simone de Beauvoir) or the history of resistance (Mary Beard). This is not to deny the importance of these two activities, but to insist that room must be left for both, and both at once, in feminist historiography. Linda Gordon comments on the difficulty of achieving this in such a way that the former is not understood as determinism and the latter as victim-blaming ('What's new in women's history?').

[18] See also Schüssler Fiorenza, *In Memory of Her*, 41.

[19] Ibid., 70; Theissen, *The Social Setting of Pauline Christianity*.

[20] Schüssler Fiorenza, *In Memory of Her*, 73f, 78ff.

That Schüssler Fiorenza recognizes both the leadership and the oppression of women is important, for her model for reconstructing egalitarianism rests on precisely this point – that early Christianity showed opposing tendencies, and that what the tradition records primarily reflects the patriarchalizing tendency rather than the egalitarian tendency. The reality of women's prominence in the Jesus movement and the earliest church has been obscured (although not erased) by the androcentricity of the transmission process. For example, whilst most of the Gospels record that Mary Magdalene was the first resurrection witness, the pre-Pauline resurrection formula 1 Corinthians 15:3-5 does not. This, says Schüssler Fiorenza, demonstrates the tendency to make women disappear.[21] In the process of defining what was orthodox Christianity over against heretical Christianity, the equality of women and the possibility of women leadership came to fall into the heretical camp:[22] it is this process that reflects Christianity adapting itself to the institutions of the Graeco-Roman state and society.

In Schüssler Fiorenza's reconstruction there are, then, two aspects to the patriarchalization process: androcentric transmission of tradition obscured the actual roles of women, and the roles of women did in fact become increasingly circumscribed as Christianity became increasingly patriarchal. The omnipresence of patriarchy requires interpreters to work with a hermeneutic of suspicion, ever alert to ideological obfuscations. It is important to note, however, that in Schüssler Fiorenza's opinion the egalitarian undercurrent remained.[23] The key question one must ask next is: how is any egalitarian strand to be disentangled from the warp and weft of patriarchal texts?

Crucial here is Schüssler Fiorenza's execution of the principles of feminist historiography in moving beyond a focus on texts 'about women' to a more holistic historical model which allows one to place women in the centre of 'historical reality and struggle'.[24] Androcentric texts are androcentric precisely because in mentioning women, they marginalize them. Schüssler Fiorenza insists that:

---

[21] It might be noted that the Pauline material is actually earlier than the Gospels in terms of compilation, so a simple chronological explanation based on increasing androcentricity does not work; the factors which allowed for the women's roles to be submerged on the one hand but discernible on the other are not clear. Clearly tradition processes will be instrumental in this, which may well be ideologically complex. It might be noted that other later material in the Pastoral Epistles contains some of the more regulative discourses on women. Capper, for example, considers this to be evidence of an early shift from private to public space. The key dynamic factor on that analysis is not increasing androcentricity but expansion, which rendered the presiding role of women still discernible in the house-church scenario problematic. See Capper, 'Public Bodies, Private Women'.

[22] Schüssler Fiorenza, *In Memory of Her*, 53.

[23] Ibid., 92.

[24] Ibid., 35.

> Biblical texts about women therefore are like the tip of an iceberg, intimating what is submerged and obliterated in historical silence. They have to be read as touchstones of the historical reality that they both repress and construct.[25]

In seeking to reappropriate a past in feminist horizons, 'what is necessary is systemic interpretation that makes the submerged bulk of the iceberg visible'.[26] One can assume that only a fragment of women's actual contribution was recorded or transmitted. This, says Schüssler Fiorenza, is either because of an implicit androcentric evaluation of what is significant, or because it was perceived as a threat. In consequence, we need to reconstruct the rhetorical aims of the biblical redactors and find ways to break the silences of the texts. In this way we may locate feminist meaning.[27] Methodologically this will involve uncovering the mechanisms of the redaction process and being alive to the incoherences and inconsistencies in the sources. In this way we can locate clues for the reconstruction of egalitarian tendencies. From the hermeneutics of suspicion, one must move forward to a hermeneutics of remembrance.

It also embodies a movement from text to historical reconstruction which is demanded not only by historiographical method, but for theological reasons also. The text may be the message: but it is not coterminous with human reality.[28] Schüssler Fiorenza concludes that the texts are not the locus of revelation: rather, the locus of revelation is the 'life and ministry of Jesus and the movement of women and men called forth by him'.[29] It is exactly this which theologically demands the development of historical-critical methods for feminist readings and this which demands movement from the text to the socio-historical context.[30]

The methodological obstacles to a feminist reconstruction of Christian origins are apparent: only vestiges of evidence are left to us. One must therefore reconstruct the 'discipleship of equals' imaginatively, and through interpretation which is creative as well as critical. This does, of course, lead to charges that Schüssler Fiorenza pays insufficient attention to textual and historical evidence and that feminist interests are taking over from critical method. Thiselton levels an accusation of this type, finding that 'social interest takes precedence over hermeneutical openness and forecloses certain possibilities before they are examined [italics removed]'.[31] In particular instances, there may be some justice in this accusation if a given interpretation fails to convince of its defensibility, but at the level of paradigm, he demonstrates only the extent to which his own principles (based on impartiality) differ. There may perhaps also a failure to grasp Schüssler Fiorenza's point: that every critical method operates with particular criteria, goals and assumptions and will therefore filter and interpret data in particular ways. A

---

[25] Schüssler Fiorenza, *But She Said*, 32; see also Schüssler Fiorenza, *In Memory of Her*, 56.
[26] Schüssler Fiorenza, *In Memory of Her*, 56.
[27] Ibid., 41.
[28] Ibid., 29.
[29] Ibid., 41.
[30] See the more detailed account of Schüssler Fiorenza's theology perspective and view of scripture in Chapter 3.
[31] Thiselton, *New Horizons in Hermeneutics*, 448.

feminist liberationist model explicitly positions itself as 'hermeneutically open' to the history of women, which may not be inscribed in historical texts except in traces. This does not 'prove' that feminist reconstructions 'actually happened' in the way argued – and nor are particular constructions beyond critique, quite to the contrary – but it opens up historical possibilities which models not using gender as a heuristic tool cannot.[32] This is exactly what drives Schüssler Fiorenza when she asserts that feminism requires a historical-critical method adapted to its own purposes. Simply wielding 'traditional' critical tools 'objectively' cannot begin to answer feminist questions because it does not ask them.[33]

Thus already we can begin to see how a feminist model of interpretation differs from 'traditional' historical-critical method. It is not merely that it asks questions about women, nor even that it asks questions about women from a point of view sympathetic to feminist concerns. It shifts the historiographical framework to one in which dynamics of gender and power are central not marginal and does not simply add 'women' as a topic to the acceptable scope of interpretation. That merely reifies the normativity of men. It opens up a space in which women can be

---

[32] Ibid., 447, who rebukes Schüssler Fiorenza for her 'gender focus'. Again, he misses the point of feminist historiography.

[33] The gulf which sometimes yawns between feminist historiography and 'traditional' historical criticism is rarely so clearly expressed as in Brook W. R. Pearson's profoundly flawed critique of Schüssler Fiorenza in his 1998 article, 'Method, Metaphor and Mammaries: The Ideology of Feminist New Testament Criticism'. Pearson reiterates the error I have just identified when he states that feminists damagingly confuse orientation with method (226). He does not appear to grasp that feminist orientation must necessarily restructure critical methodology in feminist key, or in what sense is the latter feminist at all? If male master narratives are phallic, he opines, then feminist ones might 'perhaps more realistically' be called 'mammaric' (226). He does not appear to have much grasp of the psychoanalytical and socio-symbolic history which has led to the privileging of the phallic as primary signifier (an insight common to both feminist and non-feminist interpreters, such as Freud and Lacan). His analysis of Schüssler Fiorenza begins with the comment that in 'her rhetoric, at least, she simply advocates a feminist orientation' (227). That does not seem consistent with Schüssler Fiorenza's own writings. He agrees that individual prejudice and presuppositions must be examined, but does not appear to realize that it is not simply a matter of personal bias but a structural question about methodology. He says that 'irretrievably damaging confusion' enters Schüssler Fiorenza's work when she, rejecting that oppressive texts are revelatory, moves into a realm where textual authority is in question rather than 'actual exegesis and interpretation' (228). He does not discuss this at the level of differing paradigms, but rather assumes feminist historiography is a perversion of historical-critical method. He accuses her of systematically editing out texts in the Bible she does not agree with (231) but fails to note the difference between refusing authority to a text and refusing to interpret it or excluding it from the corpus. Schüssler Fiorenza does the first, not the second. He laments the lack of evidence in Schüssler Fiorenza's historical work (232) whilst not citing once those works of Schüssler Fiorenza which are focused sustainedly and substantively on the practice of historical reconstruction. Given all this, it was unnecessary for him to conclude his article (which includes similar critique of Tina Pippin and Antoinette Wire) by pointing out that he was not attempting to paint a glowing picture of feminist interpretation.

seen resisting patriarchal structures and are not simply defined by them, whilst yet acknowledging the oppression of women. It consciously supposes that patriarchal societies will produce patriarchal texts, which do not only reflect societal ideologies but reinforce them by marginalizing women in the narratives.[34] Hence a hermeneutic of suspicion is required, and an attention to traces which does not assume that this is the only story to be told, but to the contrary, works on the assumption that there is much more that could be narrated.

These different methodological principles do not, however, exhaust the ways in which Schüssler Fiorenza's feminist historiography differs from 'traditional' methods. A particularly striking feature of her work is its explicitly rhetorical context. The goal of Schüssler Fiorenza's work is not simply to 'tell it how it was'; it is telling it to a particular audience for a particular purpose. In a pithy summary: it is history *for*, not *of*.

The discussion now moves into epistemological debate. Two issues particularly are flagged up, which are related but separable. The first is the methodological issue of objectivity: whether it is attainable or, indeed, even a goal one should aspire towards. The second is the question of 'the real' of history and whether it may be said to exist or be represented.[35] These questions shed further light on how and why feminist historical-critical paradigms may well differ from historical-criticism as such.

The Issue of Objectivity

Schüssler Fiorenza completely rejects the notion of dispassionate historical inquiry.[36] This forms part of a debate about the nature and methods of history as a discipline. Novick, for example, argues that objectivity is at the very centre of professional history. He suggests that it includes the following primary moments: a commitment to the reality of the past; to truth as correspondence to it; a sharp distinction between fact and value; a clear demarcation between history and fiction; the existence of facts and truth prior to interpretation and independent of perspective; the finding rather than construction of historical patterns. Schüssler Fiorenza's point here relates to the distinction between fact and value and the supposed ideal of approaching the past through laying aside one's own interests and perspectives. This is based on the hermeneutical position that stepping out of one's own situatedness is not only an epistemological impossibility but actually

---

[34] Schüssler Fiorenza's work increasingly broadens its theoretical focus to include not only women but other marginalized and oppressed groups whose histories are equally marginal. See *But She Said*; *Sharing Her Word*.

[35] In the discussion that follows, certain affinities between Schüssler Fiorenza and New Historicism will become apparent. New Historicism is a post-Foucauldian movement emergent in the 1980s particularly associated with Renaissance literary studies; indebted to Marxism, it focuses on the exchanges between culture and power, figured as actual and symbolic capital. As such, its impact on literature is to re-embed it into the historical socio-political complex.

[36] Novick, *That Noble Dream*, 1-2.

undesirable. History, insists Schüssler Fiorenza, is not an artefact: it is the historical consciousness for the present and future; it has rhetorical aims, whether or not these are articulated. History is always history *for* and not just history *of*. Historians are located in society and in time; any given reconstruction is dependent not only on the available evidence but also on the models of interpretation which are employed. Far from being a continuum of given facts, the past only discloses itself through specific questions. Clearly, then, our pictures of the past will depend greatly on what questions are asked: which is to say, on who is asking the questions, for whom, and why. As Spiegel says:

> In the final analysis, what is the past but a once material existence, now silenced, extant only as sign and as sign drawing to itself chains of conflicting interpretations that hover over its absent presence and compete for possession of the relics, seeking to inscribe traces of significance upon the bodies of the dead?[37]

Schüssler Fiorenza is clear on whom her history is *for*: she explicitly operates in the ideological interests of women. She considers this to be essential to the formulation of a model doing justice to women as both victims and subjects in patriarchal culture. As with all liberation theologies, it is contended that intellectual neutrality is a myth in the mind of the scholar.[38] One is ineluctably engaged either for or against the oppressed and the choice is whether one recognizes or ignores that engagement. Traditional biblical scholarship is understood to be no more 'objective' than feminist critiques and its dominant models to be simply inadequate to the task of articulating a human, rather than merely masculinist, reality. Given the partiality and bias in established scholarship, Schüssler Fiorenza considers that a feminist biblical scholarship must utilize historical-critical method to proffer up differing interpretations to public discussion and scholarly consideration.

Schüssler Fiorenza believes that a *rapprochement* between feminist biblical and academic biblical scholarship is only possible when 'biblical-historical scholarship is *willing* to shed outdated notions of "scientific factuality" and has a chance to become truly "historical consciousness"'. Feminist participation in the historiographical process should be 'actively sought' in order to 'keep "open" our unfulfilled historical possibilities'; again, this is because 'the bible is not just history *of* but history *for*'. It is this which allows the integration of biblical history and biblical theology for believing communities.

Feminist scholarship of Schüssler Fiorenza's variety, as we have seen, starts with the recognition that historical sources about women do not reflect the historical situation of women.[39] It may be that there is simply silence; in Gerda Lerner's words, the silence of 'the forgotten majority'.[40] Alternatively, it may be

---

[37] Spiegel, 'History and Post-Modernism IV', 208.
[38] Schüssler Fiorenza, *In Memory of Her*, 6.
[39] Ibid., 85.
[40] Lerner, Gerda, *The Majority Finds its Past: Placing Women in History* (New York, Oxford Univeristy Press, 1979).

that a prescriptive rather than descriptive picture of women is offered up to us in the guise of historical truth.[41]

Redaction criticism of the Gospels is dated to 1948 and arose from the awareness that the biblical writers were not neutrally or comprehensively describing situations, but writing selectively about particular interests or events. Selection by definition means that some things are said and some things are not. Most feminists argue that the biblical writers were implicitly operating with androcentric and patriarchal models of understanding.

The writing of history is not value-free: nor is scholarship itself. The problem of bias is not only inherent in the biblical source material but compounded by centuries of scholarship also implicitly operating with androcentric and patriarchal models of understanding. The selection of the canon, equally, was subject to the same implicit prejudice. A consequence has been the historical silence and invisibility of women necessitating that women's history be reconstructed from the fragments remaining. It also requires, as we have seen, that interpreters operate with a hermeneutic of suspicion. Feminism demands a radical questioning of androcentric evaluations of what is and what is not of historical significance.

Hence Schüssler Fiorenza's whole approach is underpinned by her belief that the New Testament is itself an inadequate source document because it is the product of the historical winners.[42] Feminist analysis has no alternative but to recognize that the biblical message only survives in the forms of androcentric texts. How, then, should one proceed?

Schüssler Fiorenza advocates that androcentric texts be evaluated 'theologically in terms of a feminist scale of values';[43] we shall see how this operates in Chapter 3. In terms of historiography, it is imperative to develop feminist models which might enable reconstructions excessive of the ideologies inscribed in patriarchal texts. We outlined Schüssler Fiorenza's own historical method earlier. Theologically and historically, then, it is essential to operate from explicitly feminist standpoints. This is indicative of the impossibility of objectivity (we do not approach texts and histories which are neutral), and decisive of the necessity that this should be the case for contemporary interpreters. The question is not whether one has values in scholarship but what kind of values one has and how aware of them one is.

The Issue of 'the Real'

Hence it is scarcely surprising that Schüssler Fiorenza rejects the notion of objective inquiry at the level of both theory and praxis. However, she seems to take for granted the value and possibility of reconstructive historical approaches. Her work is littered with references to reconstructing the 'reality' of women's agency

---

[41] Ibid., 85.
[42] Ibid., 55.
[43] Ibid., 60.

and women's struggle. This is despite her espousal of historiographical theory rejecting dispassionate, unbiased knowing. It is therefore necessary to glean some clarification as to how the two cohere in her work, or whether she is falling into the trap of asserting that scholarship is ideologically inflected, except for feminist practice, which finally tells the truth about women.

Historiography outside of biblical studies and theology mirrors the retreat from belief in impartial truth evident in Schüssler Fiorenza's work.[44] As Juliet Gardiner puts it, it is the loss of belief in the past 'as a jigsaw which will one day be complete'.[45] History is seen to emerge from the womb of symbolic and semiotic cultural productions; language ceases to mediate reality but becomes the medium in which the real is both constructed and apprehended. Political, institutional and social practices are read as cultural scripts, that is as discursive sets. It is in the pattern of linguistic thought from Saussure to Derrida, which suggests to us that there is no reality beside the text, each of which is wide open to interpretation. The 'real' is, indeed, nothing but a series of discourses governing all our representations of life; the material does not exist apart from its meaning. If meaning is a construct, does the real become ultimately as imagined as the imaginary?[46]

Schüssler Fiorenza's socio-historical reconstructions are sited in some respects within this trajectory. She retrospectively points out the affinities between the historiography of *In Memory of Her* and the New Historicism: 'Such

---

[44] A classic UK example of this debate is in the ongoing dialogue in *Past and Present* during 1991. The influence of postmodernism is obviously nascent, but it was an influential staking out of positions. Defences of traditional history were undertaken by Lawrence Stone and Gabrielle Spiegel. Stone expressed his anxiety that postmodern concentration on texuality meant that '[t]exts thus become a mere hall of mirrors reflecting nothing but each other, and throwing no light upon the 'truth', which does not exist' ('History and Post-Modernism', 217); this could only lead to the toppling of history as traditionally understood. For if history is only a linguistic reading, a story, based on other stories and linguistic exercises, how can it be said to guarantee anything or teach us anything about 'the real'? Spiegel argues that if texts do not mediate reality but only other texts, then historical study becomes collapsed into literary study ('History and Post-Modernism IV', 197). The crucial factor is how we understand the mediation to take place. The classical model is that of indirect connection between dual phenomena. The post-Marxist Frankfurt School rejected this analytical distinction between mediator and mediated. Or as Spiegel interprets this: 'Mediation is an active process that constructs its objects in precisely the sense that post-structuralism conceives of social construction of reality in and through language. Mediation is intrinsic to the existence and operation of a reality that it actively produces' (Spiegel, 'History and Post-Modernism IV', 199). Therefore to study history is to study the mediatory practices of the past and we can have no access to reality beyond the codes inscribed in the texts; these are peformative discourses inescably constituted by language as the mediator of human awareness. Spiegel suggests that this is to fall into error and to conflate two horizons of knowledge or action: what happened and how we know about it. However, she does not answer the question of how the former could be approached except via the latter.

[45] Gardiner, *What is History Today?*, 2.

[46] Stone, 'History and Post-Modernism', 217.

discussions do not understand history in a positivist sense but as a consciously constructive narrative, as the story of power relations and struggles.'[47] It understands its own activities as rhetorical practice rather than antiquarian science.[48] It does not conceive its task even in theory as one of distilling truths or recovering the real:

> Rather, a critical emancipatory historiography seeks to open up to historical memory what has been suppressed in traditional historiography in order to examine the exclusions and choices that constitute our historical knowledge of early Christian beginnings . . . by positioning a feminist critical historiography in the rhetorical space of the *ekklesia* of women, one is able to conceptualize early Christian history as a struggle between the dominant patriarchal discursive practices and those of the discipleship of equals. Such a positioning provides a theoretical vantage from which the problems of text and history and past and present are brought into different focus.[49]

Schüssler Fiorenza distances herself from both a positivist antiquarianism which sees texts as quarries for truths and from varieties of postmodern constructivism which reduce the past to texts alone.[50] A feminist rhetorical paradigm for historiography proceeds from both a recognition of 'scriptedness' but also of agency, and (crucially) from a commitment to the articulation of a different knowledge, a different vision. She argues that it is in fact possible to give more or less adequate accounts of 'what actually happened', although history never actually *is* that; it is rather justifications for reconstructing history in one way rather than another. Recognizing that history is performed from our own cultural locations, based on texts which only bear traces of the past, 'problematizes and denaturalizes' the real,[51] but it does not excuse us from the task of trying to let the repressed others of (real) history speak. Thereby, a better account of the past is given. Thus, whilst fully granting the perspectivalism and provisionality of historical endeavour, she does not in fact abandon claims to a relative objectivity or a relative truth to historical reconstructions. One locus for the authority to evaluate historical judgements is with the scholastic community; she stresses the importance of public consciousness and discussions. In this way it is possible for our historical narratives to be seen as not wholly either fictive or relativistic. Another is with the experience of the marginalized, which may note the dissonances and blindspots projected in particular interpretations. And, overall, both objectivity and adequacy require evaluation in light of how successfully the others of history, the subjugated, are made visible. For silence is not absence: and a critical feminist emancipatory historiography must take its point of departure from this.

---

[47] Schüssler Fiorenza, *But She Said*, 31.
[48] Ibid., 80.
[49] Ibid., 81.
[50] She equates this to the New Historicism. This is however somewhat reductionist, since the sensitivity of New Historicists and cultural materialists to patterns of power makes extra-textual materialities very much apparent in textual discourses. New Historicism is, of course, itself a very heterogeneous phenomenon.
[51] Schüssler Fiorenza, *But She Said*, 91.

Postmodernism and Politics

We have already noted that Schüssler Fiorenza distinguishes her position from the more thoroughly postmodern historiographies (by which she meant the tendency to remain with an immanent textualism in which the real is wholly reduced to representation and linguisticality), whilst yet affirming a thoroughly constructivist and culturally coded (but not anti-realist) account of historiography We also began to note that this was not only a theoretical debate about the epistemology of history, but, from the point of view of feminism as an emancipatory movement, that there are deeply political implications. On the one hand, postmodern historiographies such as New Historicism are profoundly aware of the political implications of history as metanarrative. If history is authoritative, whom does it authorize? And to do what? As Belsey argues of the New Historicism, it has thoroughly liberated itself from progressivist and liberal metanarratives of history:

> It records no heroic quests, no voyages of discovery, no dangers triumphantly overcome. On the contrary, the expeditions it describes are more commonly voyages of colonisation and ruthless conquest. It is anything but nostalgic in its account of a world dominated by power, which produces resistance only to justify its own extension.[52]

This awareness of ideological circulations and of subjugated others would seem to render postmodern historiographies of this ilk congenial to feminists. Yet, this does not go far enough. A postmodern recital of difference in which it collapses into undifferentiated *in*difference is antithetical to the thoroughly political nature of Schüssler Fiorenza's agenda. Belsey suggests that:

> The sleek surfaces of New Historicist writing propose no programme, offer a minimum of evaluations and transformations, except in so far as they transform into its opposite the grand narrative itself; and in consequence they legitimate no political intervention.[53]

The tension encountered by all forms of feminism in the postmodern vein is that feminism, like Marxism, owes much to the very Enlightenment traditions of thought which postmodernism critiques. If there is no outside to ideology, no place where one can stand to judge consciousness to be false,[54] why should 'one ideologically motivated narrative have priority over others'?[55]

Yet, as Belsey points out, postmodernism in all its heterogeneity also has a strand derived from Marxism and its account of society as a site of struggle. What was dangerously radical about Marx was his analysis of capital from the position of the Other: labour. It is this trajectory of difference as opposition which has more affinities with Schüssler Fiorenza's work, a 'historicity which tells of resistance

---

[52] Belsey, 'Making Histories then and now: Shakespeare from *Richard II* to *Henry V*', 29.
[53] Ibid., 30.
[54] Howard, 'Towards a postmodern, politically committed, historical practice', 105.
[55] Ibid., 106.

that continues to challenge power from the position of its inevitable differentiating other'.[56]

Of course in Schüssler Fiorenza's historiography her 'dangerously radical gesture' is to analyse Christian origins with women at the centre of her inquiry. Her account of women as subjects and agents as well as victims in patriarchal society takes leave of the New Historicist tendency to employ the 'subversion and containment' model. Resistance does not simply figure as the legitimation and justification of power; it is truly oppositional.[57] When the resistances produced by difference return to threaten the dominant power, its precariousness is thrown into stark relief. This deconstructs the very positing of the Other, the different, by demonstrating the frailty of the oppositions.[58] The existence of difference raises questions about power and Belsey argues that those questions 'concern a political relation, and one which, since it is an effect of difference, always inclines towards struggle'.[59] This is an echo of Schüssler Fiorenza and her constant references to the history of women as the history of struggle. Indeed, what we see here are the deeply materialist roots of Schüssler Fiorenza's theorizing. This has been noted earlier.[60]

Schüssler Fiorenza does, therefore, render a coherent account of how both constructivism and realism can operate in historiographical endeavour. The real is always constructed in particular horizons, both historically in the texts that remain and contemporaneously in efforts to move from text to world. Historiography is always in this sense rhetorical; it is not in the business of simply uncovering truths. However, in the rhetorical constructions of history, there are better and worse historical judgements to be made and more or less adequate accounts of history to be given. The extent to which such constructions answer to the demands of a critical emancipatory perspective is a defining moment in feminist evaluation of histories. This is where the political programmatic of a feminist historiography becomes most readily apparent. Ideologies of oppression must be exposed, critiqued and cracked apart to allow space for the others of history to emerge. In this way a political intervention can be made.

Feminist Historiography and the Historical-Critical Method

Thus, we have begun to chart the contours which characterize Schüssler Fiorenza's historiographical perspectives and already noted some areas where these diverge from historical-critical methodologies more generally. How then, might feminist

---

[56] Belsey, 'Making Histories then and now: Shakespeare from *Richard II* to *Henry V*', 30.
[57] Barker, 'Which Dead? *Hamlet* and the ends of history', 70, n. 13.
[58] Belsey, 'Making Histories then and now: Shakespeare from *Richard II* to *Henry V*', 31.
[59] Ibid., 44.
[60] Hennessey expresses this energetically: 'But I am arguing that feminism's radical vision of possibility for full democracy requires that our analyses be able to explain connections – between what we mean by lives and knowledges, between subjects and contexts, between particular instances and larger social arrangements' ('Women's Lives/Feminist Knowledge: Feminist Standpoint as Ideology Critique', 16).

emancipatory historiographies relate to so-called 'traditional' historical-critical method? That is the subject of the ensuing reflections, with a view to identifying what can act as defining markers for a specifically feminist historiography. This last is my interest rather than providing a map of historical-critical methods as such, as will be readily apparent, although some thoughts on the nature of historical-criticism will necessarily be offered.

The rise of historical criticism was itself, of course, something of a revolution in approaches to the Bible.[61] James Barr articulates a central question posed by historical criticism: 'Is it, as some think, basically an anti-Christian procedure which should be repudiated or at least severely restricted in its application to the documents of the Christian faith?'[62] It is ironic that feminist methodologies have generated that identical question in Christian circles. Schüssler Fiorenza's feminist historical method and historical method more generally do then have something in common, as readings of scripture which are both critical and ambivalently related to what is perceived as traditional Christianity: and the former is undoubtedly heavily indebted towards the latter. Yet mapping the relationship between the two is not always helped by Schüssler Fiorenza's own tendency to polarize historical criticism as 'positivist' and 'antiquarian'. The force of this criticism can best be demonstrated with reference to *Bread Not Stone*, in which she presents her fullest account of historical-critical scholarship and feminist-critical interpretation. This exercise will be undertaken in due course. Presently, however, I wish to contextualize the discussion with more general reference to the history and nature of biblical scholarship. Charting the history of biblical interpretation is, obviously, outside the scope of this book. However a brief synopsis of the emergence of modern historical critical method is relevant to a consideration of how feminist scholarship does or might relate to it.

It is important to bear in mind that the relationship between Christians and their scripture has always been one of renegotiation as cultural and intellectual horizons have shifted. Burrows and Rorem comment on the 'surprising multivocality through the centuries of reception and transmission' displayed by the biblical language and texts.[63] Biblical interpretation has a history, and a complex one. The genealogy of modern critical techniques is often related to the sixteenth-century reformation movements, identified as 'the necessary seedbeds of biblical criticism'. Certainly the willingness of the Reformers to depart from traditional Church teachings shares an affinity with the crucial defining factor of historical

---

[61] Throughout, I use terms such as 'historical criticism' and 'historical method' in their broad sense to include the range of scholarly methods in biblical criticism which work within a diachronous perspective. Thus various types of methodological approaches are comprehended within it: literary-historical methods, form, source and redaction criticism, tradition-history etc.

[62] Barr, Introduction to Stuhlmacher, *Historical Criticism and Theological Interpretation of Scripture*, 9.

[63] Burrows and Rorem (eds.), *Biblical Hermeneutics in Historical Perspective*, xiv.

criticism: the refusal to allow religious orthodoxy to limit inquiry.[64] It can though be argued that, whilst the Reformation overturned the priority of church tradition, it also led to an appropriation of scripture to dogmatics.[65] In this respect, critical method's characterizing principles of freedom from dogmatic constraints and open investigation of the texts made early historical criticism both a rebellion against Protestant orthodoxy and its natural legatee.[66]

The Enlightenment clearly played a pivotal role in the transition to readings of scripture which were both rationally founded and impatient of doctrinal restraint. The stress on human reason and autonomy, on evidence and historical investigation, laid the foundations for subsequent movements in biblical criticism. There arose a commitment to pursuing historical research 'objectively', on its own terms, with the goal of reconstructing 'what really happened'. The discernment of sources, authorial intention and dates of production became a keynote of modern critical scholarship, rather than the provision of theological exegesis aimed at contemporary edification. J. P. Gabler's lecture 'On the proper distinction between biblical and dogmatic theology and the specific objectives of each' was delivered in 1787. This was indicative of a move towards separating biblical interpretation from theological formulations. In the nineteenth century Strauss made the distinction between the Jesus of history and the Christ of faith; Baur attempted to formulate a historical (rather than supernaturalistic) account of Christian origins. Wellhausen, Holtzmann and Harnack abandoned the Hegelian philosophy undergirding the historical programmes of Strauss and Baur and historical-criticism became yet more divergent from theological interpretation.[67] We see from these developments the roots of biblical criticism as a pursuit which can be followed independently from systematic theological concerns.[68] This distinction

---

[64] This, indeed, could perhaps be called the key distinction between the so-called 'critical' and 'pre-critical' eras; scholars, both Jewish and Christian, had long employed rational techniques in their approaches to scripture. Josephus and Augustine are but two examples.

[65] See, for example, Hans Frei's account in *The Eclipse of Biblical Narrative*. Frei identifies a common approach to biblical interpretation in the Lutheran and Calvinistic traditions respectively, differing more in emphasis than substance (19). Both affirmed the literal sense of the Bible as primary and identified it with the inspired Word of God (37). Both saw harmony between the literal meaning, religious truths and historical accuracy (56). Duncan Ferguson sums up developments in Protestantism: 'In the years following the Reformation, Protestant Orthodoxy slipped into the practice of harmonizing biblical passages with dogmatic formulations, undercutting any genuine concerns' (*Biblical Hermeneutics*, 166).

[66] Stuhlmacher, *Historical Criticism and Theological Interpretation of Scripture*, 36-38; Barr, *Holy Scripture*, 34.

[67] Morgan with Barton, *Biblical Interpretation*, 69.

[68] It is worth quoting Barr at this point on the origins of the bifurcation: 'The change in attitude came not from historical criticism, but from a newer theological orientation, which had become critical towards its materials. When people in modern times blame 'historical criticism' for separating the university from the church, the preacher from the Bible, and the Bible from its relevance for today, they are usually not thinking of biblical criticism at all: the cause of the troubles they bewail is the different attitude of people to ultimate theological questions' (Barr, *Holy Scripture*, 122). In this respect historical

between historical research and theological interpretation should not however be overdrawn. Scholars of the stature of Schleiermacher and Ritschl moved in the worlds of both New Testament analysis and systematic theology. Grant opines that '[t]he relation of biblical interpretation to theology in the nineteenth century was very close'.[69] Nevertheless, biblical criticism and theology were increasingly travelling on divergent tracks.

Attempts to produce syntheses between historical analysis and theological interpretation have, of course, continued, emanating from both liberal and conservative perspectives. Bultmann stands out as a dominant twentieth-century figure in this respect. So too does the biblical theology movement. Morgan, however, suggests that most biblical scholars find such syntheses actually dangerous and see no prospect of integrating the two without threatening the intellectual freedom of historical research.[70] Conversely, secular critical methods can be deemed inadequate to using the Bible in the service of religious believers. In consequence, there has developed a rift 'between the rational methods and conclusions of biblical scholarship and the way that believers use their scriptures to inform and nourish religious faith'.[71] The place of historical criticism within the Christianity community hence remains uneasy. As shall be seen, it is the self-siting of historical criticism as independent and serving the ends only of scholarship which problematizes its relationship with liberationist feminism.

And yet, there would seem then to be a natural rapprochement between historical critical method and feminist scholarship. They converge in the critical manner with which both approach the biblical texts. The origins of historical-critical method in shaking loose dogmatic shackles have an obvious affinity with feminism's desire to break open ossified models of interpretation. Neither identifies the Bible and truth, whether historical or doctrinal, in a timeless and homogenizing way. That the biblical texts are produced by many hands and voices, and transmitted within and for particular communities to particular ends, is scarcely news to the historical critic. For the historian, the Bible is a set of diverse writings, whose textual form remains a matter for dispute, and which needs careful study and evaluation in light of a whole range of sub-disciplinary methodologies (philological, sociological, literary etc.). Historians employing critical methods do not approach any text as sacred icon or repository of indisputable truths. Indeed, Schüssler Fiorenza notes that she experienced historical-critical scholarship as 'liberating', releasing her from 'outdated doctrinal frameworks and literalist prejudices'.[72] She goes on to identify four further ways in which historical-critical interpretation can be seen as hermeneutically useful to contemporary Christian theologies.[73]

---

criticism can be seen as a by-product of a more generally critical theological orientation, most clearly discerned in the Enlightenment.

[69] Grant, *A Short History of Biblical Interpretation*, 123f.
[70] Morgan with Barton, *Biblical Interpretation*, 74-5.
[71] Ibid., 174.
[72] Schüssler Fiorenza, *Bread not Stone*, 94.
[73] Ibid., 130-1.

Firstly, it sets forth the meaning of the texts within its original context, destabilizing subsequent dogmatic or social 'usurpations'. This provides a measure of critical protection from ideological appropriations. A second and related point is that it makes it more difficult to assimilate the Bible to contemporary interests. Again, the freedom of the text is affirmed. Thirdly, it keeps the text 'irritating' by preserving its alienness, allowing it to challenge our own perspectives and practices. And, finally, it limits the number of interpretations with reference to those plausible in historical context. Such are the positive features which Schüssler Fiorenza discerns in historical-critical methods.

Schüssler Fiorenza herself declares that her method is a particularization of the results of historical criticism. It is not only that the Bible was written by humans: it was written by *men*. The biblical texts and subsequent interpretations are articulations of a patriarchal, androcentric society; as such they cannot be trusted as divine revelation. The Bible, indeed, continues to function as the legitimator of patriarchy.[74] As such it needs reclaiming if it is to act as a feminist resource; it is necessary to recognize the Bible as both oppressive and liberating. This dialectic is absolutely crucial. It is only because the Bible can be liberating that it can be reclaimed.[75] But it is imperative that oppressive traditions are identified and exposed. This, as we have already seen, is Schüssler Fiorenza's hermeneutics of suspicion, in contradistinction to a hermeneutics of consent. And her base starting point for this was the assumption that biblical texts and interpretations are patriarchal and androcentric, which she argued was justified by the identification of most of the biblical authors and interpreters as male and by the Bible's location in patriarchal society.

However, it is not only the case that feminism intensifies historical-critical method in a particular direction, turning it against its own 'blind-spots' to allow the androcentricity and patriarchalism of the Bible to be revealed. If this were the case, feminist method would simply be an expression of historical criticism, one which brought to light hitherto unremarked aspects of the historical data and interpretation. There is, rather, felt to be a real methodological difference and distinctiveness. The following discussion is an attempt to delineate what shape this takes, beginning from Schüssler Fiorenza's own analysis. As we shall see, the question of 'objectivity' emerges as critical to this account.

Feminism, Historical Criticism and Objectivity

We have already noted that the issue of objectivity in historical reconstructions is a vexed one and observed that Schüssler Fiorenza rejects the notion of historical inquiry as dispassionate and neutral. For Schüssler Fiorenza, this demarcates a crucial dividing line between traditional historical criticism on the one hand and feminist historical criticism on the other. This is then a pivotal issue, which in this section shall be explored further.

---

[74] Ibid., xi.
[75] Ibid., xvii.

A primary cause of the estrangement between feminist and historical-critical method is the extent to which feminists such as Schüssler Fiorenza claim that the latter is dominated by a Rankean understanding of history. 'Rankean history' – named after the important German historian Leopold von Ranke (1795-1886) – is presented as a history of events; the historian is required to describe as objectively as possible 'how it really was'.[76] Thus, Ranke stands as representative of the type of scientific, historicist worldview from which feminists such as Schüssler Fiorenza and Monika Fander[77] wish to disassociate themselves. There follows a summary of Schüssler Fiorenza's account of Rankean history.

Schüssler Fiorenza and the Rankean Understanding of History

Schüssler Fiorenza begins with a case-study which she holds as representative of a Rankean approach to history; she quotes at some length from this work, a German collection of essays on *Women in Early Christianity*. This is an extract which holds forth upon the methodological parameters within which a New Testament scholar must work for credibility:

> He [sic] may find his professional honor only in the fact that he does *not* interweave these ancient texts with the texture of modern emancipatory impulses and certainties, but rather seeks to explain them in correlation to their origin at the end of the first century A.D. . . . He must therefore be especially cautious not to explain away too quickly as conditioned by time or anachronistic all that which disturbs him today. His most important task will rather be to make felt exactly the offensive *strangeness* of these ancient expressions before the enlightened horizons of his own time.[78]

This, argues Schüssler Fiorenza, veils its 'apologetic aggression'; it claims historical objectivity, and is founded on a concept of history stemming from the nineteenth century. The assumption is that a historian can 'step out of his own time', study history 'on its own terms', and not in terms of contemporary questions and experiences.[79] Such an inquiry understands itself as dispassionately examining the past to find out what actually happened. Following Dilthey, the historian is expected to exercise empathy in reconstructing history in relation to its own

---

[76] Ibid., 94ff.

[77] See her article 'Historical-Critical Methods': 'The question remains whether an exegesis free from any pre-understanding, as Ranke imagined it, is at all possible . . .'; 'Historical scholarship in Ranke's sense confuses one's own reconstruction of history with the facticity of historical events' (216).

[78] Karl-Heinz Müller, 'Die Haustafel des Kolosserbriefes und das antike Frauenthema: Eine kritische Rückshcau auf alte Ergebnisse', in Dautzenberf, Merklein, and Müller (eds.), *Die Frau im Urchristentum* (Freiberg: Herder, 1983), 263ff, cited in Schüssler Fiorenza, *Bread not Stone*, 96.

[79] Schüssler Fiorenza, *Bread not Stone*, 96.

context and not her/his own.[80] This is in the name of a historicity which perceives the 'values, actions, and motivations' of historical agents as 'alien to the contemporary inquirer'.[81]

In the history of biblical scholarship this has meant that the task of the biblical exegete is defined as interrogating the texts to construct a picture of the events they reflect.[82] Given the methodological underpinning that history must be looked at on its own terms and not ours, a central part of the exegetical process is the discernment of authorial intention. In this way a 'true' history may be apprehended. Schüssler Fiorenza comments: '[i]f it is assumed that the New Testament texts mirror the reality of early Christian women . . . then it is the "scientific" exegete who establishes objectively *wie es am Anfang war*'.[83]

This pushes Schüssler Fiorenza to the following conclusion:

> It seems no rapprochement is possible between a feminist historical-critical and positivistic-historical understanding. Insofar as an understanding of biblical historiography prides itself on being impartial and value-neutral, objective and descriptive, scientific and antiquarian, it must reject any feminist reconstruction of early Christian history as 'ideological' and 'influenced' by present-day concerns. . . . Scholarship claiming to be 'objective' and 'realistic' is not more value-free and less ideological because it hides its 'subjectivity,' 'cultureboundedness,' and 'contemporary interests' from itself.[84]

Schüssler Fiorenza goes on to site this disjunction between 'feminist' and 'positivist' historical-critical method in the debate between 'constructionist' and 'objectivist-realist' currents in scholarship, as representing different perceptions of what can be known historically.[85] Again she labels the latter Rankean, denoting a school of thought which sees the tasks of the historian as scientifically assembling data from sources and evidence, with a view to relating 'what actually happened'. By contrast, the former lays weight upon the 'time-boundedness' and 'linguisticality' of historical knowledge, rendering it impossible for us to know the 'real past' as we would know an object in the present. On the constructionist understanding:

> Statements of historical fact do not emerge by themselves as ready-made mirrors of past events. In order to make statements of historical fact, scholars must draw inferences based in part upon their general understanding of human behavior and the nature of the world. They not only deal selectively with their historical sources in order to present a 'coherent' narrative account, but also ascribe historical

---

[80] It is interesting that Schüssler Fiorenza refers to Dilthey in the context of an objectivist model of history; Dilthey was trying to move way from historiography as 'objective' and 'dispassionate'.
[81] Schüssler Fiorenza, *Bread not Stone*, 98.
[82] Ibid., 97.
[83] Ibid., 97.
[84] Ibid., 98.
[85] Ibid., 98.

'significance' to their 'data' in accordance with the theoretical model or perspective that 'orders' their information.[86]

This leads to a relativistic understanding of historiography. That we can distinguish between modes of approaching history in (for example) the nineteenth century, the Renaissance and the Graeco-Roman world itself bears witness to the extent to which historical discourse is rooted in contemporary contexts and shifting socio-political and philosophical locations. Schüssler Fiorenza quotes with approval Mommsen's judgement that all historical judgements stand 'as it were with one foot in the self-image of a certain group in society' and that this is exactly what furnishes them 'with the meaning and relevance they have for a reader who is confronted by them as a human being whose interests are primarily determined by the intellectual context of the present'.[87]

One must question, however, whether Schüssler Fiorenza does not present a somewhat oversimplified and misleading impression of traditional historical-critical scholarship,[88] overdrawing the extent to which it inhabits a scientific-positivistic framework. Ranke himself certainly set objectivity as the historian's goal, but felt it all the more crucial to do so 'since personal limitation hinders him from attaining it'.[89] Furthermore, according to Leonard Kriege, Ranke 'acknowledged the constructive role of the subject qua historian – not merely in the sense of inevitable private limitations, but in principle'.[90] Ranke also lay stress on the particularity of history which should not be subjugated to general theories and laws, but must be allowed to speak: facts should be presented, however 'conditional and unattractive'.[91] This is surely a statement of scholarly integrity; Ranke's commitment to objectivity and factuality were in the interests of his earnest hope: 'God grant that I bring to the light the facts, I hope, as they were, without any deception whether of my own or of others.'[92]

Of course, the issue here is not whether Schüssler Fiorenza does justice to the complexities of Ranke's historiography, but whether she has adequately portrayed the pluriform heritage of historical criticism. The shortcomings of nineteenth-century biblical research were, surely, pointed out very early in the twentieth century and most tellingly prior even to that by Schweitzer, who demonstrated decisively how far apart the romantic liberal histories of Jesus were from biblical portrayals of him.[93] Thus, he concluded, 'each successive epoch of

---

[86] Ibid., 99.

[87] W. J. Mommsen, 'Social Conditioning and Social Relevance of Historical Judgements', *History and Theory* 17 (1978), 32, cited in Schüssler Fiorenza, *Bread not Stone*, 103-4.

[88] For another revisionist account of 'traditional' historical-critical method, see John Barton, 'Historical-critical approaches'.

[89] Ranke to King Maximillian II of Bavaria, Nov. 26, 1859, cited in Krieger, *Ranke*, 5.

[90] Krieger, *Ranke*, 10.

[91] Ranke, *Geschichten der romanischen und germanischen Völker*, ibid., 5.

[92] Ranke, *Nachlass*, 3:496, ibid., 5.

[93] Albert Schweitzer, *The Quest of the Historical Jesus* (London: SCM, 1981). It is of course possible to argue that Schweitzer thereafter fell promptly into a similar trap as the

theology found its own thoughts in Jesus; that was, indeed, the only way in which it could make him live'.[94] Tyrrell famously concluded that 'the Christ that Harnack sees, looking back through nineteen centuries of Catholic darkness, is only the reflection of a liberal Protestant face seen at the bottom of a deep well'.[95] Kähler argued that the Gospels should be understood as Easter confessions rather than as biographies;[96] Wrede demonstrated the extent to which Mark's Gospel was a theological document.[97] Historical criticism was taking a new direction.

The influence of contemporary context on historical research was clearly acknowledged. Schüssler Fiorenza does seem to imply that Bultmann's is a lone voice in the historical-critical tradition in his recognition that there is no understanding without pre-understanding.[98] Yet a brief sampling of methodological comments by twentieth-century biblical scholars would seem to suggest that a naïve belief in the *possibility* of unconditioned analysis is, at the very least, not uniformly held.[99]

David Stacey produced an introductory volume on *Interpreting the Bible* in 1976 and another, *Groundwork of Biblical Studies*, in 1979. As introductory texts, they deal primarily with what might be considered standard practice. In them, he explains well-established consensus views and does not engage at all with some of the more sophisticated hermeneutical theories to appear this century. He draws a clear distinction between two different aspects of biblical interpretation: deciding what it *meant* and deciding what it *means*. This might seem then to support Schüssler Fiorenza's designation of typical historical-critical scholarship as realist-objectivist, divorcing the past under examination from present horizons. With respect to deciding what the Bible *means*, Stacey stresses the role of the interpreter. '*In the realm of interpretation presuppositions are all important* [original emphasis]';[100] what is more, '[i]f the real purpose of interpretation is to apply the Scriptures to the life and thought of a particular community or individual, the circumstances of the recipient cannot be overlooked'.[101] However, even with respect to his other category of deciding what it *meant*, the role of the historian is not discounted: for this individual 'has to examine the evidence, assess it, and then construct his own account of what happened'. The historian cannot know precisely what happened; moreover, even if this were possible, the historian would still then

---

liberals with his promulgation of Jesus as an apocalyptic figure who could only be interpreted in eschatological context.

[94] Schweitzer, *The Quest of the Historical Jesus*, cited in Ferguson, *Biblical Hermeneutics*, 57.

[95] G. Tyrrell, *Christianity at the Crossroads* (London, 1909), 44.

[96] M. Kahler, *Der sogennante historische Jesus und der geschichtliche, biblische Christus*, Leipzig, 1892.

[97] W. Wrede, *Das Messiasgeheimnis in der Evangelien* (Göttingen, 1901).

[98] Schüssler Fiorenza, *Bread not Stone*, 98.

[99] Space precludes a more systematic and comprehensive survey. The eclectic selection of quotations which follows merely points to the need to evaluate generalizations about the epistemological assumptions of biblical scholars with some care.

[100] Stacey, *Groundwork of Biblical Studies*, 37.

[101] Stacey, *Interpreting the Bible*, 11.

necessarily employ personal judgement in evolving theories and hypotheses of how particular events related to each other. 'He brings to the study of history, therefore, both personal skills and personal judgement.'[102]

This seems somewhat in keeping with what Schüssler Fiorenza calls a constructivist model of history, in that it acknowledges the role of the historian in ordering data according to particular theories and perspectives. It does not suppose a pure objectivity is possible, still less that certainty could be the outcome of the scientific historiographical gaze. 'One would like certainty. Therefore one imagines it can be found. It cannot.'[103] Stacey, however, does wish to maintain a strong distinction between studying the Bible on historical grounds, to reconstruct what it meant in its time, and interpreting the Bible for contemporary communities. This distinction, as saw earlier Schüssler Fiorenza seems to want to dissolve or at the least blur.

'To the opponents of biblical criticism', comments James Barr, 'nothing is more irritating than the notion that it is neutral, objective, free from presuppositions, and in this sense scientific'.[104] Barr points out, however, how frequently biblical criticism has been quite explicitly fuelled by contemporary theological problems and how rarely by the 'positivist gospel'. The theological and confessional context of historical research on the Bible is, he suggests, well illustrated by 'biblical study of the era of Cullmann and von Rad, Hoskyns and Davey and Alan Richardson'.[105] And it is not that these scholars imported their theological presuppositions whilst supposing themselves to be working from neutral ground. They were working in the service of theology: but, for Barr, what makes critical biblical scholarship such as this objective is that 'its results are not predetermined by a given authoritative ideology'.[106] Few indeed, it would seem, are the scholars who would claim objectivity, if by that is meant freedom from personal contextuality. As we have seen, even Ranke was aware of the limitations of time and place upon the historian! Nineham talks of the *'provisional* character of historical reconstructions',[107] Hennessey of the 'inevitability' of 'subjective factors' affecting each stage of the historical process,[108] Gerald Downing of the lack of 'pure objectivity' at any point.[109] Anderson states quite flatly: 'the historian cannot escape his own presuppositions'.[110]

---

[102] Ibid., 20.
[103] Ibid., 34.
[104] Barr, *Holy Scripture*, 111.
[105] Ibid., 170.
[106] Ibid., 114.
[107] Nineham, 'Historical Criticism', 256.
[108] Hennessey, 'History', 470.
[109] Downing, 'Historical-Critical Method', 284.
[110] Anderson, *Jesus and Christian Origins*, 97. Hugh Anderson, for example, comments in 1963 with some acerbity on E. Stauffer's 'real bravado' in attempting to revive 'scientific Jesus-research'. For his part, he asserts that the New Testament itself is not interested in 'telling us *what actually happened*' (60); it is 'a memory-picture transfused with the mature knowledge of who he really was and is' (61). A 'purely photographic portrait' could be no use to faith (60).This is with a quite different agenda than Schüssler Fiorenza.

I do not suggest that Schüssler Fiorenza's criticisms have no applicability, merely that 'traditional' historical-criticism incorporates a greater breadth of perspective than she seems to imply. There is, furthermore, an important distinction in this debate that Schüssler Fiorenza does not draw out sufficiently clearly. Namely, whilst it is a feature of historical-critical scholarship to accept objectivity as a goal, this does not mean the scholars in question were not (and are not) consciously committed to ideological and theological concerns. Should those concerns, however, be permitted consciously to influence any given historical judgement?[111] Certainly it can be argued on hermeneutical and pyschological grounds that, inevitably, they do. That is not the same as accepting either that all research will be merely a projection of one's own starting point or that this would be a desirable end. That would hardly be to attain even the *relative* objectivity which Schüssler Fiorenza herself advocates. As Schüssler Fiorenza also points out, to take seriously the hermeneutical circle means that the interpreter cannot enjoy the perspective from nowhere. But nor does an interpreter enjoy the perspective *on* nowhere; there is a reciprocity and mutuality which means the interpreter's starting point can be challenged and transformed. Protecting the 'critical' component of critical scholarship is what prompted the classical statement of procedure by Mommsen (whom, as we have seen, was quoted by Schüssler Fiorenza as representative of the constructivist school):

Anderson wants to stress the significance of faith in both the production and interpretation of the New Testament. Nevertheless, his comments prefigure Schüssler Fiorenza's more generalized criticisms of nearly thirty years later in a most interesting way and I shall quote from him at some length: 'So with the determination and the sleuthlike skill of a veritable Sherlock Holmes, Stauffer pursues the *facts* in this case, as he pursues all the *facts* relating to Jesus. His whole factual reconstruction of the story of Jesus issues of course from a certain preconception of what 'history' is. Founding on the view of such nineteenth-century historiographers as Leopold von Ranke that the historian's job is simply to tell what happened (*wie es eigentlich gewesen ist*), Stauffer would eliminate every element of subjectivity on the part of the historian, and let the *facts* in their mere extrinsicality speak for themselves. But can we be so sure that this is what is meant by 'history'?' (Anderson, *Jesus and Christian Origins*, 59).

[111] Grant defines the goals of historical research very much in the way Schüssler Fiorenza critiques: as interpreting the texts in their original context, to determine their settings, purposes, and transmission (Grant, *A Short History*, 152). But he also asks: is biblical interpretation scientific? To this question, he answers with both a yes and a no. 'It is not scientific in the sense that an observer free from presuppositions and prejudices can simply analyse the biblical texts and produce a startling new and true hypothesis...'(155). However, it is scientific 'in the sense that it involves analysis before and alongside the synthesis towards which it aims' (156). But just as historical judgments influence an interpreter's theology, so an interpreter can hardly avoid the influence 'of theological concerns upon his historical ideas' (158). Already in 1948, Grant was stressing the subjectivity of exegesis: by 1963, he concluded that it hardly seemed necessary to argue for its ubiquity (160), and whilst rejecting Bultmann's demythologizing programme, concurred that prior understanding was a prerequisite for biblical interpretation (165).

Our life-nerve is research free of presuppositions: the kind of research which does not discover what it thinks it desirable to discover, for the sake of some particular aim or interest.[112]

This, it seems to me, is the kind of concern which prompted the methodological statement by Müller with which I began this section and to which Schüssler Fiorenza objected so strongly. He did not wish to consider first-century injunctions, mores and customs against the backcloth of the late twentieth century but in context of the first. This is surely the *sine qua non* of historical research which purports to tell us anything about the past. I have already mentioned that Schüssler Fiorenza criticizes the tendency of Rankean history to see the 'values, actions and motivations' of historical agents as 'alien to the contemporary inquirer' in the interests of objectivity.[113] Müller appears to articulate this tendency when he suggests that the historian's 'most important task will rather be to make felt exactly the offensive *strangeness* of these ancient expressions before the enlightened horizons of his own time'.[114] And yet I am left unclear as to why Schüssler Fiorenza finds this objectionable. She clearly appreciates the importance of contextuality; that ideologies are spun in cultural contexts. Furthermore, she herself argues that texts should always be seen in their socio-political contexts, their irritating alienness let be.[115]

My points here are twofold. One is that Schüssler Fiorenza sets up a sharp distinction between what she calls Rankean history and constructivist history. The boundaries between the two are, I would argue, rather more blurred than she allows in the very mixed bag which constitutes historical criticism of the Bible over the last 150 years. One must add further that accepting objectivity as a goal does not mean a naive subscription to its attainment. Historians have aims and presuppositions, whether or not these are articulated: but, as has already been questioned, does that justify making historical judgements on the basis of those aims and presuppositions alone? And as we saw, a *relative* objectivity was part of Schüssler Fiorenza's own critical armoury. This, I would suggest is exactly the case also for a significant strand of 'traditional' historical-criticism. Thus we can arrive in some measure at a *rapprochement*. 'Traditional' historians frequently recognize their own contextuality and feminist historiography frequently strives for 'honest' scholarship in the sense of careful evaluation of sources and attention to norms of coherence and plausibility.

Nevertheless, I do not say that Schüssler Fiorenza's brand of feminist historiography is merely a moment of 'traditional' historical-criticism or can simply be reduced to it. Rather, I want to argue that the disjunction between them has been to some extent located in the wrong place. A divide along lines of

---

[112] Cited in Morgan with Barton, *Biblical Interpretation* (1988), 81.

[113] Schüssler Fiorenza, *Bread not Stone*, 98.

[114] Karl-Heinz Müller, 'Die Haustafel des Kolosserbriefes und das antike Frauenthema: Eine kritische Rückschau auf alte Ergebnisse', in Dautzenberf, Merklein, and Müller (eds.), *Die Frau im Urchristentum* (Freiberg: Herder, 1983), 263ff, cited in Schüssler Fiorenza, *Bread not Stone*, 96.

[115] Schüssler Fiorenza, *In Memory of Her*, 60.

supposedly objective/consciously not-objective does not work. Historical criticism is too diverse and too many practitioners have for too long recognized their own contextuality and inevitable enmeshment in presuppositions. The real distinction, it seems to me, is between scholarships which seek to reconstruct the past on its own terms, and those that do so for explicit contemporary purposes. It is the question of whether history is purportedly written *of* or *for* which really divides the bulk of historical criticism from feminist historiographies of this type. And yet even this division is blurred. Materialist and ideological criticisms are not only practised by feminists. What is more, there are calls for historical criticism to be rethought such that it can once more enter into creative interplay with theology.[116] This again points to areas in which feminist method can intersect with other interest-groups and serves also Schüssler Fiorenza's own agenda: for she too is wanting to write feminist *theological* interpretations of Christian origins.

From analysis of Schüssler Fiorenza, we can see then that what is really definitive of feminist historiographies rests less with epistemological debates about constructivism and objectivity, and more with the basic structuring framework as *feminist*. It is a rhetorical practice, operating in the interests of women and, more broadly, other oppressed groups. In expression of this, feminism as a paradigm centralizes women. It renders women, the other, as normative: even where historical evidence is fragmentary and historical judgements may in consequence only be cautious and limited. It does not repeat the marginalization of women which is evidenced in historical sources. It refuses it, and brings it to notice. It retains a fierce interest in materialist concerns; past realities are not a matter of indifference but a call to remembrance. This is not a nostalgic remembering, but the memory of oppression and resistance. These themes will be taken up extensively in Chapter 6.

---

[116] Francis Watson is vocal on this front. See *Text, Church and World*; *Text and Truth*.

Chapter 3

Biblical Interpretation and the *Ekklesia*

Ekklesia is a key concept in Schüssler Fiorenza's work, articulated in increasingly sophisticated ways. The *ekklesia gynaikon* – 'women-church' – is the hermeneutical centre of feminist biblical interpretation as expressed by Schüssler Fiorenza.[1] As such, it is necessary to explore the various multifaceted dimensions to Schüssler Fiorenza's deployment of the concept, as her feminist biblical hermeneutics springs from and is answerable to this idea of the *ekklesia*. It functions in two primary ways: firstly, with reference to her historical analysis of Christian beginnings, and secondly, to designate a feminist democratic speech-community which is both partially realized and also an ideal rhetorical space.

As has been seen, Schüssler Fiorenza's historical reconstruction in *In Memory of Her* emerges from an historiographical model which places emancipatory struggles centre-stage. These submerged democratic impulses are linked by Schüssler Fiorenza to the importance of *ekklesia* as a root concept for the early Christian community, allied to the notion of the *basileia* as God's intended world. ('In sum, the well-being and happiness of everyone is the central vision of the *basileia* movement. . . . [It is] a sign of courage and hope for today and the future.'[2]) *Ekklesia* is associated with its contextual meanings of 'public assembly

---

[1] The origins of Schüssler Fiorenza's use of 'women-church' lie with her attempts to reclaim *Frauenkirche* as a positive term. The 'Women Moving Church' conference of 1981 stimulated the insight that talking of 'moving church' simply implied its relocation, not its transformation. Schüssler Fiorenza sought to reframe the discussions, arguing that the title 'Women as Church on the Move' would better express the dynamic changes being brought about by *women as Church*. The concept of *women as Church*, Schüssler Fiorenza rendered as *Frauenkirche*: Diann Neu, one of the conference conveners, translated this as 'women-church'. Schüssler Fiorenza explains that women-church had been used as pejorative label in the 1960s. She sought to revalorize it by replacing the term *Kirche*/church (etymologically dependent on the Greek word *kyriache*, 'belonging to the Lord') with that of *ekklesia* – which both signified 'assembly of the people' and is the Christian Testament word for 'Church'. The qualification of *ekklesia* with *gynaikon* stressed that, as a democratic assembly, the *ekklesia* is signally lacking unless women are fully included. See *Discipleship of Equals*, 196. As *ekklesia gynaikon*, the term is historically and politically an oxymoron: 'a combination of contradictory terms for the purpose of articulating a feminist political alterity' (*But She Said*, 130). In keeping with Schüssler Fiorenza's own practice, I will as a matter of course abbreviate this term simply to *ekklesia*.

[2] Schüssler Fiorenza, *But She Said*, 216.

of the political community' or 'democratic assembly of full citizens'.[3] As such Schüssler Fiorenza can argue that an early understanding of church as *ekklesia* derived its signification from classical concepts of democracy promising freedom and equality to all citizens.[4] In this framework women, as part of the *ekklesia*, were enabled to take on active roles in the founding and leadership of the Christian communities. This was possible within the cultural parameters because the early *ekklesia* was located in house-assemblies which undid the public/private demarcations relegating women to domesticity. Schüssler Fiorenza is careful to stress that the Christian *ekklesia* was not unique in this: 'Christians were neither the first nor the only group who gathered together in house assemblies. Religious cults, voluntary associations, professional clubs, and funeral societies, as well as the Jewish synagogue, gathered as decision-making assemblies in private houses.'[5] Thus Schüssler Fiorenza speaks of the *ekklesia* of women to refer to the 'discipleship of equals', but not cast against the negative foil of Jewish or Hellenistic context. She postulates this vision as a crucial component of Christian development in the first century. The Bible can then become the root model for the *ekklesia* of women, or, as it is translated in Schüssler Fiorenza's earlier works, 'women-church'. The gaze is then focused, not on 'malestream'[6] texts and traditions, but on women's emancipatory struggles.

Ekklesia, then, is a term which evokes continuity and connection with the early church communities. It is situated within the heritage of women as church, a heritage which the *ekklesia* seeks to reconstruct. As has been seen, this reconstruction of 'women's history' in the early Church is a key component of Schüssler Fiorenza's project. Such a move is not only a means of empowering women, but a corrective to the 'deformation of our historical consciousness that has eliminated women's and other nonpersons' victimizations and struggles from our ecclesial memory'.[7] The contemporary *ekklesia* can reclaim the *ekklesia* of women in the first century as its own biblical forebear; the Jesus movement can be contextualized within the *ekklesia*'s feminist vision.

Ekklesia is a public-political construct. Its rendering as *women-church* is misunderstood if it is then construed in relation to any conception of feminine or female identity. That would be to situate *ekklesia* within a framework organized around theories of sex/gender. Schüssler Fiorenza consistently rejects making gender theory a keynote of her work, for she considers that this would merely reinscribe patriarchal worldviews. Schüssler Fiorenza contends that only if *ekklesia* is articulated outside of the sex/gender system can cultural discourses of sex/gender be, on the one hand, named as instruments of domination, and on the other hand, subjected to deconstruction. A feminist biblical interpretation, argues Schüssler Fiorenza, 'must position itself in the public-political center of

---

[3] Schüssler Fiorenza, *In Memory of Her*, xxxii.
[4] This point shall be developed below, with the more substantive consideration of Schüssler Fiorenza's deployment of *ekklesia* as rhetorical speech-community.
[5] Schüssler Fiorenza, *In Memory of Her*, xxxii.
[6] This is a preferred term in Schüssler Fiorenza's later works, which she has gained from the sociologist Dorothy Smith.
[7] Schüssler Fiorenza, *Discipleship of Equals*, 329.

church and academy, rather than on the boundaries of feminist sex/gender alterity-constructions'.[8]

Ekklesia, then, as the locus of feminist biblical interpretation, must be situated at the centre of public-political institutions and discourses. *Ekklesia* is 'a public feminist countersphere' from which critical reading practices can emanate.[9] It is a rhetorical space. As a rhetorical space, *ekklesia* must however be construed according to a different logic than that of kyriarchy. The latter proceeds from a logic of identity, Schüssler Fiorenza argues, whilst the *ekklesia* is positioned within a logic of radical democracy.

What is the logic of identity? Schüssler Fiorenza characterizes it as follows:

> In short, the philosophical logic of identity, which in antiquity articulated the asymmetric binary dualisms of human/animal, male/female, and free/slave as "natural" differences in order to legitimate patriarchal relations of domination and subordination, is also inscribed in the discourses of modern Eurocentric political philosophy and theology. . . . This discourse emerges in various ways: it manifests itself in the Enlightenment philosophers' construction of the "Man of Reason," it surfaces in Euro-American racist discourses on the "White Lady," and in the Western colonialist depiction of "inferior races" and "uncivilized savages."[10]

It is the logic of identity which underlies the sex-gender framework. Indeed, Schüssler Fiorenza's rejection of the sex/gender system as her framework for interpretation is in fact closely linked to her espousal of radical democracy in its stead, for both are moments emerging from her analysis of 'patriarchy'. Schüssler Fiorenza's understanding of patriarchy is, then, central to her own counter-rhetoric. Therefore, the following section summarizes Schüssler Fiorenza's analysis of patriarchy.

Patriarchy

As Schüssler Fiorenza notes, most feminists employ patriarchy as a primary heuristic category, understood as 'the social structures and ideologies that have enabled men to dominate and exploit women throughout recorded history'.[11] Schüssler Fiorenza's difficulty with this is the elevation of gender oppression over against all the other varieties of exploitation on grounds such as race or class. The negative consequences of this are twofold. On the one hand, it elides oppressions which do not, or not primarily, operate on the basis of gender. On the other hand, it postulates male-female dualism as originary, thus essentializing gender difference as the source of all other divisions within humanity.

---

[8] Schüssler Fiorenza, *But She Said*, 103.
[9] Ibid., 103.
[10] Ibid., 121-2.
[11] Ibid., 105.

This debate over the theorizing of gender difference continues to be a major source of disagreement amongst feminists. So-called 'radical' feminism identifies being a woman with qualities which patriarchy has denigrated but which, it claims, ought to be valorized: pacificity, relationality, mutuality, intuitiveness and so on. The source of gender difference may be conceived of in essentialist or constructivist terms, but nevertheless, it seems that such forms of feminism challenge patriarchal construals of sex/gender but not its dualistic base. Schüssler Fiorenza places 'French feminism'[12] within a similar theoretical constellation to radical feminism by pointing to its deployment of the feminine, in particular the maternal-feminine, as alternative space. However, Schüssler Fiorenza argues that such philosophies of the feminine in American context 'tend[s] to reinscribe the cultural feminine, especially in the popular reception of religious feminists: fluidity, softness, plurality, sea, nature, peacefulness, nurturance, body, life, Mother-Goddess, as antithetical to solidity, hardness, rigidity, aggressiveness, reason, control, death, Father-God'.[13] Thus Schüssler Fiorenza's perspective is that theories of the feminine, whether grounded in essentialism, Jungian archetypes or deconstructions of phallocentrism, risk merely becoming variants on traditional patriarchal understandings of femininity. Rationality remains entombed within the citadel of masculinity, whilst the feminine is aligned with 'poetry, mysticism, magic, and religion'.[14]

What is more, and even more disturbing to Schüssler Fiorenza, is the failure of such theorizing of the feminine to take on board the increasingly global context of feminist discourse. The rise of womanist, Asian and *mujerista* voices, for example, problematizes articulations of feminism which still proceed from an analysis of oppression that only takes into account sexual difference. Schüssler Fiorenza is unconvinced that French feminism in particular has much to offer a political context. She cites, with approval, Laura Kipnis:

> The knowledge offered here is not benign. It is that real shifts in world power and economic distribution have little to do with *jouissance*, the pre-Oedipal, or fluids and that the luxury of first-world feminism to dwell on such issues depends on the preservation of first-world abundance guaranteed by systematic underdevelopment elsewhere and by the postponement, by whatever means, of a political decentering.[15]

Schüssler Fiorenza's theoretical base is rooted in materialist feminist perspective.[16] She therefore considers feminist post-structuralist theories which do

---

[12] As Schüssler Fiorenza points out, Euro-American references to 'French feminism' most frequently refer only to the work of Kristeva, Irigaray and Cixous.
[13] Schüssler Fiorenza, *But She Said*, 107.
[14] Ibid., 108.
[15] Laura Kipnis, 'Feminism: The Political Conscience of Postmodernism?', in *Universal Abandon? The Politics of Postmodernism*, ed. A. Ross (Minneapolis: University of Minnesota Press, 1988), 162, cited in Schüssler Fiorenza, *But She Said*, 108.
[16] Schüssler Fiorenza frequently cites Rosemary Hennessy's *Materialist Feminism and the Politics of Discourse* as articulating the kind of social analytic which she also wishes to embrace.

not aim to 'write the feminine', but which stress subjectivity as a site of conflicting discourses to offer a more promising account than psychoanalytically based philosophies of the feminine. Post-structuralist analyses of this kind work from the basis that societal institutions and social practices are structural, pre-existing individual subjects who are thus constituted in relationship to them. Such discursive meaning-systems have political investments, and subjectivity is marked by this in its negotiation of selfhood. Furthermore, subjectivity is formed within a nexus of competing discourses and is thus a site of conflict. Gender identity can then be conceived both politically and in terms of non-unitary discursive positioning. Schüssler Fiorenza delineates two particular reading strategies emanating from feminist post-structuralism, which she both critiques and utilizes.

The first strategy is that of Tamsin E. Lorraine.[17] Lorraine perceives the subject as both effect and shaper of its discursive locations. Subjectivity is a 'self-constituting activity', in which not only the self but also the meaning-world of the self is constructed.[18] In this navigation of subjectivity, hypostases of 'feminine' and 'masculine' represent opposing poles: the feminine pole is 'chaotic flux, beyond language, completely unique and unrepeatable', relating to the world through continuity and connection; the masculine pole is 'changeless, self-sufficient, without conflict, confusion, or motion', relating to the world in oppositionality.[19] It is impossible to live a self-strategy corresponding either to pure 'femininity' or to pure 'masculinity'. The former would not enable selfhood as such at all, for the self would dissolve into the world and into flux; the latter would produce a static, lifeless mode of selfhood. Lorraine suggests that both women and men require feminine and masculine self-strategies, but cultural discourses tend to situate women more closely to the feminine pole and men more closely to the masculine pole.[20] Lorraine's aim is to deconstruct cultural gender categories rather than to perpetuate them, by calling subjects to self-awareness in their own explorations of self-strategies. Thus, her reading model is intended to allow for self-articulation in terms which surpass culturally given gender strategies and, furthermore, incorporate the fullest possible range of perspectives and self-strategies. Subjectivity can in this framework be conceptualized as pluriform and continually transforming. Schüssler Fiorenza, then, can redeploy Lorraine's thoroughly non-essentialist vision of subjectivity as a combination of discursive effect and self-strategy within a context which deconstructs any idea of identity as fixed, unitary,

---

[17] See Tamsin E. Lorraine, *Gender, Identity and the Production of Meaning*.

[18] Schüssler Fiorenza, *But She Said*, 109.

[19] Ibid., 109. Lorraine's analysis does not extend to theological discourses: however, it can be noted that this (typical) representation of 'feminine' and 'masculine' corresponds to a polarity between the Goddess of thealogy and the traditional 'Father God' of Christian theology.

[20] Given this, I find the language of 'feminine' and 'masculine' unhelpful with relation to these abstracted polarities. It merely perpetuates the association of women with the 'feminine' pole and men with the 'masculine' pole. Whilst it may be socio-historically the case that women corresponds more to the 'feminine' and men to the 'masculine', use of such terminology naturalizes the distinction of qualities in terms of biology. Whilst the essentialist/constructivist debate is far from over, this naturalization is premature.

or given. On the other hand, Lorraine continues to situate her account within the logic of gender identity as a category: as we have seen, it is this which Schüssler Fiorenza seeks to move beyond.

Teresa L. Ebert is the second theorist discussed by Schüssler Fiorenza.[21] Ebert's interpretative model was developed through her work on romance literature and is based upon a mapping of ideological relations. To this end, Ebert utilizes Greimas's logical square, which lays out in binary terms the oppositional, contradictory or presumed relations in texts. As an example, Schüssler Fiorenza maps the logical relationship between 'man' and 'woman' such that 'man' and 'feminine', or 'female' and 'masculine' are contradictory, and 'man/masculine' sits in oppositional relationship to 'female/feminine'.[22]

These semiotic squares are a tool for indicating how contradictions and incongruities are repressed or hidden in textual landscapes, but can usefully be applied to historical and political situations when these are understood to be expressive of particular constitutions of the symbolic order. Ebert conceives of the cultural symbolic order as 'the set of discourses aimed at producing and circulating subjectivities in terms of prescriptions and prohibitions . . .'[23]; the symbolic order of patriarchy, then, has the Law-of-the-Father as its primary injunction and the phallus as its primary cultural signifier. To deconstruct gendered subjectivity requires a demystification of the phallic signifier as culturally produced rather than simply as given. The semiotic square can represent the patriarchal symbolic order in such a way that the struggle over signification is brought to the surface and thereby denaturalized.[24] This demonstrates that 'patriarchal ideology is a *misrepresentation* not because it stands in opposition to truth or is a false version of an original "real". Rather it is a misrepresentation insofar as it organizes signifying practices in such a way that the struggle over signification is suppressed.'[25]

Thus, relationships of opposition are identified between 'phallus as natural' (prescribed) and 'phallus as signifying practice' (forbidden); this mirrors the oppositional relationship between 'phallus as given' (implied in the prescription of phallus as natural) and 'phallus as construct' (implied in the positing of phallus as signifying practice). The contingent nature of patriarchal ideology's signifying practices is thus highlighted; since all signifying practices are ideological, patriarchy should hence not be seen as a 'false' representation of the 'real', but rather a falsely naturalizing representation of it. Ebert argues that to resist the patriarchal signifying order, feminist analysis must both uncover the ideological contradictions masked by patriarchal ideologies, and strive to articulate what patriarchal ideologies forbid: that is to say, the ungendered Other.[26]

---

[21] See Teresa L. Ebert, 'The Romance of Patriarchy: Ideology, Subjectivity, and Postmodern Feminist Cultural Theory', *Cultural Critique* 10 (1988).
[22] Schüssler Fiorenza, *But She Said*, 110.
[23] Ibid., 111.
[24] Ebert, 'The Romance of Patriarchy', 30.
[25] Schüssler Fiorenza, *But She Said*, 112.
[26] Ibid., 113.

Schüssler Fiorenza points out that Ebert's analysis collapses patriarchy into phallocentricism, whereby all cultural signifying practices are understood in terms of the privileging of male over female, the Other of phallocentric systems. Hence, Schüssler Fiorenza stresses that Ebert's mapping remains within the sex-gender framework, meaning that 'Third World women as the Others of the Other are doubly invisible in androcentric language structures'.[27] Patriarchal hegemony is most thoroughly destabilized when it is dissected not only in terms of gender, 'but also in terms of race, social status, and civilization'.[28] At the same time, Ebert's analysis generates some useful grist for Schüssler Fiorenza's mill. Whilst Lorraine's theorization of subjectivity yields conceptual tools for an account of self as pluriform, shifting, discursively positioned yet also negotiated, Ebert's account furnishes a more fully elaborated political dimension to subject positioning. The mapping of ideological systems betrays the contradictions and oppositions upon which they depend, both revealing and denaturalizing patriarchal constructions. Thus Schüssler Fiorenza can utilize some of Lorraine's and Ebert's insights and methodologies, whilst seeking to move beyond feminist theorizing in categories of sex/gender.

Schüssler Fiorenza considers this refusal to begin theorizing from within the sex/gender framework as an essential element of articulating a counter-logic to that of patriarchy. Whilst it is true that feminism, like other oppositional discourses, always operates from within a given system, it is incumbent upon feminism to attempt to delineate an alternative space. The sex/gender category is naturalized within patriarchal systems as a given; accepting the patriarchal parameters means that sex/gender can be revalorized, and particular constructions of it can be renegotiated: but it cannot, *as a category*, be recognized as a socio-political construction. This radical move is crucial to Schüssler Fiorenza's methodology. This shifts the site of her discourse from a basis in anthropology to a basis in socio-political formations.

Schüssler Fiorenza's point is not only that to accept patriarchal world-ordering is to replicate it. What Schüssler Fiorenza is uncovering is the ideological contradiction within feminism itself. Socialist and Third World feminists have long insisted upon the necessity of siting feminism within a broader location than simply gender oppression. However, this is not merely to say that the problem with feminism is narrowness of focus, but to point to a failure in feminist theory to recognize that *women oppress women*. It is this which fragments the 'classic' feminist representation of patriarchy as a system in which the male gender is privileged over female. This is not to say that such systemic oppression of women is not a historical and present reality, nor to argue with the contention that women are the oppressed of the oppressed. It is, rather, to deny that analyses organized in gender-dualistic terms do justice to the complexities of the world. Thus feminisms which elevate gender oppression as primary and originary both reproduce the symbolic structure of phallocentricism and fail to take sufficiently seriously oppressions along axes such as class, race or economics by privileging the axis of

---

[27] Ibid., 113.
[28] Ibid., 113.

gender. Furthermore, Schüssler Fiorenza suggests that frequently, feminisms which do wish to take into account such multiple oppressions, do so merely by 'adding them on' without allowing them to change the shape and centre of feminist discourses. But:

> Such an 'adding on' method conceptualizes the patriarchal oppression of women not as an interlocking, multiplicative, and overarching system, but as parallel systems of domination that divide women against each other. To list parallel oppressions, or to speak of a 'dual system oppression' (patriarchy and capitalism), or even of the triple oppression of women in patriarchal societies, obscures the *multiplicative* interstructuring of pyramidal hierarchical structures of ruling which affect women in different social locations differently.[29]

Schüssler Fiorenza's analysis rests on the 'historical interstructuring' of oppressions along lines of race, class, gender and nation,[30] which are not merely multiple but also multiplicative. Oppression has a compound effect. Women of colour have thus laid a challenge for feminism: can it produce a theory and practice which places at its heart these multiplicative oppressions? Can feminism account for the *different* experiences of women? Schüssler Fiorenza's answer to this takes its point of departure in a reconceptualization of patriarchy as pyramidal structure, which is oppositional to the socio-political context of the *ekklesia* as radical democracy. The *ekklesia* is then grounded in socio-political vision and critique rather than in gender identity.

Indeed, by this logic, feminism is just as concerned with the oppression of men as it is of women. Given her desire to deconstruct the sex/gender category, Schüssler Fiorenza's focus on women could appear to constitute a contradiction in her own work. However, here the dialectic between the ideal and actual comes into play. From within a phallocentric socio-symbolic order, there are common threads to the discourses of womanhood and femininity which allow for the identification of women as a collective. Yet, as has already been argued, the collective of women is anything but uniform and to do justices to the experiences of women requires a multipronged analysis based on a variety of interlocking indices of oppression. In this way, as an emancipatory and utopic discourse, feminism incorporates the oppressions of men; however, as a contextual discourse, it begins from the specificity of women's experiences. But it cannot stop at this gender-based specificity, or it fails both to take into account the differences in women's experiences and to present a discourse which is oppositional to rather than reproductive of phallocentric categorization of the world. Thus feminism theorized in this way both deconstructs sex/gender as a framing category, whilst beginning from the experiences of women framed by it.

---

[29] Ibid., 114-5.
[30] Ibid., 115.

Ekklesia as Socio-Political Construct

As indicated above, Schüssler Fiorenza suggests that patriarchy must be understood as a pyramid, rather than in terms of binary opposition. She articulates this in relation to a 'classical' model of patriarchal democracy.[31] From this analysis, her understanding of the democratic nature of the *ekklesia gynaikon* emerges as historical contradiction and as democracy in *different* horizons.

Her articulation of patriarchal Greek democracy privileges civilization and culture over the uncivilized wilderness and uncultured barbarians, public over private and free over unfree. Within this model, the highest tranches consist of free, propertied Greek males as heads of household, rulers and magistrates; and free, male, lower status citizens as citizens and electorate.

Schüssler Fiorenza uses this model to argue that ancient Greek patriarchal democracy is based not just on *patriarchal* rule, as rule of the father, but on *kyriarchal* rule (rule of the master or lord).[32] Aristotle, she insists, 'did not define patriarchy simply as the rule of men over women but as a graded male status system of domination and subordination, authority and obedience, rulers and subjects in household and State'.[33] Although groups such as women, slaves and resident aliens were necessary to the functioning of the *polis*, they were simultaneously excluded from it as participating citizens. What was more, these differential relations and stratifications were conceived by Aristotle as *natural* distinctions. In this way, Schüssler Fiorenza argues, Aristotle justified the differentiation between people (the *demos*) on grounds of gender, ethnicity, legal and economic status. According to Marilyn Arthur, it was in fact the Athenian democracy which first articulated the exclusion of women *as women* from citizenship;[34] as Schüssler Fiorenza puts it, the necessity to make explicit the specific 'natures' of subordinate members of household and state was 'occasioned by the contradiction between the social-political structures of Athenian democracy restricting full citizenship to free propertied male heads of household and the democratic ideal of human dignity and freedom first articulated in the middle-class democracy of the city-state'.[35] Hence, the theoretical vision of democracy stood in

---

[31] Schüssler Fiorenza advances her discussion of classical political philosophies in conversation with: Page du Bois, *Torture and Truth: The New Ancient World* (New York: Routledge, 1991), *Centaurs & Amasons: Women and the Pre-History of the Great Chain of Being* (Ann Arbor: University of Michigan Press, 1982); Cynthia Farrer, *The Origins of Democratic Thinking: The Invention of Politics in Classical Athens* (Cambridge: Cambridge University Press, 1988); Susan Moller Okin, *Women in Western Political Thought* (Princeton: Princeton University Press, 1979); M. E. Hawkesworth, *Beyond Oppression: Feminist Theory and Political Strategy* (New York: Continuum, 1990); E. C. Keuls, *The Reign of the Phallus: Sexual Politics in Ancient Athens* (New York: Harper & Row, 1985); A. Rouselle, *Porneia: On Desire and the Body in Antiquity* (New York: Basil Blackwell, 1988).
[32] Schüssler Fiorenza, *But She Said*, 117.
[33] Schüssler Fiorenza, *The Power of Naming*, 163.
[34] Ibid., 163.
[35] Schüssler Fiorenza, *Discipleship of Equals*, 215.

tension with its patriarchal historical realizations. The consequence of this is that the 'contradiction between the logic of democracy and its tension with historical socio-political patriarchal practices has produced the kyriocentric (master-centered) logic of identity as the assertion of "natural differences" . . .'[36] These supposedly 'natural differences' are structured not only along a gender stratification of male-female, but also male-male and female-female.[37] Schüssler Fiorenza acknowledges the changing and historically contextual nature of patriarchal formations;[38] nevertheless, she considers that the kyriarchal pyramid expressed in ancient Greece is analogous to Roman imperial/colonist forms of patriarchal democracy,[39] to the development of the Christian Church,[40] and also to the constellation of patriarchal democracy which emerged in the modern West and is indebted to its classical predecessors.

Schüssler Fiorenza suggests that the patriarchalization of Christianity occurred towards the end of the first century. It was at this point that the Church began to adapt to Graeco-Roman society and culture, and in so doing, adopted its patriarchal forms. She therefore perceives a key tension between the emancipatory elements of the early Church and its patriarchalizing tendencies. The latter are well expressed in the household codes: Schüssler Fiorenza accepts the view that these represented 'the Aristotelian political ethos of submission and domination', which were thereby codified as Holy Scripture.[41] The Roman imperial context of early Church development likewise influenced Church structures and hierarchies in a manner incompatible with the full understanding of *ekklesia* as inclusive and democratic assembly. The Protestant Reformation modified but did not transform this clerical-patriarchal model of Church.[42]

Recontextualized in the modern age, the key contradictions in patriarchal society are produced by the interaction of capitalism with democracy. Where suffrage movements have led to the extension of voting rights to adults, this has merely made 'the democratic circle co-extensive with the patriarchal pyramid, thereby reinscribing the contradiction between democratic vision and political patriarchal practice'.[43] This contradiction can be discerned in discourses of class, of

---

[36] Schüssler Fiorenza, *But She Said*, 120.

[37] Ibid., 120. Schüssler Fiorenza is drawing on the work of Elizabeth Spelman here: *Inessential Woman*, 19-56.

[38] Schüssler Fiorenza, *The Power of Naming*, 164.

[39] Schüssler Fiorenza, *But She Said*, 118.

[40] Schüssler Fiorenza, *The Power of Naming*, 165-7.

[41] Ibid., 165. See also Schüssler Fiorenza, *But She Said*, 118. It is disputable whether or not neo-Aristotelian political philosophy did indeed legitimate the patriarchal injunctions of the Christian Scriptures. There is little evidence that Aristotle's work was generally known or disseminated in the first century, and rather more to indicate that he had greater influence from the second century. A Stoic context for such injunctions would also have naturalized a social hierarchy, and hence a patriarchal world-order, since Stoic philosophies were based on the idea of divine order in the universe.

[42] Schüssler Fiorenza, *The Power of Naming*, 165-6.

[43] Schüssler Fiorenza, *But She Said*, 121.

the Man of Reason,[44] the White Lady and the noble savage.[45] Thus Schüssler Fiorenza perceives the history of democracy to be one of contradiction. Its potential valence as a society or church embodying full equality has never been realized, for it has always been undercut by structural patriarchal stratifications amongst members or citizen.

The semiotic square for modern Western democracy could thus be drawn such that 'male/elite/propertied' are set in contradictory relationship with 'the Others/Gender, race, class, culture', and the corollary of 'patriarchal democracy/quasi-equality/quasi-self-determination' over against 'radical democracy/*ekklesia* of women/domination fee/self-determination/well-being of all'.[46]

Therefore, it is Schüssler Fiorenza's contention that a liberatory feminist paradigm for biblical interpretation must position itself within 'an oppositional democratic imagination'.[47] This, then, is the *ekklesia*: a feminist rhetorical space, which can be mapped, as in the semiotic square above, in its relationship to patriarchal democracy. The *ekklesia* should not then be seen as utterly dislocated from existing socio-symbolic structures, which one could argue to be impossible: there is no non-ideologically constituted vantage point from which to critique ideologies. It is, however, articulated from within its interstices and by excavation of its forbidden spaces. It resists not only *patriarchal*, but in Schüssler Fiorenza's terms *kyriarchal*, categories, boundaries and socio-symbolism. As radically democratic, it works from a social analytic of multiplicative oppression: not according to gender-dualistic frameworks. Subject-positioning in the *ekklesia* is theorized and contextualized in terms of socio-politics: only this, it is argued, can adequately site a democratic construct which takes into account differences within as well as between the categories of 'women' and 'men'. Hence the *ekklesia* resembles the 'imagined community' of Chandra Talpade Mohanti, who argues that articulating the struggles of the Third World requires:

> political rather than biological or cultural bases for alliance. Thus it is not color or sex which constructs the ground for these struggles. Rather it is the way we think about race, class and gender – the political links we choose to make among and between struggles. Thus, potentially, women of all colors (including white women), can align themselves and participate in these imagined communities.[48]

---

[44] See Genevieve Lloyd, *The Man of Reason: 'Male' and 'Female' in Western Philosophy*; Schüssler Fiorenza, *But She Said*, 122.

[45] See the work of Gayatri Spivak and other post-colonial writers. See also Schüssler Fiorenza, *But She Said*, 122.

[46] Ibid., 124.

[47] Ibid., 124.

[48] Chandra Talpade Mohanti, 'Introduction: Cartographies of Struggle', in Mohanti, Russo, and Torres, eds., *Third World Women and the Politics of Feminism*, 1-47; see Schüssler Fiorenza, *But She Said*, 130 and *Sharing Her Word*, 47.

This is the dissolution of kyriarchal logic of identity as framing context and its replacement by the logic of radical equality.[49] The *ekklesia* is then a rhetorical space, imagined, yet also historical: 'already partially realized but still to be struggled for'.[50] It is a rhetorical democracy located in the struggle against multiplicative oppression, which is hospitable to differences and does not require their reduction to the same. The *ekklesia* is therefore a 'deliberative democracy'; it can 'enact a feminist public space, a space that attempts to keep communication between its various "denominations" (womanist, mujerista, Asian, Africana, lesbian, differently-abled, gender-feminist, liberationist feminist etc.) and its various religious audiences (Jewish, Muslim, Christian, Goddess, atheist, agnostic) "open"'.[51] 'Woman' cannot be essentialized without obliterating significant differences between women, who may have conflicting, even competing, interests and values as well as differing locations in the stratified structures of kyriarchy. At the same time, whilst differences are part of the deliberative community of the *ekklesia*, 'a feminist political discursive practice of liberation must "denaturalize" patriarchal racial, gender, and cultural status inscriptions'.[52] Not to do so would simply reinscribe kyriarchal divisions as a positive pluralism without calling their reified nature fundamentally into question. De-essentialized, the multiple discursive locations of feminists become sites for rhetorical and strategic practices which are responsive to the specific and different experiences of women in global context. The democratic speech-community of the *ekklesia* is polyphonic.

Ekklesia Gynaikon?

We arrive then, at a particular understanding of subjectivity and identity which are theorized in relationship to socio-politics rather than sexual difference and which

---

[49] Since Schüssler Fiorenza perceives the logic of radical equality to be oppositional to that of kyriarchy, she would refute the charge of Adriana Cavarero and Teresa de Lauretis that, if one does not begin from within the horizon of sexual difference, articulation of all other differences 'must remain framed in male dominant and hetero-sexist ideologies of liberal pluralism, conservative humanism, or goddess forbid, religious fundamentalism'. (Teresa de Lauretis, 'The Essence of the Triangle, or Taking the Risk of Essentialism Seriously: Feminist Theory in Italy, the U.S., and Britain', *differences* 1(2) (1989), 32). See later for a consideration of Irigaray's claim that Schüssler Fiorenza's proposals fall into the errors of liberal feminism.

[50] Schüssler Fiorenza, *But She Said*, 130.

[51] Schüssler Fiorenza, *Sharing Her Word*, 134. There is surely a tension here between the *ekklesia* as multi-faith and Schüssler Fiorenza's theological conceptualization of *ekklesia* in both the early and contemporary Church. This issue is addressed in Chapter 8.

[52] Schüssler Fiorenza, *But She Said*, 130. There is a difficulty here analagous to the positing of *ekklesia* as *ekklesia gynaikon*. The latter assumes – and incidentally rhetorically prioritizes – the category 'woman'; similarly womanist, *mujerista*, lesbian voices etc speak from locations marked out by kyriarchy, which is why they are part of the *ekklesia*, as struggle against kyriarchy, in the first place. This is the conflict between oppositional identity formation and de-essentialing, de-kyriarchalizing rhetoric. See Chapter 8.

posits an individual as positioned 'across multiple social coordinates of race, class, gender, sexuality, and ethnicity among others'.[53] And yet there seems to be here, if not a contradiction, at the very least an aporia in Schüssler Fiorenza's theoretical vision. For it seems to make little sense to argue, vigorously and consistently, that there is a need to move beyond the sex/gender framework – and then place at the very centre of one's hermeneutical reflections a phrase clearly indebted to the sex/gender framework: *ekklesia gynaikon*. Women-church. What is more, Schüssler Fiorenza's project is undoubtedly feminist to its core: how does one remove *feminism* from a sex/gender framework? And, in this radical democratic space, where do men fit in?

This aporia could be unravelled in three ways. It could be unpicked to reveal that there is in fact here simply an incoherence – a point where Schüssler Fiorenza's edifice does not hold together. If this is the case, it is a point which seriously damages, if not demolishes, her wider theories. Feminism, the *ekklesia gynaikon* and a framework *not* based upon sex/gender identity are, all three, crucial planks in the meta-structure of Schüssler Fiorenza's work. If they are incompatible elements, can the centre hold? It seems unlikely. A second possibility is that closer examination will reveal the contradiction to be spurious, and that fuller understanding or more nuanced inflection will show a more complex interlocking system to be at stake here, justifying her own rhetoric. A third might be that, whilst Schüssler Fiorenza herself does not satisfactorily resolve the problem, there could still actually be a resolution after all.

Let us turn, therefore, to Schüssler Fiorenza's texts. First of all: does the *ekklesia gynaikon* include men? This should be the simplest question to answer. However, it is complicated by the span of time over which Schüssler Fiorenza has been writing. There is continuity between her earlier works and her later ones, but as one would expect, the concepts and ideas have been subjected to a process of refinement and clarification. In her early work (1982) there is a definite strong implication that the *ekklesia* of women is just that: a movement for women, not including men. For example, she asserts that a Christian feminist spirituality 'calls us to gather together the *ekklesia* of women who in the angry power of the Spirit are sent forth to feed, heal, and liberate their people who are women'.[54] Indeed, Schüssler Fiorenza's own spirituality at this point is summed up by the 'image and vision of the people of God, of my people, who are women . . .'.[55] To the charge that the *ekklesia* does not share in the fullness of Church, because it is a church of women, she responds:

> That is correct, but neither do exclusive male hierarchical assemblies . . . In the past centuries, however, women founders and leaders of their people have arisen again and again who sought to gather communities free from clerical and monastic control. A Christian feminist spirituality claims these communities of women and their history as our heritage and history and seeks to transform them into the *ekklesia* of

---

[53] Schüssler Fiorenza, *Jesus – Miriam's Child, Sophia's Prophet*, 13, citing Hennesey, 32.

[54] Schüssler Fiorenza, *Discipleship of Equals*, 199; *In Memory of Her*, 346.

[55] Schüssler Fiorenza, *In Memory of Her*, 343.

women by claiming our own spiritual powers and gifts, by deciding our own welfare, by standing accountable for our decisions...[56]

Similarly, accused of reverse sexism, she stresses the incomparability of male exclusiveness and female exclusiveness by pointing to the power disparities. She asks why churchmen cannot understand women's need to gather together for the sake of survival both as Christians and as women. She explains that the *ekklesia* gathers as women, not over against men, but *in order* to become *ekklesia* before God, in a space not subject to male religious and spiritual control. Mutuality could only be possible if *men* relinquished their positions of authority over women and Church; women need to resist their spiritual colonization by men, reclaim their own spiritual powers, and 'exorcise their possession by male idolatry'.[57]

These are however pragmatic arguments. The 'fullness' of the *ekklesia*, she acknowledges to be a world of co-humanity, of men as well as women: but, for this vision to be realized, it is necessary for personal and structural sexism to be both overturned and repented. In her 1984 work, she explicitly states that women-church is 'the movement of self-identified women and women-identified men in biblical religion'.[58] As such, she is arguing that women-church is not after all exclusionary, but 'political-oppositional'.[59] The church of women is a manifestation of the universal Church; but one which traverses denominational boundaries and which aims to provide a feminist rather than patriarchal space. By 1994 she could not be clearer: 'I do not speak of a women's church that excludes men',[60] and in 1998, we find, the *ekklesia* 'must not... be limited to wo/men'.[61] Her development of the neologisms 'kyriarchy' and 'wo/men' contribute to this clarification. The former, as we have already seen, overturns a gender-dualistic model of oppression for one which is multiplicative and therefore includes men as oppressed and not only as oppressors. 'Wo/men' destabilizes the category 'women': in speaking of wo/men, Schüssler Fiorenza means 'not only to include *all women* but also to speak of oppressed and marginalized men. "Wo/men" must therefore be understood as an inclusive expression rather than as an exclusive universalized gender term.'[62]

Therefore, it seems conclusively the case that Schüssler Fiorenza's notion of *ekklesia gynaikon* is not exclusive of men, but uses the designator '*gynaikon*' to emphasize that it is a counter-space to kyriarchy. It underlines wo/men's visibility, participation, leadership, and autonomy over against kyriocentric theologies and structures. It brings to the fore that 'cultural "common-sense" patriarchal religion and malestream democracy have been exclusive of women, be they human or divine'.[63] The fractured spelling of wo/men, indeed, is deeply significant to this set

---

[56] Ibid., 346.
[57] Ibid., 347.
[58] Schüssler Fiorenza, *Bread Not Stone*, 7.
[59] Ibid., xiv.
[60] Schüssler Fiorenza, *Jesus – Miriam's Child, Sophia's Prophet*, 27.
[61] Schüssler Fiorenza, *Sharing Her Word*, 70.
[62] Schüssler Fiorenza, *Jesus – Miriam's Child, Sophia's Prophet*, 191, n. 1.
[63] Ibid., 27.

of debates. Schüssler Fiorenza actually intends it to highlight that she does not speak of women in essentialist or unitary terms, nor in terms naturalized by kyriarchy, ie, in terms within the sex/gender framework. At the same time, she asserts that it allows her to retain 'women' as a political category.[64] This then is the 'double-footedness' permitting one both to speak of wo/men and not to speak of women: the former being understood as a socio-political category and the latter as a naturalized or essentialist category.

Schüssler Fiorenza is self-reflective in her later work upon her continued usage of 'wo/men' and 'feminism', despite her problematization of sex/gender logics of identity.[65] It is once more her materialist commitment which prompts her to retain the category 'wo/men', lest women be utterly erased within feminist discourses, and again, she is indebted to Rosemary Hennessey for the shape of her argument. Hennessey rejects both French postmodern feminism (too apolitical, providing no resources for transformative social action) and North American feminist standpoint theory (too atheoretical, inadequate in its construction of subjectivity and language). Hennessey works from an epistemological base such that the object of knowledge is always the real as discursively produced. So reality is socially determined; it is ideological; but ideology is a material force, like the economic, like the political. Subjectivity, then, is interpellated:[66] but that does not make it 'immaterial', in either sense of the word. The signifiers 'woman', 'women', 'female', 'feminine', may be functions within discourse and effects thereof. But the discursive is included 'within the materiality out of which the social is produced'.[67] As such, the category 'wo/men' requires complexification as multiply scored and constituted, but can nevertheless be related to specific material configurations. What this means is that 'wo/men' and 'feminist' are not grounded in essentialist or naturalized projections of what a woman is, but can be recognized as ideological-rhetorical formations which are not, however, divorced from the material conditions of existence.

To return, then, to my opening questions: has Schüssler Fiorenza adequately accounted for the centre-stage which she, purportedly working outside the sex-gender framework, gives to the *ekklesia gynaikon* – with respect to her later work, rendered better (and more coherently) as the *ekklesia* of wo/men? I would argue that, largely, she has, primarily effected by the conscious destabilization of the category 'women' and its relocation in socio-political terms. Ironically, given the starting point for this discussion, the criticism which emerges is not that she

---

[64] See ibid., 191, n.1; *Sharing Her Word*, 186, n. 5.
[65] See also Tania Modleski, *Feminism Without Women: Culture and Criticism in a 'Postfeminist' Age* (New York: Routledge, 1991); Denise Riley, *'Am I That Name?': Feminism and the Category of Women in History* (Minneapolis: University of Minnesota Press, 1988); Judith Butler, *Gender Trouble: Feminism and the Subversion of Identity* (New York: Routledge, 1990).
[66] Hennessey uses Althusser's work on ideology and interpellation, whilst criticizing the latter as too inhospitable to agency. She is also indebted to Gramsci. Her analysis is thus a creative meeting of postmodernism, standpoint epistemology, Marxist thought and feminism.
[67] Hennessey, *Materialist Feminism and the Politics of Discourse*, 33-6.

remains enmeshed within a sex/gender framework. What I wish to argue is quite the opposite: that she pays too little attention to the theorization of sexual difference within the logic of radical democracy.

Schüssler Fiorenza has reprised with some cogency the reasons why it is necessary to leave behind the sex/gender framework for feminist analysis. It works on the logic of identity. It reproduces phallocentric world-ordering. It cannot adequately incorporate multiplicative oppression and it fails to take account of the multiple mapping of subjectivity. Given the non-identical nature of identity, moving to a logic of equality rather than identity makes perfect sense for a worldview taking its point of departure in emancipatory commitment. At the same time, a materialist feminism is committed to taking account of the concrete conditions of existence. So-called discursive realism, which Schüssler Fiorenza appears to accept, does not sunder the link between discourse and the material, but merely asserts that the latter is always discursively constructed. If subjectivity is pluriform and multiply mapped, and identity-logic is rejected, sexual difference ceases to be a primary, originary or unitary factor in the constitution of subjectivity. But it does not thereby disappear altogether, at least in current conditions of human existence. If theorizing and theologizing are not trans-contextual but rooted in specific historical and contextual situations, sexual difference cannot be discounted. To posit sexual difference *only* as a socio-political category neglects its connection to materiality: to bodiliness. The body is not a blank page of originary difference (sex) upon which discourse is inscripted (gender): but the body is itself inscribed within discourses of it. As such femaleness, or maleness, is *neither* simply a socio-political category *nor* simply a biological one.

Irigaray has criticized Schüssler Fiorenza on related grounds. In a review of *In Memory of Her*, with respect to the discipleship of equals, Irigaray asks: equal to whom? She argues that the *ekklesia* is merely an expression of liberal feminism. A feminist theology seeking the liberation of women should be striving for an equal share in the divine, nor just in status and rights. Irigaray wants to rewrite subjectivity such that space opens up for two sexes, rather than 'women' being written within a phallogocentric system. That does not allow for a feminine subjectivity; 'women', in their own right, cannot exist. To destabilize the singularity of male-centred subjectivity requires women to create their own speech; this, in turn, requires that women locate a transcendental horizon of their own in which women can 'become'. Thus, sexual liberation is God made a couple: 'not simply God made man'. But Schüssler Fiorenza, in Irigaray's opinion, 'describes what already exists without inventing a new subjectivity'.[68] What Schüssler Fiorenza provides is not what Irigaray is looking for in woman-centred theology: 'Sociology quickly bores me when I'm expecting the divine.'[69] Christianity reproduces phallogocentric structures of identity, which is not adequate for women: 'It does not furnish them certain needed representations of themselves, of

---

[68] Irigaray, 'Equal to Whom?', 74.
[69] Ibid., 74.

their genealogy, and of their relation to the universe or to others.'[70] Women need, not only equal rights, but rights to subjectivity and a divine identity. 'Can a claim to equality be acceptable without a fundamental respect for the subjective rights of both sexes, including the right to a divine identity?'[71]

Whilst Irigaray herself can be criticized for paying insufficient attention to the importance of socio-political equality, her argument is significant. She considers that Schüssler Fiorenza merely reproduces the phallogocentric economy by neutralizing sexuateness. This, surely, is actually the product of Schüssler Fiorenza's desire not to reproduce the kyriarchal logic of gender identity in favour of a logic of democracy. On this reading, Schüssler Fiorenza's quest to work outside the sex/gender parameters fails as a feminist undertaking, for precisely the reason that she herself thinks it succeeds. Does leaving aside the sex/gender category merely reproduce the patriarchal logic of the same, as would appear to be the import of Irigaray's critique? Or does it, in fact, radically disrupt it and set forth a framework according to a different logic than that of identity?

My argument is twofold. Firstly, I would contend that Schüssler Fiorenza has indeed successfully dismantled kyriarchal identity-logic as the framework for her work. I do not think Schüssler Fiorenza can fairly be accused of reproducing phallogocentric gender-identity and of secretly wishing, as Irigaray suggests, to become man. Her analysis is too sustainedly deconstructive of cultural gender identity constructions for that criticism to hold. But secondly, what I would argue is that she has failed to reconfigure sexual difference *outside* of that logic. Rather, she simply ignores it. This criticism is not the same as Irigaray's. Schüssler Fiorenza has dismantled kyriarchal constructions of sex/gender. This is not, as Irigaray claims, a neutralization of sex/gender, because androgyny works on an *assumption* of masculine/feminine identities which Schüssler Fiorenza rejects. Rather, what I am suggesting runs as follows: once Schüssler Fiorenza has deconstructed the kyriarchal sex-gender framework, she does not wish to reproduce it by establishing another logic of gender identity. Therefore, she suspends sex/gender as a category *at all* except in ways framed by socio-politics. Hence, she is pushed into the position where the only way to retain the category 'wo/men' is to insist that it is a political category. All too well aware of the ways in which the 'real' is rhetorically constituted, she focuses on this to the exclusion of a consideration of how the 'real' (which includes sexual differentiation) is inscribed *within* ideology and discourse. How, then, might sexual difference be framed within a logic of radical equality? That is my task in Chapter 8.

Ekklesia as Church

Schüssler Fiorenza points out that the English word 'Church' is etymologically derived from the Greek *kyriache* (belonging to the lord/master/father). The affinities of this semantic genealogy with her analysis of Church and society as

---

[70] Ibid., 74-5.
[71] Ibid., 74-5, 73.

kyriarchal are obvious. However, just as the kyriarchal democracy embodies a fatal contradiction, so too does Church as *kyriache*. For another cultural tributary feeding into the English 'Church' is the Greek *ekklesia*. This is translated by 'Church' in English versions of the Christian Testament. In terms of Schüssler Fiorenza's analytical framework, it is something of an irony that 'Church' holds together both concepts, that of *kyriache* and that of *ekklesia*. This is precisely the tension which Schüssler Fiorenza identifies in Christianity from its early formations, since she holds there to have been an egalitarian current running counter to the prevailing kyriarchal stream. *Ekklesia* as a term also holds together a dual focus, since it has also the meaning of 'democratic assembly' as well as 'Church'.

The *ekklesia* is, then, a civic as well as religious concept: 'It is not a local or static term, it is not even a religious expression; it means the *actual* gathering of people, the assembly of free citizens in a town, called together in order to decide matters affecting their own welfare.'[72] This may well be one of the reasons why Schüssler Fiorenza in her later work often uses the term *ekklesia*, or *ekklesia gynaikon*, in preference to its most common translation 'women-church': she comments that people who think the latter expression too 'churchy' or 'confessional' simply (and understandably) miss the political significance of the Greek expression.[73] However, Schüssler Fiorenza's deployment of *ekklesia* is undoubtedly (at least) double-pronged. And whilst its public-political dimension is held open on the one hand, she does also and explicitly mean to speak of *ekklesia* as Church, as 'the people of God'. Specifically, 'we have begun to gather as the *ekklesia* of women, as the people of God, to claim our own religious powers, to participate fully in the decision-making process of church, and to nurture each other as women Christians. . . .'.[74] There is then a distinctly Christian context to Schüssler Fiorenza's vision of *ekklesia*. It is somewhat unclear how this relates to the multifaith and secular articulation of *ekklesia* as radical democracy. Schüssler Fiorenza has noted that she selected the term *ekklesia* over and above *synagoge* – which might also have signified a deliberative congress – out of respect for Jewish peoples. Yet the term *ekklesia* surely remains Christocentric in the history of Western reception, even leaving aside the specifically Christian theological and

---

[72] Schüssler Fiorenza, *In Memory of Her*, 344.

[73] Schüssler Fiorenza, *But She Said*, 128. This is, again, something which receives increasing emphasis in Schüssler Fiorenza's later work. Whilst the political dimension of 'women-church' was certainly acknowledged from the outset, she seems to have concluded that 'women-church' as confessional both undermined and limited it. Hence, a distinction emerges between *ekklesia* as 'wo/men-church' and *ekklesia* as radical democracy: 'The concept of *ekklesia* of wo/men – which is best translated as 'congress' of wo/men and not as 'church' – must not, however, be reduced to 'wo/men-church' or be limited to wo/men. Rather, with this neologism I attempt to articulate a radical democratic vision as the basis and goal of feminist emancipatory struggles that seek to radically change kyriarchal society and church' (*Sharing Her Word*, 70).

[74] Schüssler Fiorenza, *In Memory of Her*, 344.

ecclesiological context of Schüssler Fiorenza's discussion of it.[75] This then requires examination in light of Schüssler Fiorenza's insistence that feminist theology is 'an *ekklesia* of ecumenical, interreligious, multicultural, and global voices'.[76]

There are three responses to this dual mapping of *ekklesia* within Christianity and exceeding it. The first is not only to acknowledge but actually to intend an explicit contextualization within the Christian paradigm as the 'proper' base for talking about the world. This would be representative of a position which affirms the truth of Christianity, which is therefore the only appropriate ground and context for deliberation – but which nevertheless values tolerance and dialogue and therefore wishes to include 'other voices' within the public-political speech-community. Schüssler Fiorenza's theoretical outlook clearly excludes this possible understanding of the relationship between *ekklesia* as a Christian expression and *ekklesia* as radical democracy in public-political key. She is clear that she speaks as a Christian theologian, but her understanding of authority[77] and rejection of positivist epistemologies would leave her position simply incoherent if she then asserted Christian truth-claims as foundational givens.

A second response would be to perceive the doubled nature of *ekklesia* as deeply problematic. Since the speech-community of the *ekklesia* incorporates wo/men speaking from differing discursive locations, not only along axes of socio-political status, race etc., but also from different cultural-religious 'home-bases', an appropriate response might be to change the terminology for the wider democratic community. *Ekklesia* as radically democratic movement within Christianity would then be a moment within a differently named broader movement incorporating a diverse spread of such 'localized' movements. Indeed, it is arguable that *ekklesia* as an outgrowth of Christianity is terminology which excludes dissenting churches such as the Brethren. Therefore each community would self-name its equivalent to *ekklesia* as emancipatory locus and form part of a broader community named in a fashion which did not reassert the dominance of any prevailing cultural-religious grouping. Schüssler Fiorenza obviously does not wish to espouse this option. As she does not discuss the relationship between *ekklesia* as a term and its incorporation of diverse cultural and religious perspectives, it is not clear why this should be the case. Possible arguments against this strategy would be, that since all our speaking emanates from specific socio-cultural and ideologically constituted locations, no neutrality of speech is possible. The speaking subject does not enjoy the 'view from nowhere'; nor is speech itself outside of cultural webs of signification. Language is invested with cultural-political significance. We cannot,

---

[75] As an ancient Greek term, *ekklesia* does not of course have Christian connotations. It is furthermore used in Greek translations of the Hebrew Bible, and could therefore be contextualized also within the Jewish tradition. However, historically, its etymological children foster the association with Christian-derived models of Church. Whilst one might speak of the Mormon Church, for example, the dominance of the Christian paradigm makes it more generally likely that the ecclesiastical and ecclesiological will be interpreted within Christian context.

[76] Schüssler Fiorenza, *The Power of Naming*, xv.

[77] See the discussion on the canon and 'women's experience' as criteria for 'truth' in this chapter and Chapter 8 respectively.

therefore, escape into an arena of communication completely transcending specificity. Therefore, any terminology employed to designate the radically democratic *ekklesia* would be 'loaded', in multivalent and dynamic manner. Here the criticism could be extended to take into account the Wittgensteinian recognition that different communities work with different language-games or what MacIntyre names as traditioned rationality. Given this, those explicitly doing Christian theology might argue that it is appropriate to employ symbols and language which relate to that particular traditioned rationality and that particular language-game. The universe is not Christian-based but their particular articulation of it is. Those doing Christian feminist theology might choose to use language which reflects and projects their own perspectives – such as *ekklesia*, as a Christian feminist rendering and reclamation of a term with a particular import in Christian history and theology.

A third response would, then, build on the recognition that rationality is traditioned and that communities play different language-games. This would acknowledge the tension between a Christian-based *ekklesia* and a global multi-cultural and multifaith *ekklesia*, whilst still choosing to retain the continuity of terms as an appropriate expression of the speaking subject's own self-positioned discursive location. It could of course still be argued that where a concept is explicitly multicultural and multifaith, a term with heavy investment in the Christian world is not only inappropriate but is in fact Christian colonialism. The only compromise here for those who take that criticism seriously is, beginning from an argument that rationality is traditioned, to put forward that *from a Christian perspective* it is appropriate to employ such terms and concepts rather than supposedly more neutral ones. However, since this is posited as a traditioned rather than universal rationality, there is no claim to monopolize the naming of movements and ideas which extend beyond the Christian parish. As such, the naming of *ekklesia* as *ekklesia* would have to be comprehended as an act within Christian theological discourse but which other discourses may choose to name differently. An objection to this as a strategy would be its fragmentation of the emancipatory democracy as a socio-political collective, albeit one which operates on an ethic of disagreement and differences. Schüssler Fiorenza, for example, remains committed to the use of the term 'feminist', precisely to avoid fragmentation and point out intersecting interests, despite her obvious affirmation of womanist, Asian and *mujerista* theologies. This may however act as a paradigm for how *ekklesia* can continue to be employed in global context. That tension between its purported naming of a trans-Christian trans-Western community and its specificity as product of Western Christianity must be highlighted, critiqued and displaced, whilst yet continuing to fulfill a meaningful function – just in the same way that the term *feminist* has been.[78]

Within the Christian context, the question emerges: how does the *ekklesia gynaikon* relate to the Christian Church as a whole? – or, more properly, to its

---

[78] It may be noted however that in my own exposition of the *ekklesia* in Chapter 8, I reject this solution and prefer the second option. At the end of the day, I do find the continuity in vocabulary to be an unnecessary act of Christian colonization.

particular institutional formations? It is after all presented as a communal phenomenon with, crucially, decision-making powers. As such it might be seen as an alternative to the existing churches rather than in relation to them. The *ekklesia* represents, for Schüssler Fiorenza, a dissolution of dualities which simply extend the kyriarchal logic of identity: in particular, with respect to the relationship between *ekklesia* and institutional Church, she understands the *ekklesia* to overcome the oft-postulated opposition between church as home and exodus-community as home.[79] This is the dichotomy between those who affirm the Church as 'household of God' and continue to find it a meaningful centre for their lives despite its androcentricity and patriarchalism, and those who either leave biblical religion for 'new' spiritualities such as Goddess feminism or constitute feminist base communities dialectically related to the patriarchal Church.[80] Schüssler Fiorenza observes that, frequently, 'women-church' does in fact represent an exodus-community, aiming to inhabit a new liberated counter-space to patriarchal religion. This may be the 'promised land' of a 'non-patriarchal' Christianity, or it may represent a feminist spirituality which is located outside of traditional religions altogether. The rise in Goddess spirituality over the last two decades witnesses to this. Contrariwise, Schüssler Fiorenza is sceptical of the possibility for truly creating a feminist 'home' outside of patriarchy, for whilst women live within it, 'feminist discourses cannot escape complicity in the patriarchal ideologies, structures, and power relationships from within which they speak'.[81] This, she concludes, is why the communities of 'women-church', believing it to be a liberated feminist space, often do not deal well with their internal divisions and conflicts. It is also why it tends to attract only women of similar experiences. Women-church can, thus, remain embedded within the logic of identity, simply providing an alternative centre for liturgy and spirituality.[82]

Schüssler Fiorenza, therefore, developed the concept of *ekklesia gynaikon* in a deliberate attempt to overcome the dualizing either/or represented by the two poles of 'church as home' or 'exodus community as home'.[83] As such Schüssler

---

[79] See, for example, Daphne Hampson.

[80] This is Rosemary Radford Ruether's conception of women-church, which has important differences from that held by Schüssler Fiorenza. See, for example, Ruether, *Women-Church: Theology and Practice*. Ruether uses the language of exodus but does not thereby mean an ideological separation and a complete break from the broader Christian Church: 'Women-Church means neither leaving the church as a sectarian group, nor continuing to fit into it on its terms' (62). She uses the idea of basic Christian communities as 'the ecclesial expression of liberation theology' (25); her feminist reworking of this construes feminist base communities as dialectically related to the patriarchal Church.

[81] Schüssler Fiorenza, *But She Said*, 127.

[82] Ibid., 127. Schüssler Fiorenza's somewhat acerbic comment is that '*women-church* is often conceived in terms of *exodus-base* communities or alternative feminist spirituality groups which tend to replicate the function of the hegemonic church as liturgical and spiritual 'service' station' (*But She Said*, 127-8).

[83] Daphne Hampson clearly misunderstands this when she states: 'many women have wished to form a semi-separatist movement within the greater body of the church, commonly known as 'womanchurch'. Such women understand themselves as being part

Fiorenza's conception of *ekklesia* needs clearly differentiating from other feminist models of women-church which are often either constituted as exodus-communities or simply represent 'cells' within the existing Church. The *ekklesia gynaikon* is intended to provide for the gathering of different feminist groups in a framework which both resists homogenization and false universalization and also refuses to be fragmented along patriarchal fault-lines. The term *ekklesia gynaikon* indicates that women are Church, and have always been Church.[84] It goes beyond this, however: it is in many respects ill-translated as 'women-church', since – as we have seen – it is intended to carry with it the public-political connotations of the Greek word *ekklesia* as democratic assembly. Thus the *ekklesia* holds together both a politic, democratic ideal and the notion of Church. Therefore, its qualifier *gynaikon* brings to the attention the failure of Church (and society) to include women.

Nor, as Church, is the *ekklesia* intended only to overcome the home-exodus dualism. Schüssler Fiorenza wants also to overcome:

> the structural-patriarchal dualisms between Jewish and Christian women, laywomen and nun-women, homemakers and career women, between active and contemplative, between Protestant and Roman Catholic women, between married and single women, between physical and spiritual mothers, between heterosexual and lesbian women, between the church and the world, the sacral and the secular.[85]

To accomplish this, the *ekklesia* must live out an ethic of solidarity, in 'a catholic sisterhood that transcends all patriarchal ecclesiastical divisions'. This is feminist biblical spirituality 'incarnated' into a liberatory movement, through emancipatory struggles in the world and through grassroots organizations. Such praxis is distinctive from but not separated from comparable struggles by secular feminists and those outside the Christian church.[86]

It would appear then that the *ekklesia gynaikon* is not co-extensive with the 'patriarchal' Church, nor co-opted into it, but inhabits a site both umbilically and critically related to it. Schüssler Fiorenza advocates a relationship of wo/men to the academic world as one of resident aliens. I suggest that this can usefully be

---

of a long line of women, stretching from the past to the present and into the future. Elisabeth Schüssler Fiorenza . . . is particularly associated with this line of thought' (*After Christianity*, 70). Quite aside from the misapprehension that Schüssler Fiorenza's notion of *ekklesia* is 'semi-separatist', Hampson's use of the term 'womanchurch' is deeply antithetical to Schüssler Fiorenza's position. Neither she nor Ruether would consider 'womanchurch' and 'women-church' to be identical terms, considering the former to be essentializing.

[84] Schüssler Fiorenza, *But She Said*, 127.
[85] Schüssler Fiorenza, *In Memory of Her*, 349.
[86] Ibid., 349. At this point Schüssler Fiorenza does not seem to be including non-Christian feminists within the *ekklesia*. This may represent a 'slippage' in usage because of the term's dual meanings, or it may be that at this stage she has not fully worked out the idea of *ekklesia* as rhetorical democratic speech-community drawing from a diverse range of those resisting multiplicative oppressions.

extended to express the relationship of the *ekklesia* to patriarchal institutions generally – be it the Church, academy, or society at large. This captures the bifurcatory experience of the *ekklesia* as insider/outsider without dualistically relegating it to one pole or the other. The next section considers this concept as a model for the structural location of the *ekklesia*.

Ekklesia: Resident Alien

Schüssler Fiorenza tells a story. The Greek goddess Athena sprang fully grown and armoured from the head of her father, Zeus. She seemed then to be motherless. Yet, in fact, this was not the case. Afraid that his child would surpass him, Zeus changed Metis, the pregnant mother of Athena, into a fly. He then swallowed her, that he might always benefit from her wisdom. This is how Schüssler Fiorenza exemplifies the so-called Athena complex, by which young wo/men scholars must prove themselves to be the daughters of their 'fathers', whilst ignorant or dismissive of their 'mothers'.[87] Thus women are assimilated into the kyriarchal family of the academy: they become sons, blessed by the 'godfathers', and may therefore inherit.

According to Schüssler Fiorenza, wo/men must, then, become resident aliens. They are becoming speaking subjects within the disciplinary discourses of academy and Church: they speak *from* those locations, which wo/men are claiming as their right. At the same time, wo/men need to occupy a position of resistance to dominant kyriarchal paradigms. As such, the concept of 'resident alien' keeps open the possibility of speaking *differently*, from the 'outside', whilst yet being simultaneously an 'insider'. The 'alien' site from which wo/men should seek to speak is of course that of the *ekklesia*, that rhetorical space for imagining radical democracy. Whilst Schüssler Fiorenza employs this analysis with respect to theological education, it would also seem suitable to operate as a model for the relationship of *ekklesia* to the institutional Church. Wo/men may take up or retain residence in scholarship, ministry, institutional Church: but those of us who do so 'must not forget that we are strangers in a land whose language, constitution, history, religion, and culture we did not create'.[88]

The risks of adopting this model are twofold. One is choosing complicity as a strategy of survival, thus becoming a collaborator, with consequent co-optation of wo/men's energies to precisely what was critiqued in the first place. This is the process of assimilation. The second danger is marginalization, a danger embodied in the very phraseology of 'resident alien'. What is alien requires spitting out of the system. It must be ejected, a foreign body, incompatible and hostile. Furthermore, the actual self-naming as resident alien may in itself perpetuate alienation. How to

---

[87] Schüssler Fiorenza, *Sharing Her Word*, 14.
[88] Schüssler Fiorenza, *But She Said*, 185. This does, of course, stand in some tension with Schüssler Fiorenza's project to reclaim history, religion and culture as the heritage of wo/men, in which wo/men were not only silent 'outsiders' but active agents within kyriarchy and struggling against it. In fact, the resident alien model could accommodate this duality by pointing to simultaneous experiences of congruence and dissonance.

articulate speaking from the margins without reinscribing that very marginalization? However, that the *ekklesia* should be figured as 'indigestible' within kyriarchy is positive. It maintains its integrity as an oppositional and resistant rhetorical space. The difficulty is conceptualizing *ekklesia* such that it will not – as alien other – be permanently spat out and therefore fail to exercise any transformative influence. My own proposal, from within the discourse of Christianity, is that the *ekklesia* requires framing within eschatological parameters, and that this is a way of rethinking the model of 'resident alien'. Eschatologically rewrought, *ekklesia* can be thought of as inassimmilable and unrealized, yet also present. This discussion must, though, await a later point, when the various threads to the eschatological hermeneutic I suggest can be woven together.

Ekklesia and Theological Authority

The importance of a socio-political framework to Schüssler Fiorenza's work has been stressed throughout. Since, however, she is expressly engaged in Christian theology, the question inevitably arises: what are the theological horizons in which she works? The theological motif which appears clearly to dominate is that of the Wisdom tradition. Indeed, one could argue that, where Schüssler Fiorenza is concerned, it is more appropriate to speak of a *sophialogy* rather than a *theology* as such. This becomes especially apparent in her later works, although the seeds of such an emphasis and focus are certainly present in her earlier writings. However, this aspect of her work receives its fullest elaboration in *Jesus: Miriam's Child, Sophia's Prophet* and *Sharing Her Word*. Sophialogy, then, I take to be the 'primary key' to Schüssler Fiorenza's theological context. The most pressing questions which arise with relation to the interaction between her biblical hermeneutics and her theology circulate around the question of authority. I shall, then, focus this discussion in two main directions: Schüssler Fiorenza's understanding of canon and biblical authority, and her christology and the normativity (or otherwise) of Jesus. Interwoven into both of these is a consideration of the *ekklesia* as locus of theological authority.

The Biblical Canon and Biblical Authority

What authority does the Bible have for the Church – or perhaps, one should ask, for the *ekklesia*? The problematization of biblical authority is hardly a feminist invention. The crisis of the so-called 'Scripture Principle' has prompted diverse attempts to consider how and in what ways the Bible can be simultaneously a collection of historical-theological writings, evidently products of particular cultural locations, not always embodying either the 'truth' (historically) or the 'good' (ethically) – and yet still be deemed the normative texts of the Christian faith. What does it mean to assert that the Bible is the Word of God? The most extreme expression of this emanates from so-called literalists who insist upon biblical inerrancy. Other theological proposals perceive a more nuanced relationship between text and revelation, yet there remains a desire to articulate some understanding of it which is still rooted in a paradigm of authority.[89] The various theological inflections of this are yet further outworkings of the logic of identity, which is driven to distill from the Bible some kind of unitary and essential truth.

Schüssler Fiorenza rejects this entire project. She stresses the process of canonization as itself a political and kyriarchal affair. 'Recognizing these harmful effects of the early Christian struggles over canonization as a means to the kyriarchal co-optation of the *ekklesia*, feminist biblical scholarship cannot remain within the limits drawn by the established canon.' To the contrary, feminist analysis must transgress such boundaries in the service of a 'different theological self-understanding and historical imagination'.[90] This is not, though, with the intention of establishing a new canon more favourable to feminists: Schüssler Fiorenza critiques the concept of canon *as such*. If the canon is imaged as an enclosed garden, then it is surrounded by a wall: erected by the 'fathers', and relegating the historical-religious world of supposedly heretical women to the outside. A 'canon' sets boundary zones according to criteria which are not timeless and everlastingly true, but relate to specific historical-theological circumstances.

Schüssler Fiorenza ponders what image might positively express the function of Scripture within the *ekklesia*. It is a scriptural image she chooses. 'It is the open, cosmic house of divine Wisdom. Her dwelling of cosmic dimensions has no walls; she permeates the whole world.'[91] Therefore, it can be argued that Schüssler Fiorenza collapses the house of authority as traditionally understood, in favour of the wide-open house of scripture. This house, then, is not fixed or closed. It is a house which is utterly permeable. Its 'authority' is that of its Latin roots, *augere/auctoritas*: nurturing creativity, fostering growth and freedom. This image may seem to dissolve 'scripture' entirely. However, I would argue that this is not so when read in context of Schüssler Fiorenza's other writings, where she identifies the Bible as 'root-model' and prototype for the Christian faith. It is my sense that the image is highlighting the openness of the text, and stripping away its exclusionary boundaries. That need not equate to displacing it from its role as root-model, merely refusing to accept it at as the one and only model, which must always be privileged over non-canonical writings. I make this judgement on the basis of her continuing self-identification within the Christian tradition and her own continuing focus on the Bible. Elsewhere, she discusses the significance of extra-canonical texts in throwing light on biblical roots. Therefore, the refusal to accept canonical limits to historical-theological reflection is an aspect of her own refocusing from biblical text to the feminist theological reconstruction of Christian origins.

---

[89] This can take the form of displacing authority from the biblical texts to history, whether the biblical '*heilgeschichte*' or the 'ministry of Jesus'; of stressing the *kerygma*; discerning criteria for evaluating the biblical texts, such as a 'canon within the canon' approach or identifying as authoritative scriptural principles (such as 'prophetic principles' of liberation).

[90] Schüssler Fiorenza, *Searching the Scriptures*, vol 2, 8.

[91] Ibid., 11.

Her 'classic' statement of biblical 'authority' is, indeed, in the distinction she draws between Bible as 'structuring prototype' and Bible as 'mythical archetype'. The former is non-absolute, open to transformation, and refutes a conception of scripture as closed authority. The latter is the polarization of impulses to reify the Bible as timeless set of truth and authority.[92] The task of the *ekklesia* is not to defend the authority or 'truth' of the Bible. 'Truth', when conceptualized according to the logic of democracy rather than the logic of identity, is articulated in polyphonic and inclusive discourses; it is not a metaphysical 'given' which can be uncovered. Therefore, within the *ekklesia*, 'scriptural truth is to be constituted in and through communicative practices'.[93] As such, it is the *ekklesia* itself, as rhetorical space, which is the centre of theological 'authority'. This is the gathering space for those, committed to emancipatory praxis, to deliberate their affairs.

This represents a considerable advance over the 'traditional' feminist appeal to 'women's experience' as truth-arbiter.[94] It is a more sophisticated inheritor which takes account of 'multiplicative oppression', differences between women, and which has at the least the potential for more sophisticated theorization as rhetorical practice.[95] Feminisms which site themselves within theoretical loci attentive to the discursive formation of world and self cannot well rely on an appeal to an unmediated and unitary conception of 'women's experience' as source and norm.

Schüssler Fiorenza does relate the authority of the *ekklesia* to theology. A critical evaluative hermeneutics, as practised by the *ekklesia*, 'derives its theological authority from the experience of G-d's liberating presence in today's struggles to end patriarchal domination'.[96] This is inspiration – the life-giving breath of Sophia-Spirit – expressed in emancipatory thought and praxis. Sophia-Spirit does not pitch her tent in texts codified in ancient times; she dwells with people. The *ekklesia* is grounded in a spirituality of 'vision and imagination', in a spirituality which envisions the world *differently* and engages with the world in the

---

[92] See Schüssler Fiorenza, *In Memory of Her, Bread Not Stone.*

[93] Schüssler Fiorenza, *But She Said*, 151.

[94] Linda Hogan's work provides the best overview and contextualization of this. She locates the feminist appeal to 'women's experience' within the Marxist tradition which liberation theology also draws on, analyzing the sources and functioning of 'praxis' within both of these contemporary theological perspectives. As she notes, putting 'women's experience' at the centre of feminist theory and practice both transforms and problematizes epistemology. In particular, like Schüssler Fiorenza, Hogan insists that an adequate functioning of 'women's experience' will be rooted in the material *differences* between women.

[95] See Chapter 8, where I consider the *ekklesia* in critical interaction with the ideal speech-community of Habermas.

[96] Schüssler Fiorenza, *But She Said*, 156. This is typical; Schüssler Fiorenza frequently identifes 'emancipatory struggles' as truth-criterion, here set in theological context. It can be noted that by *Jesus – Miriam's Child, Sophia's Prophet*, she has begun spelling God as 'G*d' in order to convey a different context than that of Jewish Orthodoxy.

engagement with God. God, Sophia-Spirit, is not apart from the world but in the world:

> Mystical-sapiental theology does not understand G-d as the totally transcendent unmoved mover, the heavenly and almighty patriarch who makes, orders and controls the world from on high. Rather, as incarnational theology, the spirituality of vision stresses the mutual indwelling of the world in G-d and G-d in the world; the saving collaboration between Christ and the believer; and the Spirit of G-d, Divine Wisdom, as a living fountain, a festal "dance of blazing love."[97]

Sophia-Spirit 'dances' in the whole world, not only in the Bible; the traces of Sophia-Spirit can be discerned in a variety of religious, cultural and intellectual traditions as people name and resist destructive systems and forces.[98] The *ekklesia* must claim its spiritual authority, assessing biblical texts in light of a critical hermeneutic of liberation.

Such a 'sophialogy' of biblical interpretation relates the critical interpretative task of the *ekklesia* to a theology of liberation. It would seem, then, that 'salvation' is viewed in this-worldly terms. Whether this exhausts Schüssler Fiorenza's soteriological vision, it is not possible to tell. Howsoever, her theological discussions may contextualize her biblical hermeneutics, but they certainly do not furnish an alternative source of external authority. The intention was not to accomplish this. For Schüssler Fiorenza, authority rests with the *ekklesia*, which may be inspired by Sophia-Spirit but which is not thereby given a direct access to divine insights. The responsibility and power for decision belongs to the *ekklesia*.

This theology of interpretation, then, does not 'solve' the 'problem' of discernment. Rather, it brings it into sharper focus, by its frank acceptance that there are neither final answers nor sure methods to arrive at such answers as can be put forward. In this respect, Schüssler Fiorenza's hermeneutics is resonant with postmodern anti-foundationalism. Of course, this does lead to certain methodological difficulties. 'Truth' becomes recognized as a very unstable thing. What place in this landscape do norms and principles have at all? The direction of movement seems to be towards relativism. Yet Schüssler Fiorenza is clearly not a relativist, for she is a feminist, who would certainly not consider kyriarchy to stand on equal ethical terms. In this sea of uncertainty, with no rocks to stand upon, what is the basis for one's theorizing? This is an issue which will be taken up in Chapter 8.

---

[97] Schüssler Fiorenza, *But She Said*, 158.
[98] Ibid., 156. Schüssler Fiorenza's phraseology is ambivalent here: the activity of Sophia-Spirit as she defines it clearly goes beyond Christianity, although she talks of the 'authority of inspiration' as given to 'the whole church'.

Christology and Normativity

We have seen that Schüssler Fiorenza rejects a notion of the biblical texts as authoritative and any approach to them which could be seen as a permutation on the tendency to set the Bible up as an archetype. Her historiographical move, indeed, is to see the biblical texts as source material which a feminist critical method of liberation can use in its theological-historical reconstructions. From this, she argues that we can discern a 'discipleship of equals' in the earliest Church, which became subject to an accelerating process of patriarchalization, but which never quite disappears. She writes the history of the early Church, therefore, as one of struggle, in which the egalitarian undercurrent remained.

It would be easy to read Schüssler Fiorenza here as postulating a 'pure' beginning, thus setting her historical account of the discipleship of equals in place of the biblical texts as such. This would simply be a shift in the locus of revelation and authority, which nevertheless still set that particular time and context apart as ultimate ground. She insists that she is not positing the 'discipleship of equals' as an edenic foundation which grounds her subsequent discourses and justifies the *ekklesia*. It has to be said that at times it would be easy to read her as though she were doing just that. Therefore, let us consider her account of the discipleship of equals, its christological context and its potential claims to normativity.

Again, it is important to set this debate in sophialogical and liberationist terms. Schüssler Fiorenza's major work on christology identifies Jesus as 'Miriam's Child, Sophia's Prophet'; Jesus is visioned as 'a prophet of Sophia who was sent to proclaim that the Sophia-G*d of Jesus is the G*d of the poor, the outcasts, and all those suffering from injustice'.[99] The movement of women and men called forth by Jesus were beginning to embody the *basileia*, which is not something locatable in the past but which comes to fruition in a pneumatologically (or sophialogically) understood history, and in eschatological horizons. It points towards future, not past. The 'discipleship of equals', then, should not be understood as a founding, finished event but a constant call and an ongoing process which has yet to bear its fullest fruit.

I would argue, hence, that the discipleship of equals does not in fact point to a pure myth of origins, as Schüssler Fiorenza consistently denies: but rather to an irruption of sophialogical intensity. Points of continuity can then be discerned with sophialogical activity both before and after, protending into the future. It is not an edenic foundation that we should be looking to, but to an ongoing process and the renewal of Sophia in contemporary contexts. Authority once again is retrieved from the past and claimed by those who would live in Sophia today.

The *ekklesia*, then, is a key element in Schüssler Fiorenza's hermeneutic theory, indeed, it sits at its heart. It represents the discursive locus of feminist communities, from which interpretation proceeds and is evaluated. The concept of the *ekklesia* is one I shall build on in Chapter 8, where I take up some of the issues raised in this chapter and develop some further reflections on the nature and constitution of the *ekklesia*.

---

[99] Schüssler Fiorenza, *Sharing Her Word*, 166.

Chapter 4

Redeeming the Text

Phyllis Trible produced seminal work in the field of literary-feminist biblical criticism. Her two major works in this domain, *God and the Rhetoric of Sexuality* (1978) and *Texts of Terror* (1984) are of interest in the context of this study for five primary reasons. The first simply relates to their importance in the development of feminist criticism of the Hebrew Bible. The second is that, in contrast to Schüssler Fiorenza, Trible's gaze is foregrounded on the 'text itself'. Historical reconstruction plays no part in her methodology. This makes her methodology an excellent foil to that of Schüssler Fiorenza. Furthermore, Trible's work also counterbalances Schüssler Fiorenza's focus on the Christian Testament and allows feminist interpretation of the Hebrew Bible to enter into the discussion. A fourth factor is the contrast between the two books under consideration. Each, as will be seen, follows a very different route and purposes, whilst the same literary method (rhetorical criticism) is employed in both. This allows for exploration of methodological issues relating to the goals of interpretation, as well as elaboration of the particular strategies themselves. And finally, Trible's work is explicitly located within theological context. She is interested in the intersection of scholarship with communities of faith – most particularly, with the feminist community.

It must be stressed that, whilst Trible's work was seminal within the literary-feminist field, she is no longer by any means the paramount figure within it. Current literary criticism of the Hebrew Bible is buoyant and diverse. Trible certainly does not overshadow the field – nor does her methodology. Literary criticism now roams through pyschoanalytical criticism, ideological criticism, reader-response criticism, deconstruction, intertextual studies, postcolonial theory, and cultural anthropological perspectives – to name a sample. Feminist criticism uses all of these methods, singly and in combination. As stated at the outset, however, it is not the goal of this study to provide an overview of current practice in feminist biblical interpretation, but rather to consider a theoretical frame in which Christian feminist interpretation might operate. Within this context, it is the very particularity of Trible's work with which I wish to engage. The contribution this can make will be seen in due course. I shall consider her two books separately for the most part, to allow their distinctiveness from each other to be fully appreciated, although there is a certain amount of interweaving for expediency since the methodologies overlap.

God and the Rhetoric of Sexuality

Trible contextualizes *God and the Rhetoric of Sexuality* in relation to events which had a profound impact on her: the assassination of John F. Kennedy; the killing of four little girls in the bombing of a black church; the publication of Sylvia Plath's *The Bell Jar*, followed by her suicide; the publication of Betty Friedan's *The Feminine Mystique*. She herself was in a period of transition, taking up a position at Wake Forest University following completion of her doctorate at Union Theological Seminary, and becoming aware that her theology was not wholly satisfactory or satisfying. From this 'convergence of crises', the trajectory leading to her work on *God and the Rhetoric of Sexuality* was established, in ways she herself found impossible to define, but which impelled her to seek 'a theological vision for new occasions'.[1] These events of 1963 were symbolic of how 'the mighty acts of God in history' had proved wanting.[2] *God and the Rhetoric of Sexuality* was put forward as *one* exercise in a marriage between biblical studies and theological perspective; there was no intention to furnish a comprehensive programme for biblical theology.[3]

The hermeneutic thrust of *God and the Rhetoric of Sexuality* is very specific. It is, in many respects, best characterized as a salvage operation. Trible seeks to recover and reclaim aspects of the Hebrew Bible which can stand as witness against dominant patriarchal inscriptions. The emphasis is on 'neglected themes and counterliterature';[4] using feminist hermeneutics, she has 'tried to recover old treasures and discover new ones in the household of faith'.[5] As she states, although 'some of these treasures are small, they are nonetheless valuable in a tradition that is often compelled to live by the remnant'.[6]

Trible's hermeneutical framework is guided by a vision of the Bible as 'a pilgrim wandering through history to merge past and present. . . . [witnessing to] the complexities and ambiguities of existence'.[7] In its wanderings, it interacts with 'struggles and perplexities' generated outside of itself, leading to 'varied applications throughout the ages'.[8] Clearly, Trible does not see the Bible as either self-contained and closed; nor does she see it as monolithic. Rather, it is diverse, contradictory and construed and reconstrued in its passage through time and place. Trible identifies three 'clues' for the study of God and rhetoric of sexuality which emerge, not from the Bible as such, but from the Bible's journeyings. These clues are hermeneutical, methodological and topical, and it is to these we now turn.

---

[1] Trible, *God and the Rhetoric of Sexuality*, xii
[2] Ibid., xi.
[3] Ibid., xii.
[4] Ibid., xii.
[5] Ibid., xii.
[6] Ibid., xii.
[7] Ibid., 1.
[8] Ibid., 1.

The Hermeneutical Clue

The hermeneutical clue subdivides; there is a hermeneutical clue within the text, but also one between text and world. Within the Hebrew Bible, single texts can appear: 'in different versions with different functions in different contexts. Through application it confesses, challenges, comforts, and condemns. What it says on one occasion it denies on another. Thus, scripture in itself yields multiple interpretations of itself.'[9] What is more, no overarching principles, no systematic perspective, can be laid upon the peregrinations of textual themes, ideas and formulations within the Hebrew Bible. The intra-biblical wanderings of texts are without a map. Such texts are also plastic; deployed differently, they change their shapes, their settings and their meanings. And meaning, of course, both then and now, is construed variously by different 'hearers'.[10]

The engagement between text and world and the way in which readers interpret the Bible reflects the way in which the Bible interprets itself: that is to say, multiply, and with reference to particular contexts. Trible cites ways in which contemporary culture and biblical interpretation intersect with reference to a variety of interests – for example, the relationship between the Bible and black experience, Marxism, ecology, American ideologies, psychoanalysis. Human sexuality is one amongst many interests prompted by questions arising from experience. Scripture is read in light of this, and present interests may then be viewed in light of readings of scripture.[11] We 'construe these traditions for our time'.[12]

What then, do the clue within the text and the clue between text and world suggest by way of hermeneutics? Trible states that:

> . . . hermeneutics encompasses explication, understanding, and application from past to present. Subject to the experiences of the reader, this process is always compelling and never ending. New occasions teach new duties.[13]

The new duty prompted by the circumstances of Trible's writing was to read in light of feminism, understood broadly as 'a critique of culture in light of

---

[9] Ibid., 4. She illustrates this claim with particular reference to a portrait of God which included the elements of both God as lover and God as punisher (Exod. 34.6-7), charting various formulations of the theme in different biblical contexts, each with distinctive emphases and rhetorical function.

[10] Ibid., 5.

[11] Ibid., 5-7.

[12] Ibid., 5-7.

[13] Ibid., 8. It is possible to discern in this definition the influence of Ricoeur, who sought to incorporate both critical explication and creative understanding in his interpretation theory. Trible does refer to Ricoeur's work in several endnotes, but does not indicate the extent to which she shares his framework. Given this, I have not attempted to 'fill in the gaps' of Trible's hermeneutic framework by assuming that she is taking her cues from Ricoeur.

misogyny'.¹⁴ So feminism, understood in this way, is explicitly the perspective from which she interprets in the application of her 'hermeneutical clue'.

The Methodological Clue

Her second clue is methodology: hermeneutics, as 'a total process of understanding', employs a variety of 'acceptable' methodologies.¹⁵ The methodology preferred by Trible is a literary one, rhetorical criticism. This is in keeping with her view that the Bible is a literary form. This is not a matter of perceiving the Bible as *either* literature *or* sacred writings, and her choosing to see it as the former: she does not see literary and religious perspectives as oppositional to one another, but rather as fusing in the interpretative act. She argues that the Bible is scripture and the Bible is literature, regardless of whether one accepts it as one's own sacred text or how one evaluates its literary merits.¹⁶

The distinguishing marks of literary criticism¹⁷ emanate from its emphasis on the text rather than 'on extrinsic factors such as historical background, archaeological data, compositional history, authorial intention, sociological setting, or theological motivation and result'.¹⁸ At the same time, she is careful to note that such considerations can impinge upon a literary reading: she does not posit a complete divorce between the two, but rather is identifying the primary focus of literary criticism in contradistinction from critical methods which may be interested in, for example, reconstructing historical and cultural formations at the postulated time of the text's origins.¹⁹ The emphasis on the final form of the text is

---

¹⁴ Ibid., 7.

¹⁵ It is important to draw attention to the fact that Trible does not speak of *understanding* as total, suggesting that texts could be known, thoroughly, once and for all, without remainder: but rather she refers here to the *total process* of understanding. The implication is that she simply means the overall activity of understanding necessarily relies upon specific methodologies; a different interpretation would have her suggesting that the aggregate of acceptable methodologies leads to a complete textual knowledge. However, this is unlikely given her view of Bible as wandering pilgrim: this leaves the process of interpretation always inevitably open and incomplete. What is interesting here, though, is the question of what might count as an 'acceptable' methodology. This, Trible unfortunately does not address. She notes that different interpreters may prefer one amongst these 'acceptable' methodologies over another but does not discuss what criteria would be used to select the possible range of appropriate options.

¹⁶ Ibid., 8. Trible here refers to the convergence of aesthetic and religious discourse: 'Since the word *scripture* itself means writing, it is difficult to set it over against literature'. Ibid., 27, n. 40.

¹⁷ Trible is critical of the confusion in biblical studies between literary criticism as practised in the field of literature studies and literary criticism as source criticism. She means the former. Ibid., 26, n. 36.

¹⁸ Ibid., 8.

¹⁹ In this way Trible distances herself from the literary movement, new criticism, which is completely ahistorical. She agrees with James Barr that this would be a reactionary turn

what Trible means when she labels rhetorical criticism an 'intrinsic reading'. This is a significant point because so easily misunderstood to imply that she claims her hermeneutics to be entirely rooted in and confined to the text. Trible is not disdaining insights from other critical disciplines as always irrelevant to a literary analysis;[20] furthermore, as has already been seen, Trible recognizes the role of the reader and cultural context in the interpretation process.

The brand of rhetorical criticism employed by Trible is that which analyses the 'interlocking structures of words and motifs'.[21] Such an approach recognizes the intrinsically literary nature of the biblical texts; as noted, for Trible, scripture is literature. It also lays stress on the inseparability of form and content; the medium is, in fact, the message.[22] Meaning cannot be mined from the semantic 'container' of the text; nor do the stylistic and structural features of texts have an existence independent of their subject matter. In this organic unity of form and content, the boundaries for analysis of a given text are determined by the interpreter, who decides what constitutes a literary unit and what will be examined.

Texts are understood to be a mixture of the unique and the typical. Whilst, for example, the Grimm brothers' recension of 'Sleeping Beauty' is recognizably the same story as previous and subsequent versions, it is nevertheless a unique literary creation. Conventions and typologies contribute in part to a given text but do not constitute its whole. 'The clue as text, then, involves both the typical and the unique.'[23] Rhetorical criticism focuses on the unique properties of a given text, in contrast to form criticism which focuses on the genric.[24] Within the genric category of hymns, for example, each hymn is unique and differs from the others: so in literary study more generally, the words used and the ways they are put together 'make every unit a new creation'.[25] Thus, rhetorical criticism pays careful attention to nuances of literary and stylistic features.

However, whilst the methodology of rhetorical is critical and rigorous, it is to be conceived as an artistic endeavour. 'It uses critical tools but is not determined by them.'[26] Guesswork and intuition have a part to play, yielding surprises. Its critical base does not lead it to arrive at an absolute, objective meaning. This is particularly the case given that 'all methodologies are subject to the guiding interests of individual users'; multiple interpretations are thereby inevitable.[27]

---

in biblical studies, since it would cut all connections to historical biblical scholarship. Ibid., 27, n. 41.

[20] Ibid., 8-9.

[21] Ibid., 8. She specifically does not mean by 'analysis of structure' what a structuralist would mean. She refers to surface textual structures rather than deep abstracted ones (26 n. 37). The method is that pioneered in biblical studies by Trible's mentor, James Muilenburg.

[22] Ibid., 9.

[23] Ibid., 10.

[24] Ibid., 11. She is careful to point out that form criticism is a sociological and historical method as well as a strictly literary one (28 n 52).

[25] Ibid., 11.

[26] Ibid., 11.

[27] Ibid., 11.

The multiplicity of interpretation does not, though, lead Trible to advocate an infinite free play of readings. Different readings can co-exist, 'but not all interpretations are thereby equal'.[28] The criterion by which she distinguishes between interpretations is the text itself. 'The text, as form and content, limits constructions of itself and does, in fact, stand as a potential witness against all readings.'[29] Presumably, this is what lies behind her statement that '[p]roper analysis of form yields proper articulation of meaning'.[30] The question here begged is obvious. If rhetorical criticism is the 'proper analysis of form', yielding 'proper analysis of meaning', what actually constitutes 'proper'? This might appear to imply that Trible does in fact suggest the existence of a single right meaning, which can be mined from the semantic container of the text if the right method is used. This sits so ill with her acknowledgement of readerly input and the non-objectivist nature of rhetorical criticism that it bears further examination.

Two points may be noted. Firstly, 'proper' is subtly different from 'right'. The latter suggests 'true'; the former has more the connotations of 'appropriate'. This is important; the criteria for discerning what is 'true' and what is 'appropriate' may not be the same. Trible has identified the text as a criterion for 'proper' interpretation. It makes a difference if she is claiming that attention to the text, through rhetorical criticism correctly applied, will yield the true meaning of the text – or, if she is rather claiming that rhetorical critical method, applied using the critical principles appropriate to scholarly endeavour, will produce a meaning which can be justified with reference to the form and content of the text – and is therefore appropriate. Of course, what is 'appropriate' is a judgement particular to the discursive locus of reading production. Trible does not make explicit the norms and criteria she employs, with the exception that she names the text itself as a control. This point, and its problematic, will be discussed further below. However, her acceptance of the importance of reader and context in the construction of meaning makes it probable that she does not in fact postulate universal absolutes as arbiters for what might or might not be appropriate. The corollary of her position is that a text could be read in any number of ways, but not all of those would be equally acceptable to reading communities dependent on the principles and criteria operative. Trible does not consider this implication of her stance, although it is a decisive factor in considering how judgements between different interpretations can be made.

However, in one respect, as indicated, Trible does suggest a universal norm: the one criterion for arbitrating between different interpretations she explicitly identifies – the text. Trible sheds a little further light on the relationship she

---

[28] Ibid., 11. Trible's endnote to this comment refers to Paul Ricoeur's *Interpretation Theory* (Fort Worth: Texas Christian University Press, 1976), 79. See the discussion below.

[29] Trible, *God and the Rhetoric of Sexuality*, 11. She refers in an endnote (29 n. 62) to James Barr, who himself designates the text as potential witness against any given interpretation. Barr argues that historically, it was the very givenness of the biblical text which opened up the possibility of change. Interpretations could be challenged with reference to it. 'The mere existence of the text therefore keeps open the possibility of a challenge to its accepted interpretation' (*Old and New in Interpretation*, 137).

[30] Trible, *God and the Rhetoric of Sexuality*, 8.

perceives between text and interpretation in a passing reference to Ricoeur: 'The text is like a musical score and the reader like the orchestra conductor who obeys the instructions of the notation.'[31] Trible adds further clarification to this issue in *Texts of Terror*. Here, she explains that 'stories live not without us'; storytelling is 'a Trinitarian act that unites writer, text, and reader in a collage of understanding'.[32] Although she comments that the three participants are 'unequal', she does not elucidate in what manner the asymmetry is conceived. It is also interesting that she includes the writer in her 'trinity' of interpretation: as we have already seen, her literary-critical method is expressly disinterested in authorial intention or contextual origins. One would surmise that methodologies of this ilk would perceive interpretative interaction to be between text and reader alone – or possibly a 'trinity' of text, reader and world. Still, it remains apparent that Trible does indeed recognize the role of the reader (although within what parameters is unclear):[33] she also recognizes that rhetorical criticism is not something that emerges, intrinsically, from the text; the conventions of literary analysis, she notes, vary across time and from critic to critic; rhetorical criticism is brought to bear 'upon' the text, it may offer an intrinsic reading, but that does not indicate intrinsic to the text in the sense of 'within' it, but rather wholly upon it.[34] Trible is well aware that theories of language and literature exert formative influence upon readings.

In what sense then, might the text be said to act as a 'control'? Trible's underlying argument seems to be that certain interpretations will correlate to the textual structures more faithfully than others, and the readings which most consistently and carefully take account of the features of the text will be better readings. This does not necessarily require a belief that texts have singular meanings which the task is to discover. To build on the musical analogy she adopts from Ricoeur, there may be many different renderings of a given musical score, such as the *Moonlight Sonata*, but one which sounded more like *Chopsticks* would be labelled 'wrong' – as a rendition of that particular piece, whatever its merits on other grounds.

---

[31] Ibid., 9; Ricoeur, *Interpretation Theory*, 75.

[32] Trible, *Texts of Terror*, 1.

[33] Trible cites Paul Ricoeur with reference to her statement that, alone, a text is 'mute' and 'ineffectual' (*Interpretation Theory*, 75), and Wolfgang Iser with respect to the role of the reader (*The Act of Reading: a theory of aesthetic response*).

If she follows Iser, the reader would complete or actualize the potential effect of the text, on the basis of presuppositions, textual prompting, and creative construals. Therefore, the interaction between text and reader is a 'productive matrix' which causes the text to be meaningful differently in different contexts. Polyvalency is not however never-ending: not, at least, if the reader is competent and able to discern textual features and patterns. Iser has been criticized for embracing the poles of both text as given and reader as determining 'meaning'. It is unfortunate, however, that Trible does not indicate the extent to which she is in agreement, or otherwise, with Iser. This would assist in clarification of Trible's own position on these issues.

[34] Trible, *Texts of Terror*, 3.

That seems, *prima facie*, to be a reasonable account of the nature of textuality. However, digging deeper, it leaves untouched some crucial issues which must be addressed if an adequate account of text/reader relations is to be posited. If this is indeed the model of textuality operative in Trible's hermeneutics, it imports certain difficulties into her work which are not only unresolved but unexamined. The most serious of these is her failure to deliberate in this context upon the distinction between text and text-as-interpreted. The 'text' as such, as a given object in the world, cannot act as a control of readings of it. Textual structures and features may be constant, but they are only discerned in the act of reading the text. Therefore, the 'text' may – as she says – be a *potential* witness against particular interpretations of it, but the text requires actualization through being read. In the actualization, the text ceases to be text as given object in the world and becomes text-as-interpreted. What counts as a 'faithful' reading of the text, and whether faithfulness to it is in fact the goal, are all discursively constituted. The relationship between text and interpretation then becomes one of infinite regress, with no possibility of arriving at a foundation to interpretation which is not itself an interpretation. This does not eliminate the place of textual structures as givens in the interpretative process but it does problematize the manner in which a text can be set forth as a control for interpretation. The recognition of discursive location of text-as-interpreted profoundly destabilizes the notion of 'text' as something which can simply be appealed to in the struggle for interpretation.

In evaluating exercises in rhetorical criticism as interpretations, this is a fundamental point. Of all the literary methods, rhetorical criticism rests on the tightest possible fit between textual structures and features and the articulation of meaning. Crucially, however, the parameters in which the nature and goal of interpretation are understood are extra-textual. It is this which is the controlling frame, and only within the rules and logic thus implicitly or explicitly laid out that the 'text' can speak. So, within Trible's methodological clue lies an ambiguity with respect to the role and function of the 'text' in interpretation, which, as we shall see, may return to haunt her.

The Topical Clue

Her third 'clue' is topical, and acts as her 'reading lens'. It relates to her chosen subject matter of God and the rhetoric of sexuality. She selects the text of Genesis 1:27 as her topical frame – noting that she is not postulating any 'historical, philological, literary, or intentional links' between it and rest of the Bible:[35]

> And God created man in his image;
> in the image of God created he him;
> male and female created he them. (Gen. 1:27)

---

[35] Trible, *God and the Rhetoric of Sexuality*, 29 n. 75.

The context of the text is the 'liturgy of creation that moves in orderly fashion from chaos to cosmos (Gen. 1:1-2:4a)'.[36] Within this narrative, the creation of humanity is uniquely presented: only human creatures are made in the image of God; only they are specifically identified as sexual beings. What is more, these two aspects are linked: 'this specific reference pertains not to procreation but to the image of God'.[37] Trible's analysis of Gen. 1:27 highlights the co-equivalence of male and female in the creation process. She notes particularly that translations often fail to take account of the importance of Hebrew being grammatically gendered; apparently masculine references in Gen. 1:27 can then be understood to include both male and female throughout: God created humanity in his image; in the image of God he created it; male and female he created them.[38] She stresses that the text supposes harmony between the two sexes who are, as humanity, in original unity as well as original differentiation. No distinctions are made of worth or role. Furthermore, 'male and female' is, through parallelism, perceived to be the vehicle of a metaphor in which 'image of God' is the tenor. The distinction between 'God' and 'image of God' points to the transcendence of God and the difference between Creator and created.[39] With these provisos, and pointing out that 'sexual differentiation of humankind is not thereby a description of God',[40] Trible can say:

> To describe male and female, then, is to perceive the image of God; to perceive the image of God is to glimpse the transcendence of God.[41]

It is the metaphor of the image of God, male and female, which guides Trible's interpretation as her topical clue. Humanity is both like and unlike God, but its similarities and dissimilarities are jointly held by the differentiated unity of sexed humanity. As a reading clue, it operates in two ways: firstly, it draws attention to the incompleteness of metaphors for God based on either the image of God male, or the image of God female. It also underscores the imbalance in the Bible in favour of male imagery. Hence, the topical clue provides 'hermeneutical impetus' to investigate female metaphors for God.[42] In *God and the Rhetoric of Sexuality*, Trible uses variants on womb/compassion/mercy to image God, to hold up to the light this metaphor for God's compassion and creative activity which is rooted in the wombs of women.[43] The second function of the topical clue is to

---

[36] Ibid., 12.

[37] Ibid., 13.

[38] Trible argues that the shift from singular to plural pronouns demonstrates that the *adam* is not one entity. As such it is best read with its generic meaning. Trible in fact retains the translation 'him' for the singular masculine accusative pronoun; I translate this as 'it' here to highlight the difference it makes when grammatical gender is neutralized.

[39] Trible, *God and the Rhetoric of Sexuality*, 20-21.

[40] Ibid., 21.

[41] Ibid., 21.

[42] Ibid., 22.

[43] Focus on the root metaphor *rhm* is also supplemented by poetical depictions of Yahweh as pregnant, in labour, giving birth, nursing.

bring into focus instances where male and female feature in comparable contexts. Hence, attention is brought to bear upon traditions which are thought to embody this more inclusive rhetoric of sexuality. Trible considers that this can be discerned in Genesis 2-3, Song of Songs and Ruth. These constitute the remainder of *God and the Rhetoric of Sexuality*, and between them (she argues) encompass tragedy, ecstasy and the struggles of daily life.[44]

Trible's topical clue is indicative of a vital difference between her reading practices and Schüssler Fiorenza's. Whilst Schüssler Fiorenza has sought to push her work forward beyond the boundaries of the sex-gender framework, it would seem that Trible remains within it. It is her 'topical clue' which gives this away: the image of God male and female. This not only retains 'male and female' as stable and central analytic categories, but divinizes them.[45] Gender identity becomes the primary lens for her interpretations and the key metaphor for the image of God. Sexuality is a 'human clue' to divine transcendence.[46]

Trible's efforts to locate 'female' imagery for God in the Hebrew Bible, to balance the 'male' and fulfill the promise of her topical clue, may not be entirely felicitous. The association of 'uterus' with God's compassion could be perceived as projecting gendered stereotypes into the divine. Anselm comments that Jesus and Paul are 'Fathers by your authority, mothers by your kindness. Fathers by your teaching, mothers by your mercy.'[47] Trible's meditations on the links between motherhood and compassion could be seen to strengthen essentialist accounts of gender.

She recounts the story of two women, standing before the king, each claiming that the same child is her own.[48] The women are named as harlots. The situation is at an impasse: as the king comments, 'The one says, "This is my son that is alive, and your son is dead"; and the other says, "No; but your son is dead, my son is the living one"' (RSV; 1 Kings 3:23). The king cuts through the deadlock: 'Divide the living child in two, and give half to the one, and half to the other' (RSV; 1 Kings 3:25). The woman whose son it was said to give the child to the other woman, and on no account to slay it – because her 'compassion' grew warm. The other said to divide the child, that neither woman should have it.

Trible sees in this story a 'transcendent love' allowing the word *mother* to appear in the narrative (v. 27); the story tells that 'the presence of a love that knows not the demands of ego, of possessiveness, or even of justice reveals motherhood'.[49] This is the story she uses as her paradigm for understanding the relationship between the biblical metaphor of womb to connote mercy.

---

[44] Trible, *God and the Rhetoric of Sexuality*, 162.
[45] Although it must be noted once more that Trible asserts the *difference* between Creator and created.
[46] See Trible, *God and the Rhetoric of Sexuality*, 21.
[47] *The Prayers and Meditations of St. Anselm*, tr. B. Ward (Harmondsworth: Penguin Classics, 1973), 152-4; cited Hampson, *Theology and Feminism*, 94.
[48] Trible, *God and the Rhetoric of Sexuality*, 31-33.
[49] Ibid., 33.

> To the responsive imagination, this metaphor suggests the meaning of love as selfless participation in life. The womb protects and nourishes but does not possess and control. It yields its treasure in order that wholeness and well-being may happen. Truly, it is the way of compassion.[50]

This sounds remarkably like the romanticized accounts of motherhood and femininity which one might find in the writings of cultural feminists. It bolsters the association between femaleness, selflessness and indifference to justice. As such it can only create suspicions of an essentialism which many feminists seek to reject. Trible strengthens further the link between God and the wombs of women in the Hebrew scriptures, by tracing the stories in which female barrenness/fertility are causally connected to the actions of Yahweh in closing or opening wombs.[51] The womb 'is a physical object upon which the deity acts. Control of it belongs neither to women nor to their husbands, neither to the fetus nor to society. Only God closes and opens wombs in judgment, in blessing, and mystery.'[52] It is also God who shapes the child in the womb (Jer. 1:5; Job 31:13-15) and brings it forth (Jer. 20:14-18; Job 10:18-19). She then comments on the texts which speak of God's figurative 'labour pains' (Deut. 32:18; Isa. 42:14b).

From a feminist perspective, such rhetoric is double-edged. On the one hand, it might seem to connect femaleness positively to the divine, in which women embody the creative activity of God. On the other hand, it might disconnect women from their own bodies altogether, ascribing women's creative activity to the Father God. Trible summarizes: 'God conceives in the womb; God fashions in the womb; God judges in the womb; God destines in the womb; God receives out of the womb . . . .'[53] Women, then, would appear to figure simply as the physical container for the womb. Trible neglects to place her discussion in the context of gendered power dynamics. She acknowledges the dominance of male-based metaphors for the divine. Given this, the association between God and female-based metaphors can appear in two lights, both negative. The first sees the female-based metaphors as a significant affirmation of female sacrality, testifying to a theology which is either remnant or marginal;[54] but given the relative proportionality of male as distinct from female imagery for God, the latter can only seem supplementary, unimportant, or actively minimized. The second sees the female-based metaphors as significant, but only within kyriocentric logic. God is presented in predominantly male terms; associating God with female-based imagery of birth may not valorize the female, but appropriate the 'birthright' into a male-dominated paradigm. If the womb is an object on which God acts, the power

---

[50] Ibid., 33.
[51] Ibid., 34-35; She cites, as examples, Gen. 20:1-18; Gen. 29:31-35; Gen. 30:22; 1 Sam. 1:1-20.
[52] Trible, *God and the Rhetoric of Sexuality*, 34.
[53] Ibid., 38.
[54] By 'remnant', I mean to allow for the possibility that female imagery might once have been considerably more important, but in the codified tradition has been minimized; by 'marginal', I mean to indicate a use of female imagery which was always less popular and significant than male imagery.

to give birth is removed from female bodies and appropriated to the Father. If, throughout the Bible, God is explicitly Father and implicitly Mother, does this not simply incorporate maternity into paternity? Into the phallus symbol is absorbed everything of cultural value. Hampson here has a perceptive comment:

> This suggestion that the masculine God should be understood in a more female or feminine way is however not without problems. The effect of such imagery is to enrich or enlarge our concept of the male, or of what may truly be said to be 'masculine'. God (who is basically seen as male) is portrayed as nurturing and caring, Christ as feeding and protecting. It may well be said that the patriarchal understanding of what it means to be male is abandoned. But such a move does nothing for women, or for the concept of the feminine *per se*: it expands our understanding of what is to be considered authentically male.[55]

Issues of female subjectivity are taken up and discussed in Chapter 8; at this point, I simply register a problematization of Trible's topical clue. More pertinent to the analysis at this stage is an emerging conflict between Trible's 'clues'.

The first and the third provide the discursive frames for Trible's work: texts have different meanings in different contexts, Trible's context is feminism, and her topical clue is her very specific reading lens 'the image of God male and female'. Her second clue pulls in a different direction. Methodologically, she wants to talk of 'proper' articulation of meaning and the controlling status of the text in interpretations. This places a cracked stone at the foundation of her readings. We shall see how this plays out in practice. It is the case that use of rhetorical criticism, as a text-based methodology, can best be considered in relation to particular interpretations of particular texts. As such, there follows an account of Trible's application of rhetorical criticism to Genesis 2-3.

The purpose of this is to elucidate the manner in which rhetorical criticism is wielded in Trible's hands. Given the density of Trible's argument (it occupies seventy detailed pages), close focus will be directed only onto Genesis 2:18-24 and a broad-brush outline given of the remainder. Thereafter, examples of criticisms levelled against Trible's exegesis, and a number of alternative interpretations, will be noted. However, although judgements may be made where appropriate, the aim is not to arbitrate between competing exegetical accounts of Genesis 2-3[56] with a view to identifying the 'correct' or 'most sustainable' reading. In going over these various interpretations, the points I seek to make are hermeneutical.

As a case-study for feminist interpretation, Genesis 2-3 is a particularly rich hunting ground. The reasons why a feminist might consider these texts especially deserving of consideration are manifest. The prevailing understandings of this text have characteristically seen in the tale of our beginnings what amounts to a mandate for sexism and the identification of the male as the normative human

---

[55] Hampson, *Theology and Feminism*, 94.
[56] This would require a lengthy study in its own right; the volume of literature on Genesis 2-3 is now enormous, and deeply contradictory.

being.[57] Trible sketches in the shape of 'traditional' interpretations, which she holds to be common both to those who 'applaud' it and those who 'deplore' it.[58] This narrative 'proclaims male superiority and female inferiority as the will of God. It portrays woman as "temptress" and troublemaker, who is dependent upon and dominated by her husband.'[59] Given this and the burgeoning of interest in gender issues, it is hardly surprising that the interpretative history and possibilities of Genesis 2-3 have been critically re-examined from feminist perspectives. As the site of multiple conflicting interpretations, these texts comprise an immensely fertile ground for the consideration of feminist methodologies. Trible's own analysis of Genesis 2-3 may indeed justly be called seminal and its influence remains large.

However, Trible's statement of aims in relation to her reading of Genesis 2-3 seem somewhat confused. On the one hand, she claims she is merely setting out 'to contemplate it afresh as a work of art; for, literary study of Genesis 2-3 may offer insights that traditional perspectives dream not of';[60] she is not trying to 'defend' the narrative against the prevailing views (although admits she is tempted to do so, and may sometimes yield).[61] This could appear rather disingenuous; if Trible is really suggesting that literary methodologies will produce alternative readings, whilst not specifically aiming to refute the dominant 'misogynous' ones,[62] it is extraordinarily fortuitous that rhetorical criticism in her hands performs exactly that manoeuvre. It also ignores the framing of the study within her own broader purposes, stated textually in advance as an attempt to 'recover old treasures' and 'discover new ones' from an expressly feminist vantage point.[63] It has the effect of implying that a fresh look at Genesis 2-3 as art, as literature, will proceed from a purer starting point not infected by 'traditional' perspectives. And yet the traditional perspectives to which she objects are not those emanating from the historical-critical school as such, which is after all a modern phenomenon, but those readings which seek to expound the meaning of the story in terms of its ontology of gender whilst inhabiting a patriarchal/androcentric worldview. Indeed, it could be argued that synchronic interpretations of Genesis 2-3, as narrative, have historically been the norm rather than a recent incursion.[64] In those terms,

---

[57] As documented in, for example, Merlin Stone, *When God Was a Woman* (New York: Dial Press, 1976), 5-8, 198-233; Bal, *Lethal Love* (1987), 109-112.

[58] Trible, *God and the Rhetoric of Sexuality*, 73. I make no attempt here to detail the history of interpretation, although it may be less monolithic than Trible supposes.

[59] Ibid., 73.

[60] Ibid., 74.

[61] Ibid., 74.

[62] Ibid., 73.

[63] Ibid., xii.

[64] I do not suggest that past methods of reading the Bible anticipate rhetorical criticism as a method. Rather, the somewhat erroneously labelled 'pre-critical' paradigms of biblical interpretation assumed a coincidence between *historia*, theology and narrative; as such the narratives themselves were the object of reflection. In this respect interpretation was text-centred, because it did not posit a disjunction between text and reality. Figural readings deepened the connection between text and reality by taking interpretation to a

considering the Genesis 2-3 texts without asking questions relating to 'extrinsic' factors, and as a work of narrative art, may be less far from 'traditional' methodologies than Trible supposes.

The ingredient which makes Trible's reading genuinely fresh is not, in fact, her use of rhetorical criticism. It is her feminist perspective. This, she happily acknowledged in her introduction: its disappearance at this juncture as the reading context contributes to the suspicion that Trible is in fact attempting to state that her interpretation is (objectively) the more accurate. The suspicion is fostered by Trible's claim that 'traditional interpretations of male superiority and female inferiority' are 'simply not present in the story itself'. In fact, such interpretations 'fail to respect the integrity of this work as an interlocking structure of words and motifs with its own intrinsic value and meaning. In short, these ideas violate the rhetoric of the story.'[65] This implicit claim to providing a more objective, more accurate reading is significant when it comes to evaluating Trible's own interpretation.

Paradise Found: The Redeeming of Genesis 2:18-24

Genesis 2:18-24 is normally placed within the broader narrative episode of Genesis 2-3. For Phyllis Trible, as Table 1.1 shows, Genesis 2-3 is a tale of the movement from Life (Eros) to Death (Thanatos) and from joy to tragedy. Genesis 2:18-24 falls into what she designates as Scene One – the Development of Eros. Life means 'unity, fulfillment, harmony and delight': albeit a fulfillment which includes limits, distinctions and hierarchies.[66]

We are told in the introductory verses 2:4b-7 that the earth was barren: no plant was yet in the earth and no grain sprouted because God had not caused it to rain and because there was no human to serve or till the earth. In verse 2:7, this lack is remedied with the creation of *'adam*. There is a play on words here in typical Hebrew fashion, which is rather lost in the RSV translation. We see in Table 1.2 how Trible's own rendering points up the similarity between the Hebrew used for human and for earth.

---

less obvious plane. Similarly, midrashic readings frequently rested on close readings of texts. Whilst this is no way equates to modern literary methodologies, there are nonetheless resonances. My argument is that close reading of narrative units pre-dates twentieth-century literary criticism, although differing significantly from it. Such readings were, of course, specifically related to particular Jewish or Christian theological interests. It is, to say the least, questionable whether Trible's reading is not.

[65] Trible, *God and the Rhetoric of Sexuality*, 73.
[66] Ibid., 74.

Table 1.1 Genesis 2-3: from Eros to Thanatos

2:4b-7	Introduction moving from cosmos to earth.
2:7-24	The development of Eros Entrance into a garden Yahweh creates the plant, animal and human worlds
2:25-3:7	The act of disobedience The plant world as symbol of disobedience The animal world as temptation to disobedience The human world disobeys
3:8-24	The disintegration of Eros Expulsion from a garden Yahweh disrupts the plant, animal and human worlds

Table 1.2 Genesis 2:7-8

7 Then the LORD God formed man out of dust from the ground, and breathed into his nostrils the breath of life; and man became a living being. 8 And the LORD God planted a garden in Eden, in the east; and there he put the man whom he had formed.

RSV Genesis 2:7-8

And Yahweh God formed *ha-'adam* [of] dust from *ha-ʰadama*
    and breathed into its nostrils the breath of life
        and *ha-'adam* became a living *nephesh*.
And Yahweh God planted a garden in Eden in the east
    and put there *ha-'adam* whom he had formed.

Phyllis Trible Genesis 2:7-8

The assonance between *ha-'adam* and *ha-ʰadama* prompts Trible to translate *'adam* as 'earth creature', thus retaining some of the flavour of the original Hebrew. This also, of course, highlights her contention that sexual differentiation has not yet been created. *'Adam* is grammatically masculine but 'grammatical gender . . . is not sexual identification'.[67] For Trible, '[a]lthough the word *ha-'adam* acquires ambiguous usages and meanings – including an exclusively male

---

[67] Ibid., 80.

reference – in the development of the story, these ambiguities are not present in the first episode'.[68] The earth creature is, in fact, unsexed.[69] Trible emphasizes that because *'adam* is not sexually identified, the creation of humanity is seen as a process; at this stage, the tale is still being told.

Verses 2:9-17 develop the story by showing the responsibility of the earth creature for the earth; its job is to till and keep the garden. Then in verse 2:18, Yahweh God says, 'It is not good for *ha-'adam* to be alone.' Isolation is identified as a problem. The earth creature, although created from earth and in harmony with it, is also set apart from it. It is from the earth but other than it. So Yahweh God aims to remedy this lack: 'I will make a companion corresponding to it.'[70]

The Hebrew word *'ezer*, which Trible translates as 'companion' is more usually translated as 'helper'. However, the English word helper suggests an assistant or subordinate; Trible argues that these connotations of inferiority are missing from the Hebrew word. In fact, the word *'ezer* is often used of God: for example, Exod. 18:4, Deuteronomy 33:7, 26, 29, Psalm 33:20 etc. The whole phrase used in the Hebrew text is *'ezer k^{e}negdô*. *K^{e}negdô* may be translated as 'corresponding to' or 'opposite to', and suggests a being separate but equal, on the same level. Therefore taking the phrase as a whole, *'ezer k^{e}negdô* is taken to suggest mutuality and equality rather than the domination of either sex.

The importance of *'adam* finding a companion corresponding to it is stressed by the structure of this episode. The lack has not yet been fulfilled: the animal world does not contain a suitable being. Indeed the animal world is shown to be explicitly subordinate to the human world because the earth creature is given the power of naming the animals. The animal world is, then, distinguished from the human world in status, but the similarities between them are also brought out. The animals are also living *nephesh* made from *ha-'^{a}dama*. As with the relation of humanity to the plant world, there is hierarchy, but not conflict.

However, human loneliness has still not been alleviated. The delay is building up towards the climax of this section, with verses 2:21-24 and the creation of sexuality.

Again the section has a circular design, with the word for flesh (*basar*) marking the beginning and end of the unit. This word, flesh, occurs once at both the beginning and end of this section, twice in the middle, and nowhere else in the whole story, pointing to its significance as a motif. The four parts of this episode in 2:21-24 correspond structurally to the four parts of the previous episode in 2:18-20. In the first two parts of each, Yahweh God is the subject; in the last two parts, the earth creature dominates and Yahweh God is not mentioned. The solution in 2:21-24 mirrors in structure the setting out of the problem in 2:18-20.

The first part, verse 2:21, points to the activity of Yahweh God and the passivity of the earth creature. The creation of the woman, like the creation of the earth creature is dependent upon God's activity.[71]

---

[68] Ibid., 80.
[69] This is a development from Trible's earlier work in which she postulated an androgynous first creature.
[70] Trible, *God and the Rhetoric of Sexuality*, 88ff.
[71] Ibid., 94ff.

The second part, verse 2:22, points to the distinction of the woman from the rest of the created order. Everything else has been created from the earth, and the earth creature, also created from the earth, stands over and above the plant and animal worlds in a position of power and responsibility. The earth creature has power over that which was created from earth. The woman is unique in creation because she is built from the earth creature's own self: a rib is the raw material and Yahweh God builds it into a woman.

Trible compares 2:22 with 2:19. In 2:19, Yahweh God brought every beast of the fields and every bird of the heavens to the earth creature to see what it would name each one. No such reason is given in 2:22; it simply states, Yahweh God brought her to *ha-'adam*. Trible sees in this omission a crucial distinction between the status of the animals and the status of the woman: specifically, the earth creature is not given power over the woman.

The flesh of the earth creature has itself been altered by the creation of woman. Sexual difference has now been created: the *ha-'adam* who speaks after the creation of the woman is a different creature from the *ha-'adam* of before. And for the first time, we hear the words of *ha-'adam*: 'This, finally, bone of my bones and flesh of my flesh. This shall be called woman because from man was taken this.' The poem is an expression of delight at the being of the woman. She is strongly emphasized by the repetition of the word 'this' at the beginning, the centre and end of the poem.

For the first time, *ha-'adam* identifies itself as male: *'is*. Again we have a play on language in the Hebrew between *'is* and *'issa*, which English can reproduce in man and woman. The word *ha-'adam* acquires a second usage. In preceding episodes, sexuality had not been created: the earth creature was neither male nor female, nor androgynous, but unsexed. Now the creature is transformed and the words *'is* and *'issa*, man and woman, enter the story for the first time. *Ha-'adam* has also now acquired sexual reference, which is used often but not exclusively for the male. Trible notes that the story is building ambiguity into the word *ha-'adam*.[72] There is both continuity and discontinuity between the first creature and the male creature. In a similar way, because she was fashioned from the rib of the original *ha-'adam*, there is both continuity and discontinuity between the first creature and the female creature.

There is also both similarity and dissimilarity between the female and the male. Whilst distinguishing *'issa*, the woman, from *'is*, the man, she is also 'bone of my bone and flesh of my flesh'. These words, say Trible, 'speak unity, solidarity, mutuality and equality'.[73]

The distinction between the woman and the animal world has already been mentioned. She is not made from the earth and Yahweh God did not bring her to *ha-'adam* for her to be named. However, in verse 23, we have *ha-'adam* exclaiming 'This shall be called woman.' Is the man here expressing his power over the woman in the same way in which *ha-'adam* expressed his power over the animals by naming them?

---

[72] Ibid., 98.
[73] Ibid., 99.

Phyllis Trible says no, by pointing out certain differences she perceives between the earth creature's naming of the animals and the man's exclamation that 'This shall be called woman.' She postulates the existence of a naming formula: 'the verb *call* by itself does not mean naming; only when joined to the noun *name* does it become part of a naming formula'.[74] So the earth creature called the names of the animals. In verse 23, the earth creature does not call the name of the woman; the earth creature exclaims, 'This shall be called woman.'

Furthermore, the word for woman is introduced into the story before the earth creature uses it; *ha-'adam* is not determining who the woman is by exclaiming 'this shall be called woman'. Rather, the man is playing with language to rejoice in the mutuality and similarity of *'is* and *'issa*; he is not suggesting her subordination to him. As *'issa*, woman, was taken from *'is*, man, so was *ha-'adam*, the earth creature, taken from *ha-'ᵃdama*, the earth. Trible concludes: 'Finally, woman is not derived from man, even as the earth creature is not derived from the earth. For both of them life originates with God. Dust of the earth and rib of the earth creature are but raw materials for God's creative activity.'

The creation of woman has fulfilled the creation of humanity. In 2:20, we have: 'But as for *'adam*, it did not find a companion corresponding to itself.' In 2:24, we find the culmination of this whole episode: 'Therefore a man leaves his father and his mother and cleaves to his woman and they become one flesh.' The pattern is circular; we begin with the flesh of the earth creature which was differentiated into two; but we end with the two once more becoming one flesh. Trible also notes that although the man calls the woman 'his woman', he does not control her: 'he moves towards her for union'.[75] As she explained earlier: 'Loneliness, then, is overcome not by something other than humanity but by distinction within one flesh.'[76]

From this promising start, however, Trible's story moves towards tragedy. It is not, though, a movement which casts a negative light upon the role or status of the woman. Rather, in Trible's reading, the woman is able to represent the couple: when the serpent beguiles her, 'to capture her is to capture the man, for the two are bone of bone and flesh of flesh'.[77] The serpent, in fact, addresses the woman as the spokesperson of the couple. She is 'intelligent, informed, and perceptive. Theologian, ethicist, hermeneut, rabbi, she speaks with clarity and authority.'[78] She is independent of mind, evaluating the advantages of eating from the forbidden tree – it is good for food, it appears attractive, it makes one wise. In contrast to the woman – 'intelligent, sensitive, and ingenious' – the man is 'belly-oriented', 'passive, brutish and inept'.[79] The woman, accused, does not seek to cast blame on the man or on God for placing the serpent in the garden; rather she accepts that she was beguiled. The consequences of their joint disobedience, though, are the fracture of the original harmonious relationships in the garden. Yet this is not

---

[74] Ibid., 99.
[75] Ibid., 104.
[76] Ibid., 103.
[77] Ibid., 108.
[78] Ibid., 108.
[79] Ibid., 113.

understood to be a punishment from God, but rather the outcome of the disruption of creation:

> Three separate judgments have described the outcome of their actions: the good earth is cursed; plants give way to thorns and thistles; fulfilling work has become alienated labour; power over the animals has deteriorated to enmity with the serpent; sexuality has splintered into strife; human oppression prevails. With such consequences, a happy ending to the story is impossible; only the aftermath of disaster remains.[80]

Where God does act is in driving them from the garden, that they may not eat of the tree of life. And now, an original joy, unity, equality and harmony has disintegrated into oppositions and hierarchies. As Trible tells it, Genesis 2-3 is 'a love story gone awry'.[81] It culminates in tragedy, part of which is the corruption of relations between male and female such that the woman comes to occupy a position of inferiority and subordination. But in the plenitude of creation, the woman was fully equal to the man. That is the 'lost coin' which Trible believes she has recovered from Genesis 2-3 and impels her, at the end of her search, to 'join that ancient woman, who, having found the lost coin, called together her "friends and neighbors, saying, 'Rejoice with me, for I have found the coin which I had lost'" (Luke 15:9, RSV).[82]

... And Paradise Lost: Genesis 2:18-24 Reread

Not all Trible's readers find cause for rejoicing in Genesis 2:18-24. Some think that she is too optimistic in parts;[83] others, such as James Kennedy, think she is completely wrong and there is nothing redeemable about this text for a feminist who considers the female to be as normative as the male. Says Kennedy, 'There is nothing in the text to indicate that the woman is considered as equal in value and worth to the man.'[84]

Against Trible's interpretation is the fact that *ha-'adam*, the earth creature, remains *ha-'adam*, the man, after the creation of the woman. Surely, scholars such as David Jobling argue, this is evidence that *ha-'adam* is to be considered male from the beginning. Susan Lanser, similarly, draws on speech act theory to argue that conventional processes of inference would lead one to suppose that the *'adam* was male from the outset: 'Let me postulate that when a being assumed to be human is introduced into a narrative, that being is also assumed to have sexual as well as grammatical gender.'[85] Logic is on Trible's side: a biological male is

---

[80] Ibid., 132.
[81] This is in fact the chapter heading, 72-143.
[82] Trible, *God and the Rhetoric of Sexuality*, 202.
[83] Amongst whom, David Jobling, Mieke Bal, Susan Lanser.
[84] Kennedy, 'Political Allegory in Genesis 2-3', 8.
[85] Lanser, 'Applications of Speech-Act Theory', 72. Lanser's primary argument is that Trible's formalist approach ignores the importance of inference in literary readings. By

anomalous without a biological female, but Jobling argues that the text affirms the creation of maleness before femaleness against logic.[86] Even agreeing with Trible that *ha-'adam* was originally unsexed does not resolve a feminist's problems with this text. The unsexed *'adam* becoming a male *'adam* still, through the continuity of terms, identifies the male with original humanity and the female with derivative humanity. As Elizabeth Sarah says: 'by staying in the picture *adam* has not only become identified with "man", but defined "woman" in relation to *himself*'.[87]

Furthermore, altogether lacking in Trible's analysis is any consideration of how the sexually undifferentiated earth creature becomes male. How does the removal of part of *ha-'adam's* side constitute the creation of male sexuality? The interesting question of the significance of the rib, or side, is perhaps bypassed by a purely intratextual approach and requires socio-historical consideration. This is a limit to rhetorical criticism: if the function of an isolated trope is obscure, rhetorical criticism cannot illuminate it.[88]

Various suggestions have been put forward to explain this enigmatic 'rib'. In the cuneiform script of the Sumerians, the same character denotes both 'rib' and 'life'; thus a connection is seen between a hypothetical Sumerian myth and the Hebrew text's designation of the woman as Eve, or 'living', and her formation from a rib.[89] Graves and Patai suggest there is a pun on the word *tsela*, the Hebrew for rib: although the woman was intended to be a help, she proved to be a stumbling block or misfortune: again, *tsela*.[90] Neither of these suggestions shed any light on how the removal of the *'adam's* rib, or side, might be instrumental in engineering male sexuality. In the absence of any such explanation, we may choose between two flawed proposals: either maleness was created prior to the intention of creating femaleness, against logic, and the original *'adam* is indeed to be understood as male; or, there is an aporia in the text and the unsexed *'adam* becomes a male *'adam* by unspecified means.

On the subject of the woman as helpmate, *'ezer k^{e}negdô*, David Clines argues that a helper is always to be understood as secondary to the one helped.[91] However esteemed, the helper's identity is defined in relation to the one being helped, rather than as an autonomous being. Clines considers that what Eve does to help is reproduce – thereby enabling human society. In this way the isolation of *ha-'adam* is overcome.[92] Does the woman's designation as *'ezer k^{e}negdô* after all

---

operating only at the level of surface propositions, this type of criticism does not consider the significance of the context of language use in the production of meaning.

[86] Jobling, *The Sense of Biblical Narrative* 2, 41.
[87] Sarah, 'The Biblical Account of the First Woman', 53.
[88] Although it should be borne in mind that Trible herself is not averse to introducing extra-textual considerations where she considers it appropriate; however, she makes no attempt to do on this occasion.
[89] Gaster, *Myth, Legend and Custom in the Old Testament*, 21.
[90] Graves and Patai, *Hebrew Myths*, 69.
[91] Clines, *What Does Eve Do to Help*.
[92] This reductive interpretation of the woman's role is contestable; it also assumes the procreativity of the human couple prior to the Fall. Sam Dragga, for example, argues that only after eating of the tree of knowledge do the couple possess sexual knowledge. As a

connote subordination? In itself, suggests Anne Gardner, $k^e negdô$ simply 'denotes a complementary creature, one of the same species'; it does not indicate respective status in relationships.[93]

One could also question whether Trible's idea about there being a naming formula is correct – or is the man, in fact, portrayed as naming the woman as an expression of her subordination to him? Lanser points out that the authority of *ha-'adam* to name has already been established; given this, the 'illocutionary act of naming has already been evoked; the surface propositional content of 2.23 simply re-evokes the same illocutionary act'.[94] Ramsey also argues that Gen. 2.19 and Gen 2.23 should be understood to have the same nature.[95] Even granting that 'this shall be called woman' is not a formal assertion of male authority, the story remains plainly androcentric in that it is told from the male's point of view. Whether the earth creature became male only with the creation of the woman or whether the earth creature was always male, it is the reaction of the man we hear about in Genesis 2: 23-24. Moreover, the woman is referred to as 'his woman', but the man is not referred to as 'her man'.

A more general objection to Trible's argument is that, given the social context of ancient Israel, it would fit for the text to be androcentric and patriarchal but strike an incongruous chord for the text to accord with feminist principles.[96] Nevertheless, Jobling argues, 'positive' notes are struck – but precisely because the patriarchal mindset is tying itself in knots 'trying to account for woman and femaleness in a way which *both* makes sense *and* supports patriarchal assumptions'; there is, though, no 'feminist consciousness' being expressed.[97] Given the context of production and reception, it must be asked: 'why is it acceptable to patriarchal assumptions, indeed how does it subserve these assumptions?'[98]

The Limits of Rhetorical Criticism

Thus, as an exercise in rhetorical criticism there are several points at which the sustainability of Trible's case is called into doubt. As an interpreter who affirms

---

consequence comes the prohibition against eating of the tree of life and expulsion from the garden: the potential for personal immortality is lost in favour of fertility. Dragga, 'Genesis 2-3: A Story of Liberation'.

[93] Gardner, 'Genesis 2.4b-25', 5.
[94] Lanser, 'Applications of Speech-Act Theory', 73.
[95] Ramsey, 'Is Name-Giving an Act of Domination . . .?'. Ramsey, however, then goes on to argue that this does not signify an act of domination, but rather of discernment.
[96] It can of course be argued that original historical context does not determine 'meaning'; however, since Trible sets centuries of interpretation over against the 'text itself', there is an implicit appeal in her work to an original, non-patriarchal intentionality in the production of this text. On those grounds, the objection is lodged within Trible's own terms of reference.
[97] Jobling, *The Sense of Biblical Narrative*, 43.
[98] Ibid., 42.

that the text sets boundaries on its own constructions, her work is open to the criticism that she does not herself pay sufficient attention to where those boundaries might be. The playing field for interpretation she has established means that other persuasive constructions of the 'text itself' can undermine her entire argument.[99] Her method makes much of small detail to wring a feminist construction from the text, whilst other details or possible constructions are passed over in silence.[100] That is the nature of interpretation, but it undercuts any claim that Genesis 2-3 can simply be pronounced a counter-voice in the biblical tradition. It may indeed be possible to argue that elements within the stories support a reading more congenial to feminism; but it seems just as clear that there are elements within the stories which lend themselves to substantially different readings. Even on its own premises, the kind of rhetorical criticism which Trible uses cannot produce a consensus reading of this text as 'non-sexist'; Lanser argues that a 'theory of language use that understands the role of inference in the construction of meaning *could not* yield the reading of Genesis 2-3 as a non-sexist text [emphasis added]'.[101]

Lanser's argument undercuts the principles upon which Trible's methodology rests. She presses the point that Trible's literary-critical method depends upon an understanding of language as formal code. Meaning is then posited as a function of the semantic and grammatical properties of textual form. However, Lanser argues that such formalist readings, in stressing the surface codes of the text, are blinded to inferential context. She demonstrates how a literary reading informed by speech-act theory can undercut many of the structurally articulated 'gains' identified by Trible's close reading.[102] The real difference at stake here is how language is understood to operate:

> As speech act theory understands language, the basic unit of communication "is not, as has generally been supposed, the symbol, word or sentence," but rather "the production or issuance of the symbol or word or sentence in the performance of a

---

[99] Indeed, reflection upon this point problematizes its very premise: it surely destabilizes the notion that the 'text itself' provides boundaries for 'proper' interpretation, when different interpreters draw their boundaries for 'meaning' differently.

[100] One could, for example, draw attention to the structural similarities between the .'*adam* being created for the benefit of '*ªdama* and '*issa* being created for the benefit of '*is*, and the mirroring of this in the eventual punishments: 'if the earth-creature is created 'to till and keep' the earth (Gen. 2:15), then the linguistic relationship between '*ish* and '*ishshah* could mirror a correspondingly hierarchial relationship of primacy and servitude beween the first and second created humans. I would similarly point out that this structure is mirrored again in the distribution of punishments, as the man's punishment relates back to the earth from which he was taken, and the woman's punishment relates to the man . . .' (Rutledge, *Reading Marginally*, 36-37).

[101] Lanser, 'Applications of Speech-Act Theory', 76.

[102] Some examples of this have already been given - namely, the questions of whether the original '*adam* is male or unsexed and whether or not the man's naming of woman signifies an asymmetrical relationship between them. Lanser's analysis is based on speech-act theory as developed by philosophers such as J. L. Austin, H. P. Grice and John R. Searle. Ibid., 70.

speech act" (Searle 16). Meaning is therefore a function of the *context* in which linguistic communication is performed. When people speak, they are assuming a complex system of what Searle calls "constitutive" rules – rules that do not simply govern but actually create the meaning of a particular utterance.[103]

Thus, the process of communication is undergirded by unarticulated contextual assumptions, an uncodified body of culturally constructed rules which means that meaning exceeds semantic propositions. The question is not whether or not one reads 'in context', but *what* context, explicitly or implicitly, one supplies. As Lanser comments, this should not be understood to imply that the distinction between formalist language theories and theories of language use indebted to speech-act theory (and Wittgenstein) is one between models of reading dependent on textual rather than extra-textual factors. Semantic properties of grammar and vocabulary are just as much, or as little, extra-textual as the silent body of conventions upon which interpretation depends.[104] Again, the axis of criticism against Trible here is her claim to be basing her reading on the 'text itself'; she is simply supplying a different, implicit context of interpretation, which depends upon screening out inferential context as an explicit factor in the determination of meaning.

Initially, Trible asserts that:

> If the story is simple, it is not, at the same time, neat and tidy. Abrupt, terse, elliptic, tentative, its language carries a plurality of meanings. From beginning to end the narrative is riddled with ambiguity. Embodying tension, connotations, hints and guesses, it compels multiple interpretations, as centuries of exegesis amply demonstrate. The task is not to circumscribe meaning but to enlarge it . . .[105]

Yet it is possible to argue that circumscribing meaning is precisely what Trible does, by presenting a univocal reading of texts which she acknowledges to be ambiguous. She does indeed try to make all neat and tidy, painstakingly 'explaining away' all possible textual forms which might suggest the expression of a patriarchal worldview. Plurality and ambiguity play little role in Trible's interpretation of Genesis 2-3. That, in itself, is not a criticism. One can acknowledge potential plurality of meanings, then argue for one particular reading as most appropriate according to whatever frame of interpretation is employed – whilst knowing well that this is one argument amongst a plethora which could be advanced. However, there is sleight of hand when plurality of interpretation is accepted in principle, then one particular reading put forward as the one demanded on the basis of the *text itself*. This is the working out in practice of the hermeneutical contradiction noted earlier: Trible's hermeneutic framework stretches so far it breaks in its attempt to incorporate the role of readers, cultural contexts, and multiplicity and dynamism of meaning into a theoretical model

---

[103] Lanser is citing John R. Searle's *Speech Acts: An Essay in the Philosophy of Language* (London: Cambridge University Press, 1969).

[104] As Lanser argues, 'Applications of Speech-Act Theory', 71.

[105] Trible, *God and the Rhetoric of Sexuality*, 72.

which rests on the assumption that the text itself can act as control and that particular meanings are or are not 'present' in 'the story itself'.[106]

To stay with Genesis 2-3 as an interpretative example: let us consider – what *does* Genesis 2-3 mean?

It is a story of liberation.

> It describes the origins of the human family as comic and heroic. It pictures the man and the woman developing as human beings, from timid dependence to aggressive irresponsibility to courageous maturity. It displays the woman choosing fertility and the man joining the woman, together forfeiting personal immortality, blessed and cursed with the ability of creativity, proud of their choice, and given their liberty by a sympathetic creator.[107]

It is a text in a state of tension. There is not one story being told here, but two: that of creation and fall, and that of resolution of a problem: there is not a man to till the earth.

> Our text presents us with a paradox at the narrative level. . . . Gen 2.4b-3.24 is a unit, and one expects thematic unity. But its major theme does not (or its major themes do not) unify it – rather it is unified by a superficially minor theme. The programme 'a man to till the earth' has been overtaken or upstaged by other themes – especially the theological theme of the fall, and to a smaller extent the social theme of marriage – which have captured the narrative interest.[108]

These two models are in a relationship of tension and lead to a failure to produce a coherent sense.[109] Rather than unity and univocality, we have 'a dominant narrative, that of the fall, presented in a way which creates deep problems and an alternative, "recessive" narrative which undermines but fails to replace the dominant one'.[110]

It is a political allegory.

> The creation account of Genesis 2-3 describes a basic social contradiction facing the Judahite royal élite, namely the struggle between royal social and economic interests and the peasant class. . . . The narrative of the couple's revolt against Yahweh is a literary expression of the social threat of peasant unrest and rebellion.[111]

It is about the daughter's desire to acquire the father's knowledge and power through the (phallic) sign denied to her. The father has erected an invitation to transgress, simultaneously desiring and forbidding the transgression which he will punish. With the transfer of the fruit to Adam, the potency and privilege pass

---

[106] Ibid., 11; 73.
[107] Dragga, 'Genesis 2-3: A Story of Liberation', 12-13.
[108] Jobling, *The Sense of Biblical Narrative 2*, 27.
[109] Ibid, 17-43.
[110] Ibid, 40.
[111] Kennedy, 'Political Allegory in Genesis 2-3', 11.

from father to son; because of this displacement of paternal power mediated by the woman, the son passes from his father's control.[112]

It is about the emergence of the female character.[113]

It is about the nature of interpretation: logocentricism falls prey to language.[114]

It is about . . . and the list multiplies, proliferates, interpretations spinning out with abandon.

What I wish to emphasize here is threefold. The first is direct commentary upon Trible's objectives. I would argue that 'recovering' old treasures, based on the 'text itself' is not a viable strategy. This is a hermeneutical point based on the nature of textuality. There is no 'text itself' which can act as a control on interpretation based on the meaning 'present' in the text. All of the criticisms levelled against Trible's reading, and the brief indications of alternative readings, base themselves on what is 'present' in the text and they all take different directions. At this point I must make again a vital distinction between the 'text-itself' and the 'text-as-interpreted', because I do not suggest that the text cannot play a controlling role in interpretation: but that it will always be the text-as-interpreted which acts in this manner, within the interpretative construct of the discursive community. The latter is the real control, for it is that which determines what role the text plays and what actually constitutes a reading 'based on the text'. Interpreters sharing a scholarly and literary paradigm will generally agree on certain principles of consistency, coherence, and taking account of textual features within synchronic horizons, but will not thereby agree in their analysis of what constitutes a 'good' or 'justifiable' interpretation. Indeed, the argument against Trible here moves in two directions: that interpretations are never made on the basis of the 'text-itself' but on the basis of 'text-as-interpretation' within particular reading paradigms; and that, within a scholarly paradigm of exegetical principles, there is a strong case that her particular interpretation is unconvincing. This latter point only serves to underline the difficulty in claiming that her interpretation is based on the 'text-itself', which can appear as a naturalized relationship if one particular reading paradigm is hegemonic and 'obvious'.

This leads me to my second point. Trible's work is very valuable to the feminist community. This is precisely because it undercuts and destabilizes the 'naturalized' relationship between patriarchal interpretations and the text of Genesis 2-3. As argued, I do not think Trible has plausibly 'reclaimed' Genesis 2-3 as an egalitarian myth; however, she has undermined dominant patriarchal interpretations and in the very act of doing so has pulled the threads of some

---

[112] See Rashkow, *The Phallacy of Genesis*.

[113] Bal, *Lethal Love*.

[114] This is a reductive account of David Rutledge's fascinating and multifacted reading in *Reading Marginally*, which highlights the manner in which Yahweh's own commands are 'fatally vulnerable to the vagaries of language' (190) and in which both Yahweh and the serpent 'seemed to speak plainly, but neither of whom apparently said what they meant' (195). He then contextualizes his reading within a post-structuralist theory of language, from which perspective "the conflicts dramatised in the text' appear as conflicts that stem from the intersection of langue, interpretation and power' (196).

inconsistencies which could be unravelled in a way rather fruitful for the feminist interpreter. The readings of Bal, Jobling, Lanser and Rutledge intensify this point, each of which in their different ways focuses on tensions and the very failure of Genesis 2-3 to produce consistent readings. I shall cite here Mieke Bal as exemplary of a reading based on tensions, which she locates in the function of the myth as legitimation:

> The burden of domination is hard to bear. Dominators have, first, to establish their position, then to safeguard it. Subsequently, they must make both the dominated *and* themselves believe in it. . . . Traces of the painful process of gaining control can therefore be perceived in those very myths.[115]

Bal's emphasis is on the need to explode the 'realist fallacy'.[116] Realist representation works powerfully in the perpetuation of values;[117] myth is another form of realist representation through its positing of what is as what has always been; myth defends the interests of the dominating groups whilst wrapped in its false mantles of sacred origin and permanence.[118] Like Jobling and Rutledge, Bal reads the text in a different key from the usual creation and fall model and looks at it from the point of view of the development of character. Indeed, her chapter heading sums up her approach: 'Sexuality, Sin, and Sorrow: The Emergence of the Female Character'.[119] Bal is interested in the subject as site of tensions; more particularly, the female subject who 'has been repressed or made guilty of all that did not fit'.[120] With regard to the story of Eve, Bal believes it possible to defend a reading that implies neither Eve's secondary existence not her temptation. But her reading is not, she claims, presented as a better reading, a master reading. Its intention is to undercut the dominance of established ways of interpreting particular texts and thus to demonstrate their precariousness. Her interests lie more with the poetics of dominance *per se*: 'the attractiveness of coherence and authority in culture, that I see as the source, rather than the consequence, of sexism'.[121] Therefore she presses forward difference as a means of deconstructing the androcentricity of prevailing interpretations.

This is a shift from reclaiming texts by reinterpreting them in order to produce a more congenial and *correct* reading, towards reclaiming texts as a strategy to destabilize dominant interpretations and thereby undermine them. It is a

---

[115] Bal, *Lethal Love*, 110.

[116] Ibid., 4.

[117] The interpretative history of Genesis 2-3 demonstrates only too well both how meaning changes and that meaning is not innocent. Bal suggests that the point to the story is creation by differentiation, of humanity, of character; (Bal, *Lethal Love*); how poignant that the differentiation into *difference* (Other) has been so often perceived as the 'point'. The step from difference to subordination is small and for many it has been only too congenial a step to take.

[118] Bal, *Lethal Love*, 4f.

[119] Ibid., 104.

[120] Ibid., 5.

[121] Ibid., 3.

shift which can be played out in two ways. Texts can be re-read, and it can be argued that a plausible and justifiable interpretation is hence produced with respect to whatever paradigm is inhabited (historical-critical, literary-critical, social anthropological...and so on). Or texts can be re-read with the conscious intention of subverting dominant readings and disrupting the ideological codes discerned.[122] Such readings may be 'against the grain', consciously *resisting* prevailing understandings of texts or dominant ideologies discerned in texts, and exploiting aporia, difficulties, and inconsistencies in textual interpretation. Reading against the grain then has a close affinity with deconstructive approaches, although not confined to that. It can simply be a refusal of a particular presentation of the world as 'true'; it is an aspect of the hermeneutic of suspicion.

In some respects, this resonates with Trible's own broader agenda. It has already been noted that Trible is not a 'biblical feminist'; she does not seek to 'depatriarchalize' the Bible as such, but simply to present her 'lost coins', as non-patriarchal strands within the Bible. Trible reflects on her work:

> Clearly, the patriarchal stamp of scripture is permanent. But just as clearly, interpretation of its content is forever changing, since new occasions teach new duties and contexts alter texts, liberating them from frozen constructions. Moving across cultures and centuries then, the Bible informed a feminist perspective, and correspondingly, a feminist perspective enlightened the Bible. Shaped by a rhetorical-critical methodology, this interaction resulted in new interpretations of old texts; moreover, it uncovered neglected traditions to reveal countervoices within a patriarchal document. It did not, however, eliminate the male-dominated character of scripture; such a task would have been both impossible and dishonest.[123]

Thus we can move to an understanding of reading as discursively constructed, of texts as plastic. Different reading communities discursively actualize textual potential *differently* within their own reading matrices. Then, as with Mieke Bal's analysis, it is the *difference* which can be pressed forward, as a destabilizing tactic. This does not, as Trible notes, remove the patriarchal stamp of scripture. It does however negotiate new pathways and readings, both denaturalizing more established interpretations and opening up different and potentially more fruitful understandings.

---

[122] I am indebted for this phraseology to J. Cheryl Exum, whose own strategy is to 'disrupt some of the cultural and ideological codes in selected biblical narratives in order to construct feminist (sub)versions of them' (*Fragmented Women*, 11).

[123] Trible, *God and the Rhetoric of Sexuality*, 202.

Chapter 5

The Terrors of the Text

Phyllis Trible's contribution to feminist interpretation goes beyond *God and the Rhetoric of Sexuality*. If, there, the focus was on positive readings, in *Texts of Terror* we are presented with a quite different set of interpretations. In this book, Trible deliberately sets out to read some of the most horrific tales in the Hebrew Bible, and by so doing, lays out some interesting possibilities for feminist hermeneutics. Is it possible to find constructive strategies for reading such texts, or rather, must we reject them out of hand?

Walter Brueggemann wrote the preface to *Texts of Terror*. As he comments, the great merit of Trible's interpretations is that her method 'lets us notice in the text the terror, violence, and pathos that more conventional methods have missed ... What now surfaces is the history, consciousness, and cry of the victim, who in each case is shown to be a character of worth and dignity in the narrative. Heretofore, each has been regarded as simply an incidental prop for a drama about other matters.'[1]

Nevertheless, the perils of embarking upon feminist interpretation are evident in Brueggeman's approving comment on Trible's work: that, here, there is 'no special pleading, no stacking of the cards, no shrillness, no insistence'.[2] One wonders at the gendered ideological investment in pejoratives such as 'shrill' – and perhaps too in the commendation of Trible's method for not being 'assertive'.[3] It is also interesting that Trible's work is exempted from the charge of 'special pleading'; feminists such as Schüssler Fiorenza might refute this terminology as negatively loaded, but argue that, in fact, feminist works are properly rooted in advocacy of a particular worldview. Indeed, Schüssler Fiorenza would contend that all interpretative endeavour emanates from particular ideological matrices, and as such is a rhetorical activity. That may be another way of saying what Brueggeman disparagingly labels as 'special pleading', but devoid of negative undertones and applied to all rather than simply to feminists. In any event, it seems that, from a feminist point of view, Brueggeman does Trible an injustice in his praise: she identifies her perspective as feminist, and clearly does not see this as a disengaged

---

[1] Brueggeman, Preface to *Texts of Terror*, x.
[2] Ibid., x.
[3] Ibid., x.

standpoint: rather it is a prophetic one, 'pronouncing judgment and calling for repentance'.[4]

What, then, does Trible claim for her methodological hermeneutics in *Texts of Terror*? Her reflections are brief, confined to the preface and introduction which together total six sides. In common with *God and the Rhetoric of Sexuality*, the springboard for interpretation is 'a feminist perspective, a literary critical methodology, and the subject matter of female and male in the Hebrew scriptures'.[5] Yet, whilst her earlier work was a time to 'laugh and dance', this later set of readings is a time to 'weep and mourn'.[6] What dominates the study, she states, is terror.[7] The minimalization of theory is intentional: storytelling is sufficient for her purposes, for stories 'are the style and substance of life'.[8]

Trible herself places more emphasis on the reader than Brueggeman would lead us to expect. Brueggeman does no service to the theoretical coherence of Trible's methodology when he notes that she 'proposes to get the interpreter/expositor out of the way so that the unhindered text and the listening community can directly face each other'.[9] This comment betrays a faith both in the primacy of the text and passivity of its 'listening community', and in a potential transparency of interpretative processes such that the text (unmediated) could shine through. It is an extraordinary comment, because one does not need to be an adherent of reader-oriented or ideological criticism to perceive that, in reading secondary literature, the very thing one is not doing is confronting the primary text directly. Furthermore, he privileges rhetorical criticism as methodologically 'natural' to the text: apparently, it 'makes very little, if any, imposition' upon it.[10] This is all the stranger for Brueggeman's recognition of ideological bias in the biblical-critical methods prevalent at the time of writing.[11]

Texts of Terror consists of four 'sad stories': the tales of Hagar (Gen. 16:1-16; 21:9-21), Tamar (2 Sam. 13:1-22), an unnamed concubine (Judges 19:1-30), and Jephthah's daughter (Judges 11:29-40). Particularly of interest in Trible's context of interpretation is her desire to relate these tales to contemporary experience: 'Ancient tales of terror speak all too frighteningly of the present.'[12] In the deft hands of Trible, they certainly do: she tells these stories in dialogue with incidents from the modern world, intersecting the one with the other. She describes how she came to light on these particular biblical narratives:

> ... hearing a black woman describe herself as a daughter of Hagar outside the covenant; seeing an abused woman on the streets of New York with a sign, "My name is Tamar"; reading news reports of the dismembered body of a woman found

---

[4] Trible, *Texts of Terror*, 3.
[5] Ibid., xiii.
[6] Ibid., xiii.
[7] Ibid., xiii.
[8] Ibid., 1.
[9] Brueggeman, Preface to *Texts of Terror*, ix.
[10] Ibid., ix.
[11] Ibid., x.
[12] Trible, *Texts of Terror*, xiii.

in a trash can; attending worship services in memory of nameless women; and wrestling with the silence, absence, and opposition of God.[13]

Trible's prose is passionate. She is concerned to do justice to these narratives, and seeks to avoid what she labels 'Christian chauvinism'. By this she means tendencies to set an Old Testament God of wrath over against a New Testament God of love, or to see these stories as products of an inferior past. She also wants to ensure that the suffering in these stories is not trivialized or passed over through trite strategies which subordinate the suffering of the women to the cross or negate it in the resurrection. 'Their passion', she states firmly, 'has its own integrity'.[14]

Those are the pitfalls: what reading method does Trible advocate? Firstly, it is rooted in a particular conception of scripture, which is seen to reflect both the 'holiness and horror' of life.[15] Reflections in and of themselves can neither 'mandate nor manufacture' change: but they can inspire repentance and thus, from sad stories, may come new beginnings.[16] We can see then that for Trible, engagement with text and engagement with world are related activities. The text may illumine the world (sometimes, as here, by casting upon it a dark shadow), and the world may shed light of a certain shading upon the text.

So text and world are reciprocally related: the scriptural texts can also be engaged reflexively. Scripture can interpret scripture. Trible anticipates the intertextuality of later literary readings in her creative setting of one scriptural story in the frame of another.[17] Thus the Suffering Servant of Deutero-Isaiah constitutes a recurrent motif, as do the passion narratives and the Pauline Eucharistic corpus. As we shall see, this is a destabilizing mechanism; the contexts in which Trible applies these familiar themes provoke unfamiliar allusions: specifically, for example, the representation of biblical women as figuring Christ, or the Suffering Servant. This intertextual usage of scripture to interpret scripture 'undercuts triumphalism and raises disturbing questions for faith'.[18] This is an important feature of a reading which takes the texts as both scripture and literature. Historico-critical readings are unable legitimately to read an earlier text in light of a later one, with no postulated historical connection, but simply a desire to solicit different angles on textual interpretation. A literary reading of scripture can engage its texts with other texts, both intra- and extra-canonically, for the purpose of creatively expanding upon its meanings or setting it off in a particular way.[19]

---

[13] Ibid., 2.

[14] Ibid., 2.

[15] Ibid., 2.

[16] Ibid., 2.

[17] She also anticipates the value of intertextuality as brushing alongside each other both similarity and difference, or either/or. The application and process are selective. Ibid., 6 n. 7.

[18] Trible, *Texts of Terror*, 3.

[19] Although here Trible operates intra-canonically, she explicitly considers that material from outside the Bible, from throughout history, can illuminate scripture. Ibid., 6 n. 6.

Trible employs the same perspective (feminism) and the same literary methodology (rhetorical criticism) as she does in *God and the Rhetoric of Sexuality*; however, there is a profound difference in the aims of *Texts of Terror*. Here, she is offering sympathetic readings of abused women *in memoriam*: through telling these stories, which are not only sad but stories of outrage, she aims to reclaim a neglected history on behalf of its female victims, 'to remember a past that the present embodies, and to pray that these terrors shall not come to pass again'.[20] It is unclear what Trible is implying by her expressed desire to recover 'history'; it would seem unlikely that she should mean this in historical-reconstructionist terms, and make rather more sense if it is literary history to which she refers.[21] However, this is an inference from the overall context of Trible's method – since it would, from a historical-critical point of view, seem naive to suppose an equivalence between textual representation and 'what really happened', and it would also fit ill with Trible's avowed decoupling of the texts from the moorings of originary historical context.

An account of Trible's methodological approach in *Texts of Terror* would not be complete without reference to the story which she identifies as paradigmatic for encountering terror. This is the tale of Jacob's wrestling at the Jabbok (Gen. 32:22-32). Jacob limps as he leaves the Jabbok after that strange night and eventual blessing. This story, says Trible, offers sustenance for the textual journey she is undertaking:

> To tell and hear tales of terror is to wrestle demons in the night, without a compassionate God to save us. In combat we wonder about the names of the demons. Our own names, however, we all too frightfully recognize. The fight itself is solitary and intense. We struggle mightily, only to be wounded. But yet we hold on, seeking a blessing: the healing of wounds and the restoration of health. If the blessing comes – and we dare not claim assurance – it does not come on our terms. Indeed, as we leave the land of terror, we limp.[22]

Trible's writing cannot be evaluated on its theoretical underpinnings as abstractly stated. Precisely as literary criticism, it is directed towards the texts, and it is in the embodiment of her critical principles that the strengths and weaknesses of her method can be appreciated. As such, there follows a summary of her engagement with 2 Samuel 13:1-22, the story of the rape of Tamar. It must be noted, however, that even following her argument quite closely could not possibly do justice to Trible's own rendering. The dazzling quality of Trible's prose style cannot easily be conveyed in digest form.

The leitmotif for her chapter on Tamar is: '*a woman of sorrows and acquainted with grief*'; its subtitle, 'The Royal Rape of Wisdom'. This is a story of royal and incestuous rape. 'He [Amnon] is a prince to whom belong power,

---

[20] Ibid., 3.

[21] Trible insists always that literary judgements supersede historical claims. This is so even in the ordering of the material, which is shaped for dramatic effect: from 'rejection to rape to dismemberment to sacrifice'. Ibid., 4.

[22] Ibid., 4-5.

prestige, and unrestrained lust. She [Tamar] is a princess to whom belong wisdom, courage, and unrelieved suffering.'[23] Trible excerpts the story of Tamar from the David court history as self-standing.[24] She examines literary structure and compositional technique as she attends to Tamar, the one female character.

Trible identifies an overall chiastic structure, in which three episodes lead to the rape and three follow inversely from that. The rape hence stands at the centre of the chiasmus and at the heart of the plot structure.

The initial ring composition sets up the tensions in a nutshell. To Absalom, son of David, a sister beautiful, with the name Tamar, and desired her Amnon, son of David. We have here three children of David, the daughter caught between two brothers. 'As the story unfolds', Trible explains, 'they [the brothers] move between protecting and polluting, supporting and seducing, comforting and capturing her'.[25] The stress on familial relations is highly significant. Tamar is sister to both Absalom and Amnon, and hence the daughter of David. Yet this family relationship is a gap in the text. Amnon is son of David, Absalom is son of David, Jonadab is nephew of David: Tamar's relationship to him is left as absent presence. Even more inauspicious is 2 Samuel 13:2: Now only one brother surrounds Tamar in the literary circle, signifying 'total danger'.[26]

Through skilful use of repetitions, the story moves forward with ever-increasing tension. Jonadab advises Amnon to deceive David, to act ill and request the presence of his sister Tamar; Amnon follows this advice. Whereas in vv. 4-5, Amnon informs Jonadab that 'Tamar, sister-of-Absalom my brother, *I*-desire', in Amnon's duplicitous speech to David, it is 'Tamar my sister' of whom he speaks.[27]

Tamar's repeated textual place is 'before Amnon's eyes'; the audience knows this a dangerous space for Tamar to inhabit; Amnon 'wants more than illicit sight; he desires forbidden flesh'.[28] This approaches fulfillment in Amnon's words 'come lie with me, my sister'. In this central unit (13:9d-18), Trible claims 'form and content yield a flawed chiasmus that embodies irreparable damage for the characters':[29]

---

[23] Ibid., 37.

[24] This is arguable: see later for the discussion of the difference this might make.

[25] Ibid., 38.

[26] Ibid., 39.

[27] Trible reads that David has 'unwittingly' sealed Tamar's fate (ibid., 42). However, other literary critics question whether we are to suppose that David is deceived by this fraternal wish. Dijk-Hemmes suggests that in fact the text hints at David's unspoken complicity. Amnon makes a significant alteration from the speech that Jonadab had prepared for him. What Amnon asks for is not healing food, but the ambiguous 'lebiba' cakes. A pun on the Hebrew word for heart, these could be translated as 'heart cakes'; Bekkenkamp, indeed, suggests that 'libido' cakes captures well both the Hebrew and the nature of Amnon's desire. Dijk Hemmes therefore asks the question: are we to suppose David has been given warning in the text of Amnon's true desires, a warning which he ignores? Dijk-Hemmes, 'Tamar and the Limits of Patriarchy', 141.

[28] Trible, *Texts of Terror*, 43.

[29] Trible, *Texts of Terror*, 43.

a Amnon's command to the servants and their response (13:9de)
b Amnon's command to Tamar and her response (13:10-11a)
c Conversation between Amnon and Tamar (13:11b-14a)
d Rape (13:4b-15b)
c'-b' Conversation between Amnon and Tamar:
Amnon's command to Tamar and her response (13:15c-16)
a' Amnon's command to a servant and his response.

And here Tamar claims her voice. Her reasoned response contrasts the wisdom of Tamar with the folly of Amnon, who would do this foolish thing which is not done in Israel. And thus Amnon would be like one of the fools in Israel. As Trible notes, Tamar acknowledges the position of herself as a woman: she works within the existing structures. She knows David would not deny her to Amnon, but pleads for the proper forms to be followed. 'Yet in this story victory belongs to the fools.'[30] Amnon did not want to hear her voice; he raped and laid her. In this way desire turns to hate and Amnon cannot get rid of Tamar quickly enough. But again, Tamar speaks. Trible stresses her firmness and clarity of speech. Sending her away, she insists, would be an even greater evil. Again, Amnon would not listen to her. 'The words of this wise woman he spurns a second time.'[31] He has her ejected: 'Send this away', he commands – and 'bolt the door after her'. No longer do we hear of Amnon my brother, Tamar my sister; the relationship has fractured; moreover, until she is out from the presence of Amnon, Tamar has lost her name.

The narrator poignantly introduces the information that 'upon her was a long robe with sleeves', of the sort worn by virgin daughters of kings; the servant puts her outside and bolts the door after her. Tamar ritualistically heaps ashes on her head and tears the virgin robe as indeed she herself was torn by rape. 'A woman of mourning, Tamar goes away weeping.'[32] Amnon did not listen to her words; desolate, she dwelt in the house of Absalom.

Absalom counsels Tamar who had spoken wisely to be quiet; Trible perceives this to be a pragmatic expedience masking a plan for revenge.[33] Tamar's desolation, though, cannot be reversed: 'She lives in death . . . Raped, despised, and rejected by a man, Tamar is a woman of sorrows and acquainted with grief.'[34] David, the King, did nothing, and it is significant that his royal status is mentioned in this context. Trible lays stress on a contrast between David and Absalom. To be king is to be responsible, to have an obligation over and above the obligations of a father to a daughter. His neglect of that relationship, is of course, embodied in the text through its very absence as an explicit reference. Furthermore, according to the Greek Bible, he did not rebuke Amnon his son because he loved him. If in the Judges' narratives, we are repeatedly told that such things could happen because

---

[30] Ibid., 46.
[31] Ibid., 48.
[32] Ibid., 50.
[33] An alternative feminist reading would emphasize the inadequacy of Absalom's response: even this supposedly sympathetic textual perspective could be perceived as projecting an androcentric field of vision. 'Do not take it to heart': do words such as this really offer sustenance to victims of violence?
[34] Trible, *Texts of Terror*, 52.

there was no king in Israel and each man did what was right in his eyes, here there is a king in Israel, but royalty does right in its own eyes.

The end-stress of the unit belongs, however, to Tamar: 'but Absalom hated Amnon on account of the deed that he raped Tamar his sister'.[35] Absalom's hate is left, festering and unresolved. Two years later, Absalom murders Amnon: the rape of Tamar is cited as the cause. And 'there were born to Absalom three sons and one daughter: her name was Tamar' (14:27);[36] Thus, '[f]rom aunt to niece have passed name and beauty so that rape and desolation have not the final word in the story of Tamar'.[37]

Hence Trible's reading suggests that, with respect to the portrayal of Tamar as female subject, she is the victim of the plot, but not of the narrative. That is to say, the sequence of events, the plot, is against her: but she and her plight are sympathetically presented in the narrative. Bringing women to visibility is one of the tasks of feminist interpretation; here Tamar is clearly visible. The literary devices are employed to emphasize the horror of her situation, not to pass over it in indifference or silence. And it is with Tamar, ironically, that the voice of wisdom lies. Tamar's speech is directed towards keeping order, maintaining societal codes. Amnon violates both them and her in this incestuous rape.

Trible's literary interpretation can therefore encompass a more nuanced perspective then simply demonstrating the perfidious manner in which women are used and abused in the Hebrew Bible. It can of course be argued that Trible over-estimates the extent to which the narrative accords Tamar subject-status. Placing 2 Samuel 13:1-22 in its broader literary location, might for example, cast a very different shading upon it. The rape of Tamar is preceded by David's appropriation of Bathsheba and murder of her husband, and followed by the murder of David's first-born son, an uprising by another of his sons (Absalom), the public rape of ten of David's wives, and a further revolt from Sheba in the north. This could be seen as an intertwined literary set, in which the disorder inscribed on individual women in the shape of rape is played out in ever-increasing circles. There is a pile-up of disorder, emanating from an initial disorder in David's illicit desire for Bathsheba. This might also usefully be set in context of the fortunes of the House of David. The court history of 2 Samuel is far from presenting David as an ideal figure. The adulterous taking of Bathsheba and the murder of her unfortunate husband, Uriah, are a crucial pivotal point in the narrative. Nathan the prophet brings to him words from Yahweh which do not augur well: 'I gave you your master's house . . . I gave you the house of Israel and of Judah.' Following this evil, 'a sword will not turn aside from your house, a lasting sword . . . Behold, I am raising up evil against you from your house.'[38] David's family history in 2 Samuel 10-20 is intertwined with political history. Gunn and Fewell locate this within the context of approaching stability: 'As one house (the house of Israel) is secured, another (the house of the king) begins to crumble.'[39] If this reading in terms of broader literary location has

---

[35] Ibid., 54.
[36] Cited in ibid., 55.
[37] Ibid., 55.
[38] 2 Samuel 12:8-11.
[39] Gunn and Fewell, *Narrative in the Hebrew Bible*, 167.

merit, the story of Tamar is circumscribed if taken in isolation. On the other hand, reading it in terms of context undercuts the emphasis on Tamar as a character, who then becomes (like Bathsheba) appropriated to a story about male power-plays and political manoeuvres.

Such a reading would be double jeopardy for these biblical women. Firstly, they are assigned the role of victim; they figure as the objects of rape and of violent abuse. Secondly, even their rapes are not their own; it would seem that even the rape of women is not really about women, it is about men – power-struggles between individual men and, on a broader scale, in the socio-political ordering. And indeed, exposing the ideological obfuscations and manipulations which operate against women in textual strategies is a significant aspect of feminist interpretation, and I would argue a crucial one.

However, to limit an exposition to that would, I believe, itself be a violence against biblical women. The interpreter and interpretation would perpetuate the relegation of women to liminality, to invisibility, where they are not female subjects but wholly and only objects in male-oriented narrative ploys. The texts can support considerable diversity and what appear to be ideological contradictions. As part of this diversity, women can appear as both subject and object, user and used, within patriarchal ordering and subverting or overturning it. Therefore, Trible's reading is powerfully subversive of monolithic readings of 'women in patriarchy'; she draws from the narrative a reading which makes it a story about Tamar, rather than a story about David. Of course, these are not mutually exclusive strategies: such divergent readings can co-exist, both/and rather than either/or, the one not necessarily subordinated to the other but lying alongside it.

This study of Tamar is typical of Trible's approach in all four stories. Her accounts analyse the articulation of form and content in readings which revolve around the main female characters. Partly then, this literary retelling is a challenge to conventional readings simply because it privileges the woman's point of view, highlighting the shocking nature of these particular tales. She does not have any obvious vested interest in portraying the biblical narration as either 'misogynist' or 'sympathetic', since her judgement as to scriptural representation of women is contextually determined. Sometimes, as in the case of Tamar, she seems to think that narrative art is employed to draw attention to the female character's plight. At others, as in the case of Jephthah's daughter, she is deeply critical of scriptural representation of the father as faithful hero, and scriptural neglect of the fate of the daughter.

Her own vivid rhetoric on the texts' rhetorical formations cast new and interesting light on plot, character and textual perspectives. But what really breathes vitality into Trible's expositions is the constant challenge she posits towards both domestications of biblical outrages and to contemporary attitudes. In all four chapters, she reflects upon the broader implications of her literary explorations and sets past as inscribed in the texts in dialogue with the present. Trible is not universalizing on the basis of a common 'human essence', nor suggesting that there is equivalence of experience which is simply culturally transportable and thereby enables modern readers to find a timeless transcript of their life-stories in biblical texts. Rather, she tells her biblical tales, then sets them in creative interplay with contemporary circumstances, allowing parallels and analogies to emerge from the interrelation. Whilst the practice of Trible's method has been exemplified with respect to just one 'text of terror', it is illuminating to case the net more widely the better to discern just how her hermeneutic relates past and present.

Firstly, then, Hagar, the 'desolation of rejection', she who 'was wounded for our transgressions' and 'bruised for our iniquities'.[40] Hagar, read with contemporary eyes, depicts oppression in three familiar forms: nationality, class and sex. And here, the only way to do justice to Trible's narrative, is to quote her at some length.

Hagar symbolizes the oppressed:

> She is the faithful maid exploited, the black woman used by the male and abused by the female of the ruling class, the surrogate mother, the resident alien without legal recourse, the other woman, the runaway youth, the religious fleeing from affliction, the pregnant young woman alone, the expelled wife, the divorced mother with child, the shopping bag lady carrying bread and water, the homeless woman, the indigent relying upon handouts from the power structures, the welfare mother, and the self-effacing female whose own identity shrinks in service to others.[41]

She is the prototype of mothers in Israel, the first woman to hear an annunciation, to receive a divine promise of descendants, to weep for her dying child. She is the site of contradictions. In bondage, she flees from suffering: God may be the God-who-sees, but it is Hagar, the Egyptian slave woman, who is afflicted: 'bruised by the iniquities of Sarah and Abraham', she bears the 'chastisement that makes them whole'.[42] She experiences 'exodus without liberation, revelation without salvation, wilderness without covenant, wanderings without land, promise without fulfilment, and unmerited exile without return';[43] in this subversion of the story of Israel, is terror. To ignore the theological challenge she presents is to 'falsify faith'.[44]

Trible places the story of Tamar in context of the 'strange woman' of Proverbs – she who is loose, an adventurer of smooth words. Call on sister wisdom, Proverbs 7:4-5 advises the young man. Amnon does call on his sister, who speaks wisdom, yet there is no strange woman temptress in this story, but only Amnon's own lust. Trible demands, 'If sister wisdom can protect a young man from the loose woman, who will protect sister wisdom from the loose man, symbolized not by a foreigner but by her very own brother?'[45] Israel is found wanting, and so, concludes Trible, '*so are we*'.[46]

---

[40] Trible, *Texts of Terror*, 8.
[41] Ibid., 28.
[42] Ibid., 28.
[43] Ibid., 28.
[44] Ibid., 29.
[45] Ibid., 57.
[46] Ibid., 58.

Trible's third story of outrage is that of an unnamed woman, representing the 'extravagance of violence', whose 'body was broken and given to many'. In the absolute applicability of the latter phrase, is terror. This is a story of 'betrayal, rape, torture, murder, and dismemberment'; a story we wish to forget, but 'are commanded to speak'.[47] We may not pass by on the other side, although in Trible's view, scriptural tradition overwhelmingly does.[48] 'Direct your heart to her, take counsel, and speak', commands the text.[49] Yet 'to speak for this woman is to interpret against the narrator, plot, other characters, and the biblical tradition because they have shown her neither compassion nor attention'.[50] And moreover: what response could be adequate?

What we can do, says Trible, is recognize that 'violence and vengeance' to this day 'infect the community of the elect'. To direct one's heart to this story is to recognize its contemporaneity. 'The story is alive, and all is not well.' Never again, we must say, and to ourselves: 'Repent. Repent.'[51]

Fourthly, we have the tragedy of Jephthah's daughter, 'an inhuman sacrifice'. Trible prefaces this chapter with the question: 'My God, my God, why hast thou forsaken her?'[52] Forsaken indeed is this daughter of Jephthah, whose father is exalted in Israel.[53] This daughter is 'an unmistakable symbol for the courageous daughters of faithless fathers'.[54] Her story 'evokes the imagination'.[55] Scripture can provide a model for suitable response. In 2 Samuel 1:19, David mourns for Saul and Jonathan:

> Thy glory, O Israel, is slain upon thy high places!
> How are the mighty fallen!

---

[47] Ibid., 65.

[48] Ibid., 86.

[49] Trible notes how the story fails to do so (ibid., 83): the response of Israel is to obliterate the Benjamites, killing 25,000 men, all women, all children, all animals. The only survivors were six hundred men who fled; in an effort to restore the tribe, Israel then sacks Jabesh-Gilead, and takes captive four hundred virgins and murders all other inhabitants; still two hundred short, they abduct two hundred virgin daughters of Shiloh as they come out to dance at the yearly festival of Yahweh. The rape of one has become the rape of six hunded.

[50] Ibid., 86.

[51] Ibid., 87.

[52] Ibid., 92.

[53] Ibid., 107-8. She comments on the shift in the Jephthah cycle of story from private sacrifice to public victory (Judges 12:1-7). Jephthah receives an exemplary epitaph (12:7), and in the Christian Testament letter to the Hebrews, Jephthah is credited with victory 'through faith' (11:32-34). This is a 'sciptural violation' of the story, in Trible's eyes. She notes that in the story itself, there is some measure of mitigation of the fate of Jephthah's daughter through the women's practice of ritually mourning her.

[54] Ibid., 108.

[55] Ibid., 108.

Trible concludes this chapter and this book with a literary offering of her own:[56]

> Thy daughter, O Israel, is slain upon thy high places!
>   How are the powerless fallen!
>
> Tell it in Ammon,
>   publish it in the streets of Rabbah;
> for the daughters of the Ammonites will not rejoice;
>   the daughters of the enemies will not exult.
>
> Tell it also in Gilead,
>   publish it in the streets of Mizpah;
> for the sons of Israel do forget,
>   the sons of the covenant remember not at all.
>
> Ye valleys of Gilead,
>   let there be no dew or rain upon you,
>   nor upsurging of the deep,
> for there the innocence of the powerless was defiled,
>   the only daughter of the mighty was offered up.
>
> From the tyranny of the vow,
>   from the blood of the sacrifice,
> the unnamed child turned not back,
>   the courage of the daughter turned not away.
>
> Daughter of Jephthah, beloved and lovely!
>   In life and death a virgin child,
> Greeting her father with music and dances,
>   facing his blame with clarity and strength.
>
> Ye daughters of Israel, weep for your sister,
>   who suffered the betrayal of her foolish father,
>   who turned to you for solace and love.
>
> How are the powerless fallen
>   in the midst of victory!
>
> The daughter of Jephthah lies slain upon thy high places.
> I weep for you, my little sister.
> Very poignant is your story to me;
>   your courage to me is wonderful,
>   surpassing the courage of men.
>
> How are the powerless fallen,
>   a terrible sacrifice to a faithless vow!

I give prominence to this poetic conclusion because this aspect of Trible's hermeneutics has, I would argue, received insufficient attention. The postscripts to

---

[56] Ibid., 108-9.

her chapters seem to be perceived as insignificant comments after the *real* reading has been done. This is an inference from absence: there is little mention of the importance of creativity and imagination to Trible's hermeneutics. Yet the closing paragraphs to each chapter are where she confronts the challenge of each story and reflects upon it with a view to forging a theological and contemporary response. This is surely a crucial component of Trible's hermeneutics: the reading itself is a moment in a broader task.

Part of this, as has been noted by Carol Smith, is Trible's refusal to occupy the paradigm of objectivist scholarship.[57] She names herself as a feminist, then goes on to present emotionally laden interpretations of these horrific texts. Her own powerful prose is directed towards eliciting a response of passion from her audience. This could be seen as part of feminist rejection of neutral objectivity and insistence upon the ethical dimension to reading. With such stories as these, it is surely the affective horror of the texts which most fully calls out an ethical response.

In memoriam: that was the sign under which Trible read these texts. As a feminist strategy, this links in with Schüssler Fiorenza's hermeneutic of remembrance, which shall be explored much more fully in Chapter 6. Where scriptural texts offer no possibility of redemption, of liberating openings, one must ponder in what sense they might contribute towards feminist theological readings. And yet in a sense, these texts remind us that reading the Bible may not be about receiving liberating answers, but might also sometimes be an invitation to share the story of a struggle. As holy scripture, these texts occupy a limit-position. We ought perhaps to pay more attention to these narratives on the margins, which subvert dominant understandings of what scripture is or might be about, and instead demand us from a response. That is what Trible calls for in her intersecting of these texts with contemporary situations. Hear, participate, be shocked, she says: and then act. The action called forth is to be directed towards contemporary situations; in remembering these scriptural stories, we should be impelled to a response of ethical praxis.

---

[57] Smith, 'Challenged by the Text'. See Brenner and Fontaine, *A Feminist Companion to Reading the Bible*.

Chapter 6

Towards an Eschatological Hermeneutic

Remembrance, destabilization and hope: these are the three themes emerging from my analysis of Schüssler Fiorenza and Trible which I wish to explore with respect to their value for a feminist hermeneutic paradigm. The movement of my argument in this chapter is as follows.

Memory: we have seen how remembrance plays a significant role in the hermeneutics of both Trible and Schüssler Fiorenza, although it is in the latter's work that it receives a fuller articulation in theoretical terms. Initially, therefore, there is an extended discussion of Schüssler Fiorenza's foregrounding of memory in historiography in interplay with the historical materialism of Walter Benjamin. Benjamin was a German Jew whose writings have made a significant contribution to diverse fields, including literature, art and critical theory. Reading Schüssler Fiorenza in light of Benjamin, I argue that a feminist materialist historiography and hermeneutic must foreground remembrance as a strategy of resistance.[1] Although I concentrate on Schüssler Fiorenza because of the theoretical locus of the argument, it should not be forgotten to what extent Trible's literary textual analyses provide a practical demonstration of how readings *in memoriam* can be haunting, subversive, and empowering matrices for emancipatory action.

Destabilization: the work of both Schüssler Fiorenza and Trible is of such value to feminist communities because they read *differently*, against the grain of kyriarchal discourses. Again, this is an act of resisting reading. This should not, I argue, be reductively conceived in terms of a hermeneutic of 'redemption' or 'reclamation', set in false opposition to recognizing the text as 'sexist'. Rather, a destabilizing hermeneutic is one which refutes the notion of 'fixed meaning' in texts, because textual valence is located in discursive communities. Destabilizing readings can be related to Derridaen *différance*, in which meaning is differed and deferred, never coming to closure.

Hope: if to remember is to remember oppression, and destabilization is to set readings adrift, we must find ways to move forward to a hermeneutics of hope. For the former might ossify interpretation into reiteration of a hostile past, and the latter might lead to readings spinning endlessly and ultimately ineffectively, with

---

[1] I use 'materialist' here in the sense employed by Schüssler Fiorenza, derived from Hennessey; this is distinguishable from 'materialist feminist' used as a synonym for 'Marxist feminism'. This is because class contradictions and analysis are not held to be central over against other materially grounded contradictions (such as race, sexuality or imperialism). Nor is a mechanical theory of human progress embraced.

no resources for political action. This is where the eschatological impulse comes into play. It orients readings. Readings are not simply *of*, they are readings *for*. They are attuned towards a future vision of justice which reaches out from time unrealized, and draws time in the process of realization into its ambit. Thus for the remembered past there is the possibility of redemption, and for the free-flowing streams of interpretation there is the possibility of channeling towards eschatological visions.

Eschatology, indeed, provides my entrance into the dimension of hope. For as I shall argue in the next chapter, to articulate a philosophy, a hermeneutic, is necessarily to articulate a theology. Arising from my hermeneutic analyses also comes the question of what kind of God can cohere with the interpretative strategies and frameworks I suggest. The answer, I begin to intimate, must take its point of departure in a rethinking of the nature of being and an eschatological metaphysics.

But let us begin with memory.

Memory

'The struggle of man against power', wrote Milan Kundera, 'is the struggle of memory against forgetting'.[2] History can be forgetful. This, as we saw in Chapter 2, is the springboard for the recent surge of interest in so-called women's history. For historiography, always selective, has operated with a pronounced gender bias. History, it is ironically said, has been just that: his-story. Yet historical silence is not to be confused with historical absence. This is – as so often – well expressed by the poetry of Adrienne Rich:

> Silence can be a plan
> rigorously executed
>
> the blueprint to a life
>
> It is a presence
> it has a history   a form
>
> Do not confuse it
> with any kind of absence[3]

Feminist theologians, working from a theoretical framework comparable to that of women's history, have subjected the texts and traditions of theology to analysis from the point of view of gender dynamics. The biblical texts and traditions have of course been seen as central to any such enterprise. We have already observed the emergence of remembrance as a prominent theme. Phyllis Trible, we saw, draws on this strategy as a way of approaching biblical texts of

---

[2] Cited in Hewitt, *Critical Theory of Religion*, 147.
[3] Rich, 'Cartographies of Silence', *The Dream of a Common Language*, 17.

terror. Faced with codified stories of barbarism such as the sacrifice of Jephthah's daughter, or the rape, murder and dismemberment of the concubine in Judges 19, she suggests that we continue to tell these stories *in memoriam* and as a spur to contemporary praxis. Remembrance as a hermeneutic theme, though, is perhaps most obviously present in the work of Schüssler Fiorenza. That remembrance as a motif is a major strand of her hermeneutics is in fact immediately clear from the evocative title of her first major book: *In Memory of Her*. This title is a reference to the story of a woman who anoints Jesus, as told in the Gospels of Mark (14:3-9) and Matthew (26:6-13). Jesus is reported to have said, 'And truly I say to you, wherever the gospel is preached in the whole world, what she has done will be told in memory of her.'

The following discussion takes Schüssler Fiorenza's hermeneutic of remembrance as a springboard. We shall, then, trace again in brief the role it plays in her method overall. One aspect of her stress on remembrance is that traditions about women require recovery and placement at the centre (as distinct from the margins) of scholarship. Yet such a move is not only in the interests of a more comprehensive scholarship, although Schüssler Fiorenza is undoubtedly correct to assert that a 'richer and more accurate perception of early Christian beginnings' results. The nature of her agenda, as we saw, is expressly political. The significance of this will become clear in the forthcoming discussions. *Remembrance* carries far more import than simply filling in the missing gaps in historical records.

The experience and struggle for liberation of contemporary women is at the heart of Schüssler Fiorenza's feminist reconstruction of Christian origins; she seeks not only to undermine patriarchal religious structures but to empower women in their struggles against those very same oppressive structures. Indeed, feminist hermeneutics must claim this liberation struggle of contemporary women as its 'locus of revelation' whilst also reclaiming 'its foresisters as victims *and* subjects participating in patriarchal culture'. Heritage, it is said, is power. Remembrance is certainly not simply an additive historiographical solution.

The importance of remembrance to oppressed groups is clear in this statement by the historian Bernice Carroll, speaking of colonized peoples:

> The search to understand collective conditions and the relations of race to the dominant society has enabled blacks to locate their strengths, their social importance, and the sources of their oppression. Furthermore, this process has provided an analytical framework for recognizing their unity through historical experience, rather than simply through their racial difference from the ruling caste.[4]

Heritage and remembrance, then, are implicated in narratives of oppression and resistance. Marsha Hewitt draws illuminating parallels in this respect between Schüssler Fiorenza and the critical theorists Walter Benjamin and Johann Baptist Metz. Although it is Metz who features explicitly in Schüssler Fiorenza's hermeneutic theory, Hewitt contends that it is Walter Benjamin whose work has most in common with hers.

---

[4] Carroll, *Liberating Women's History*, 83f.

It is the perceived articulation between history, memory and social transformation which places Schüssler Fiorenza and Benjamin within the same theoretical constellation. In the words of Hewitt:

> What Benjamin and Schüssler Fiorenza share is a concept of memory laden with redemptive and emancipatory potentialities that are released when history is brushed 'against the grain' of the false and falsifying perspectives of the rulers' and oppressors' accounts of the world. The sparks generated by this brushing against the grain of hegemonic historical discourses in turn reveal as 'authentic' history the history of the oppressed victims.[5]

Schüssler Fiorenza, like Benjamin, resists the historical amnesia of the silenced. This is an overtly politicized act, based on a deep-rooted connection between memory and emancipation – or, in Benjamin's terminology, redemption. It is necessary to remember what history from the dominant perspective has forgotten, for the victims of history are also the makers of history: to forget this is be prey to false consciousness. If history remains captive to the 'historical winners', then the past injustices and structures of domination can only be perpetuated into the future.

Moreover, the past is incomplete: we meet the past only in the horizons of the present and it is never finished, never over, but rather remains open to us as a resource. For Benjamin and Schüssler Fiorenza, it is a resource that creates possibilities for liberation and transformation on the socio-political plane. In reclaiming the memories of women in early Christian history, Schüssler Fiorenza is not only striking a blow at false consciousness and banishing 'false' memories which tell predominantly of women residing at the margins. She is also subverting the ideological interest which robs the Gospel of its tensive political edge; like liberation theologians in general, she insists on the socio-political character and implications of the Jesus tradition.

Benjamin was a secular theorist, but his *Theses on the Philosophy of History* are steeped with theology. He himself declared that history could not be understood without it[6] and described the relationship of his thinking to theology as a blotter to ink:[7] 'It is soaked with it.' If left up to the blotting paper, there would no trace of what had been written. However, as Tiedemann comments: 'The historico-philosophical theses demonstrate that it is not up to the blotter. Apparently there are reasons beyond the control of thinking that make it let some theology remain, make it readable again.'[8] Critics such as Kittsteiner find the infusion of theology into Benjamin's historical materialism to be 'shockingly

---

[5] Hewitt, *Critical Theory of Religion*, 150.
[6] 'Although in the *Arcades Project* as well as in drafts of the theses, Benjamin himself wrote of an experience 'that prevents us from fundamentally understanding history without theology' (V, 589; 1235)', cited in Tiedemann, 'Historical Materialism or Political Messianism?', 72.
[7] V, 588; 1235. Cited in Tiedemann, 'Historical Materialism or Political Messianism?', 84.
[8] Tiedemann, 'Historical Materialism or Political Messianism?', 84.

imposed'.⁹ This does violence to Benjamin's conceptualization of historiography. His very first thesis expresses the value of theology to historical materialism:

> The story is told of an automaton constructed in such a way that it could play a winning game of chess, answering each move of an opponent with a countermove. A puppet in Turkish attire with a hookah in its mouth sat before a chessboard placed on a large table. A system of mirrors created the illusion that this table was transparent from all sides. Actually, a little hunchback who was an expert chess player sat inside and guided the puppet's hand by means of strings. One can imagine a philosophical counterpart to this device. The puppet called 'historical materialism' is to win all the time. It can easily be a match for anyone if it enlists the services of theology, which today, as we know, as wizened and has to keep out of sight.[10]

What this expresses is a theological subtext to historical materialism. Theology is a submerged substratum without which historical materialism cannot do. At the same time, theology is subordinated to the purposes of historical materialism. The latter is supposed to 'win all the time'. The question is whether or not it will actually do so. Theology enhances its chances of success.

Tiedemann thinks it strange and paradoxical that Benjamin should attempt to reorient historical materialism to revolutionary praxis by reaching beyond philosophy to theology. He comments: 'Granted, it is still historical materialism 'that is to win,' but to be *able* to win, it is to require the services of the most spiritual of all disciplines.'[11] This reveals more about Tiedemann's conception of theology than it does about Benjamin's. Tiedemann assumes that praxis is divorced from theology. It can by means be assumed that Benjamin shares this understanding, most especially since 'theology' for him seems to indicate a secular messianism. Benjamin is certainly concerned with praxis. His historiography is no abstract affair, but deeply rooted in the concrete conditions of oppression in a conflictive society.

Benjamin's vision of history is one of an accumulation of devastation. The debris of history reaches to the skies. An appalled dismay leaves the historian with nothing to say, no language to express the horror.[12] This is the shocked and silent gaze of Benjamin's Angel of History:

> A Klee painting named 'Angelus Novus' shows an angel looking as though he is about to move away from something he is fixedly contemplating. His eyes are staring, his mouth is open, his wings are spread. This is how one pictures the angel of history. His face is turned toward the past.[13]

It seems most probable that Tiedemann is correct to identify this angel as the "true' historian, the historical 'materialist' who has stripped himself of all

---

[9] Ibid., 72.
[10] Benjamin, *Illuminations*, 255.
[11] Tiedemann, 'Historical Materialism or Political Messianism?', 87.
[12] Benjamin, 'Über Das Grauen', Theodor Adorno's Benjamin-Archive, Frankfurt, MS 807 (unpublished), cited in Tiedemann, 'Historical Materialism or Political Messianism?', 73.
[13] Benjamin, *Illuminations*, 259.

illusions about human history'.[14] History lies in shards, a chaos of the smashed and the dead. Where we see 'a chain of events', the angel sees 'one single catastrophe which keeps piling wreckage upon wreckage and hurls it in front of his feet'. For Benjamin, the idea of 'historical progress' is all too frequently pernicious, resting on an anthropology of 'infinite perfectibility' and on a dogmatic claim to inexorable advancement. Progress is a storm which propels the angel 'into the future to which his back is turned'. His wings are pinioned open by the violence of the storm. As Benjamin says, 'The angel would like to stay, awaken the dead, and make whole what has been smashed.' But the storm of progress propels him irresistibly onwards. This storm is blowing from Paradise.

This reference to Paradise is interesting in the context of Benjamin's secular messianism. Given this, he clearly cannot be postulating an otherworldly elysian realm. Tiedemann's interprets it thus as a positive and inspiring force: 'If anything still propels humanity onward, it is the memory of the lost Paradise. This utopian strength is an *impulse* which has not yet expired.'[15] This does not however take account of the negative rendering of the storm which blows from Paradise. It is the storm of progress, which Benjamin sustainedly critiques. Nor do Benjamin's writings betray a nostalgia for some postulated plenitude, and what else could a 'memory of the lost Paradise' be taken to imply? I would suggest that Benjamin's allusion to Paradise here be read as critical, which accords better with the passage as a whole. Understood in this way, the most likely target is dogmatic systems which postulate regimented progress in the name of false utopias.

This point is important. Yet there is certainly a utopic dimension to his historiography, expressed through messianic imagery and language. However, I would argue that redemption is linked, not to remembrance of a 'lost paradise', but to remembrance of past oppression. This surely lies behind Benjamin's statement that 'only a redeemed mankind receives the fullness of its past – which is to say, only for a redeemed mankind has its past become citable in all its moments'. Redemption is important here. For Nietzsche, the catastrophe of history required a commitment to affirmation to it in the shape of the eternal return of the same. For Benjamin, that history is in a permanent state of emergency requires its redemption. Key to this is Benjamin's understanding of the past as incomplete. His thought developed here in dialogue with Horkheimer, who wrote to Benjamin as follows:

> I have long been thinking about the question of whether the work of the past is complete. . . . The pronouncement of incompleteness is idealistic if it does not incorporate completeness as well. Past injustice is done and finished. Those who have been beaten to death are truly dead. Ultimately you are making a theological statement.[16]

To this, Benjamin replied:

---

[14] Tiedemann, 'Historical Materialism or Political Messianism?', 76.
[15] Ibid., 74.
[16] Correspondence, March 1937.

> Your excursus on the completeness or openness of the work of the past I find very significant . . . Victory bears its fruit in a way much different from the manner in which consequences follow defeat.[17]

So past happiness and past suffering stand differently in relationship to the historian. 'Remembrance can make the incomplete (happiness) complete, and render the complete (suffering) incomplete. That is theology.' The apparent closure imposed by suffering, oppression and death can be broken apart in theological perspective. The past can be redeemed, transformed, by the present generation – which, like all preceding ones, is endowed with a 'weak Messianic power'. That is to say, each generation is endowed with a limited capacity for transformation. For Benjamin, 'our image of happiness is indissolubly bound up with the image of redemption . . . The past carries with it a temporal index by which it is referred to redemption.'[18] The past has a claim to our weak messianic power. To the historical materialist this is a serious concern.

This is exactly because the dead are not beyond reach of the historical materialist and because the wreckage upon wreckage of the past is not beyond redemption. The fight for the dead is no small matter: '[o]nly that historian will have the gift of fanning the spark of hope in the past who is firmly convinced that *even the dead* will not be safe from the enemy if he wins'.[19]

For Schüssler Fiorenza also, the dead are not beyond our reach: the subversive and dangerous memory of women's religious suffering allows 'for a universal solidarity of sisterhood with all women of the past, present and future who follow the same vision'.[20]

The concept of solidarity is important. It is not just a vague idea of empathy and identification, which appears to be how Daphne Hampson understands it in her critique of Schüssler Fiorenza.[21] It is a political act translating into political action. Hewitt describes how the concept operates in Benjamin's political messianism:

> The present generation redeems the past in an act of anamnestic solidarity with all who suffered at the slaughter-bench of history. There is no possibility of redemption, neither for them nor for us, if we allow the annihilation of their very memory.[22]

The praxis of the past generations should not be lost for all time. The praxis of historiography is a way through which this can be achieved. That is one of the points which separates the historical materialist from the historicist. For the former, the writing of history is itself historical praxis.

Walter Benjamin draws a distinction between historicism and historical materialism which evinces marked parallels with Schüssler Fiorenza's distinction between Rankean history and feminist history. 'Rankean history' is so named after

---

[17] Correspondence, March 1937.
[18] Benjamin, *Illuminations*, 256.
[19] Ibid., 257.
[20] Schüssler Fiorenza, *In Memory of Her*, 31.
[21] Hampson, *Theology and Feminism*, 33-37.
[22] Hewitt, *Critical Theory of Religion*, 153.

the important German historian Leopold von Ranke (1795-1886) whose name we had cause to invoke in Chapter 2. 'Rankean' history is presented as a history of events; the historian is required to describe as objectively as possible 'how it really was'.[23] For Benjamin, '[T]o articulate the past historically does not mean to recognize it 'the way it really was' (Ranke).' That is historicism. The task is, rather, 'to seize hold of a memory as it flashes up at a moment of danger'. The same danger affects both the tradition and its receivers, and the danger is this: 'becoming the tool of the ruling classes'.[24]

This is akin to Schüssler Fiorenza's notion of 'historical consciousness'. History, insists Schüssler Fiorenza, is not an artefact: it is the historical consciousness for the present and future; it has rhetorical aims, whether or not these are articulated. Like Schüssler Fiorenza, Benjamin believes that the truly historical is history *for* not history *of*. For, 'no fact that is a cause is for that very reason historical. It becomes historical posthumously, as it were, through events that may be separated from it by thousands of years.' A historian who realizes this 'stops telling the sequence of events like the beads of a rosary. Instead, he grasps the constellation which his own era has formed with a definite earlier one.'[25]

Indeed, Benjamin derides the additive methods of historicism, its mustering of data to fill 'the homogeneous, empty time'.[26] Nothing could be more distinct from the methods of materialistic historiography:

> Materialistic historiography, on the other hand, is based on a constructive principle. Thinking involves not only the flow of thoughts, but their arrest as well. Where thinking suddenly stops in a configuration pregnant with tensions, it gives that configuration a shock, by which it crystallizes into a monad. A historical materialist approaches a historical subject only where he encounters it as a monad. In this structure he recognizes the sign of a Messianic cessation of happening, or, put differently, a revolutionary chance in the fight for the oppressed past.[27]

This is brushing history against the grain. It is refusing the dominant ideology. History can simply mimetically repeat the gestures of historical winners. Historical materialists interrupt this continuity, for 'the continuum of history is that of the oppressors'.[28] The task is not to allow the oppressed access to tradition: but to construct it anew. Historical materialists look for the rough edges, the points which could offer a handhold to those who seek to get beyond established tradition. Historical materialism thus has its deconstructive moments. It is the 'exploding' of historical continuity which gives historiography its critical edge.[29]

---

[23] Schüssler Fiorenza, 'Remembering the Past in Creating the Future: Historical-critical scholarship and feminist biblical interpretation', 44ff.
[24] Benjamin, *Illuminations*, 257.
[25] Ibid., 265.
[26] Ibid., 264.
[27] Ibid., 264f.
[28] Ibid., 92.
[29] Tiedemann, 'Historical Materialism or Political Messianism?', 93.

Schüssler Fiorenza does not speak of the arrest of thought, nor of the historical subject as monad, but there are nonetheless also significant resonances between Benjamin's materialistic historiography and Schüssler Fiorenza's feminist historiography. In her determined reconstruction of the discipleship of equals, what else is Schüssler Fiorenza doing but seizing the 'revolutionary chance' to reclaim from a feminist perspective the oppressed past? Every time women's voices are heard through the cracks of androcentric history, the past is torn away from its oppressors. Schüssler Fiorenza argues that the 'remembrance of women's suffering and their history of patriarchal oppression must be kept alive as an inner moment in a feminist Christian history and biblical theology'.[30]

For Schüssler Fiorenza, an obvious corollary is that the biblical texts themselves must be demythologized. Whilst Benjamin seeks to 'wrest tradition away from a conformism that is about to overpower it',[31] Schüssler Fiorenza seeks to wrest biblical tradition away from its patriarchal codifications, of which the Bible itself is a prime example.[32] Benjamin writes:

> There is no document of civilization which is not at the same time a document of barbarism ... barbarism taints also the manner in which it was transmitted from one owner to another.[33]

Schüssler Fiorenza would, one suspects, concur with this statement as applied to the biblical texts and conventional history, and also with the conclusion Benjamin draws from it: that the task of the historical materialist is 'to brush history against the grain'.[34] For history, as both Schüssler Fiorenza and Benjamin know, can be tyranny.

The political implications of the past for the present cannot be avoided by the historical materialist. The historian, in grasping the constellation of the present era with a former one, 'establishes a conception of the present as the "time of the now" which is shot through with chips of Messianic time':[35] that is, enables the moment of insight which is a breakthrough in understanding and a prerequisite for the possibility of action. Benjamin calls this apprehension of the present through the past the 'tiger's leap' into history. For him the question is whether this leap takes place in an arena where the ruling classes give the commands, or whether it takes place in the 'open air of history'; in the latter instance, the leap is a dialectical one.

Presumably it is only the dialectical leap into the past which enables one to perceive the genuine historical image, which flares up but briefly.[36] Whilst historicism believes with Gottfried Keller that '[T]he truth will not run away from

---

[30] Schüssler Fiorenza, *In Memory of Her*, 32.
[31] Benjamin, *Illuminations*, 257.
[32] Schüssler Fiorenza, *In Memory of Her*, 32.
[33] Benjamin, *Illuminations*, 258.
[34] Ibid., 258.
[35] Ibid., 265.
[36] Ibid., 258.

us',[37] for the historical materialist, 'every image of the past that is not recognized by the present as one of its own concerns threatens to disappear irretrievably'.[38] That, says Benjamin, is where historical materialism cuts through historicism.

If that is where historical materialism cuts through historicism, it is easy to identify where feminism cuts through historical materialism. The historical materialist rejects the 'bordello' of historicism, and the 'whore' called 'Once upon a time'. The historical materialist is 'man enough' to blast open history. Yet:

> The good tidings which the historian of the past brings with throbbing heart may be lost in a void the very moment he [sic] opens his mouth.[39]

It is apparent how a feminist can appropriate this sentiment and give it a feminist gloss. The need for the wheel to be reinvented in every generation is a point well made by feminist historiographers. Nevertheless the shared ground between feminist historiography and historical materialism should now be clear. A materialist hermeneutic is absolutely crucial to the feminist enterprise because of its praxis base and rootedness in concrete conditions of existence. Benjamin's marriage of historiography to remembrance provides a useful rhetorical framework for articulating the relationship of feminism to the patriarchal past. At the same time, feminist theory cannot be subsumed into Marxist, materialist or any other conceptual schema. At stake here is the contest for what feminism is or ought to be.

De Beauvoir repudiated the label 'feminist' until 1972, when, finally, she considered feminism to have advanced beyond the merely 'reformist and legalistic'.[40] Just as Marx thought that communism would neutralize the problem of religion by removing the need for it, so de Beauvoir considered that socialism would automatically resolve the problems of women by creating an equitable society. Basically, she was rejecting a form of feminism which construed itself only in terms of women's issues: she argued that the fight to change conditions for women should occur 'in association with the class struggle'.[41]

De Beauvoir's insight cannot be ignored. Feminism arose from a concern with sexual politics. It frequently authorizes itself with reference to 'women's experience' as source and norm. But the very fragmentation of women's experience as a category points to the complexity of social location. A narrow, topical focus on 'women' fails to take account of this heterogeneity and the differences *between* women. That feminist critique requires articulation in relation to a wide range of indices of exclusion or oppression is increasingly taken as read. Class, ethnicity, geography and economics are amongst the structures which position us societally. That is why Schüssler Fiorenza coined the term 'kyriarchy' in her quest for 'an analytic concept of patriarchy that . . . could express the changing social relations of domination/subordination which are structured by the

---

[37] Cited in Benjamin, *Illuminations*, 257.
[38] Ibid., 257.
[39] Ibid., 257.
[40] De Beauvoir, *Simone de Beauvoir Today: Conversations with Alice Schwartzer 1972-1982* (London: Chatto, 1984), 29.
[41] De Beauvoir, *Simone de Beauvoir Today*, 32.

economic political discourses not only of gender but also of race, class, and colonialism'.[42] As we saw in Chapter 3, this replaced a binary conception of patriarchy simply in terms of the relationship of men to women with, in Schüssler Fiorenza's terms, 'a multifaceted heuristic theoretical model'.[43]

According to Toril Moi, 'Marxist-feminist criticism offers an alternative both to the homogenizing author-centred readings of the Anglo-America critics and to the often ahistorical and idealist categories of the French feminist theorists'.[44] Therefore those critical theories informed by historical materialism and neo-Marxist analyses would seem to accord well with contemporary feminist desire to analyse society in a multiplicative manner. However, a note of caution must be sounded. Marxism and critical theories parasitic upon it are not merely sex-blind, but actually phallocentric. Concepts such as 'class', 'labour', and 'alienation' are based on productive wage labour. Hence, women only become theoretically and politically relevant when they inhabit the male world of paid work. There is no reference in Benjamin's work or in critical theorists in general to the morphology of the sexed body as a horizon for lived experience. Feminism needs to develop not only critiques of masculinist theory, but also to generate conceptual alternatives.

This is where Schüssler Fiorenza's historiography takes its point of departure from Benjamin's historical materialism. The hermeneutic of remembrance ties both together in a materialist framework, but revisioning that framework as feminist implies considerably more than simply including women as a group oppressed by material forces. It changes the whole shape of the analytic through its discursive relocation and the demand for a different constitution of subjectivity, as shall be explored more fully in Chapter 8.

So the relationship of historical materialism to feminism requires theorizing. So too does its relationship to theology. Peukert provides us with an eschatological reading of Benjamin's historiography.[45] His aim is to revise Habermas' theory of communicative action. Habermas, having diagnosed the pathology of modernity, postulates an ideal speech situation as the locus for social consensus. This is, of course, difficult to envisage: it would require a universal intersubjectivity. So pragmatically, Habermas' theory may lead to paralysis rather than resources when it comes to social action. Peukert goes further, arguing that logically, the theory of communicative action embodies a paradox. This is introduced by the fact of temporality. The past and future must perforce always be excluded from the ideal speech situation. This, for Peukert, de-idealizes the ideal. To obliterate our debt to

---

[42] Schüssler Fiorenza, *In Memory of her*, xviii.

[43] Ibid., xix.

[44] Moi, *Sexual/Textual Politics*, 95. Moi is critical of French feminist apparent political paralysis or indifference. She cites the instance when one of Cixous' students connected Cixous's politics with her habit of appearing at the University of Paris dressed in 'dazzlining ermine', the 'sovereign center of a decorous, eminently caressive body', splintering the 'archaic scene in which the king would have his wives circulate about him'. Toril Moi's response to this is caustic: 'Ermine as emancipation: it is odd that the women of the Third World have been so ludicrously slow to take up Cixous's sartorial strategy' (126).

[45] Peukert, *Science, Action and Fundamental Theology*.

those who have gone before undermines the concepts of intersubjectivity and solidarity as preconditions for a humane humanity. But to acknowledge our debt to them is to speak of the impossibility of universal justice and happiness. Our civilization is built upon annihilations. Peukert articulates this paradox thus:

> Anamnestic solidarity marks, then, the most extreme paradox of a historically and communicatively acting entity; one's own existence becomes a self-contradiction by means of the solidarity to which it is indebted. The condition of its possibility becomes its destruction.[46]

Peukert suggests that religious affirmation is the only escape from this paradox, which can only be attained if the dead live in God. In this way a communal existence not dominated by relations of power can be eschatologically affirmed. As he says:

> The practice of universal anticipatory and anamnestic solidarity, the solidarity finally demanded by the theory of communicative action, is possible without paradox only if there is a God who calls the dead to life.[47]

Peukert attempts to use this insight as a foundation for theology, which, as Milbank points out, is a 'new version of the Kantian idea that practical reason must "postulate" God's existence, because only if there is a just God can the requirements of justice be perfectly fulfilled and justice be harmonized with nature in a realm beyond the present natural order'.[48] This is an attractive idea, stumbling, as Tilley argues, over the question of theodicy. Tilley, furthermore, criticizes the assumption of both Habermas and Peukert that a universal dialogue would be the route to a just world. This is because, as a process, it would involve 'colonization of other lifeworlds by demand for commensurable, translatable, universal language'.[49]

Furthermore, as Hewitt notes, the early Frankfurt School did not manage to develop a theory of intersubjectivity, partly because its emancipatory potential was undermined by its own 'intrinsic irrationality, situated in its inability to negate the reified image of woman carried over from Hegel, Marx, and Freud'.[50] The challenge for Habermas, she identifies as constructing a model attentive to 'gender-specific features of domination', and rooted in concrete speaking (or non-speaking, or silenced) subject positions.

It seems that Peukert's theological rendering of Benjamin in order to rescue Habermas' project will not hold. How then might theology relate to a historiography of remembrance? Schüssler Fiorenza's historiographical project is in itself by constitution theological. She insists that for feminists to repudiate

---

[46] Ibid., 209.
[47] Tilley, *Postmodern Theologies*, 14f.
[48] Milbank, *Theology and Social Theory*, 239.
[49] Tilley, *Postmodern Theologies*, 16.
[50] Hewitt, *Critical Theory of Religion*, 184.

biblical texts and Christian history is self-defeating:[51] rather, feminists must reclaim androcentric texts and patriarchal history and not allow the history and theology of Christian women to be cancelled out.[52] In this way, through the remembrance of women's sufferings, the 'emancipatory power of the Christian community' may be set free. This power is 'theologically rooted neither in spiritual-sexual dimorphism nor in patriarchal ecclesial dominance, but in an egalitarian vision and in altruistic social relationships that may not be "genderized"'.[53]

One might expect the Christian theological roots of emancipation to have some connection to the death and resurrection of Christ. It is interesting to compare Schüssler Fiorenza and Metz at this point. Whilst for Benjamin the idea of the Messiah is only an image, an analogy,[54] for Metz, the *'memoria passionis, mortis et resurrectionis Jesu Christi'* is the 'dangerous memory of freedom', anticipating the 'future of those who are oppressed, without hope and doomed to fail'. In this way memory 'breaks through the magic circle of the prevailing consciousness' that sees significant historical meaning residing only in the actions of the rulers and politicians.[55]

Schüssler Fiorenza uses Metz's concept of 'dangerous memory' and *'memoria passionis'* in a significantly different way:

> A feminist Christian theology, in my opinion, has as primary task keeping alive 'the *memoria passionis*' of Christian women as well as reclaiming women's religious-theological heritage.[56]

And, once again:

> . . . a feminist biblical hermeneutics has the task of becoming a 'dangerous memory' that reclaims the religious suffering and engagement of the dead. Such a 'subversive memory' . . . also allows for a universal solidarity of sisterhood with all women of the past, present and future who follow the same vision.[57]

For Hewitt, it is one of Schüssler Fiorenza's great merits that she cuts loose from the soteriology and eschatology of Metz and the weaker political messianism of Benjamin. In a Christian theological hermeneutic, that is not necessarily a virtue. Indeed, the hermeneutic of remembrance as articulated in Schüssler Fiorenza's work is a way of relating to the past; it provides a corporate solidarity which allows for projection into the future but it is not as such future-oriented. I would like to set a hermeneutic of remembrance to play in interaction with an orientation to the future. This dialectic between past, present and future can be cast in eschatological terms. As such Metz's dangerous memory of Christ can once

---

[51] Schüssler Fiorenza, *In Memory of Her*, 29.
[52] Ibid., 36.
[53] Ibid., 92.
[54] Hewitt, *Critical Theory of Religion*, 155.
[55] Metz, *Faith in History and Society*, 90.
[56] Schüssler Fiorenza, *In Memory of Her*, 36.
[57] Ibid., 31.

more enter into the hermeneutic, if we see Christ as uniquely related to the eschatological horizon.

However, the hermeneutic of remembrance teased out and illuminated by comparison with Walter Benjamin's work has great potential for the location of feminist meaning in a frequently hostile past. Yet, if to remember is to remember oppression as well as resistance, one must also consider how to move forward from a theology of remembrance to a theology of hope. Dangerous memory is two-dimensional, encompassing both hope and suffering.[58] In this respect, one might wish to revise Benjamin's concept of the angel of history. Benjamin's historical materialist is turned towards the past, in horror. In Christian theology, as I have already indicated, there is surely also an eye towards the future. Perhaps remembrance, then, does indeed need to stand in dialectical relation to the eschatological.

Mark C. Taylor argues that the present must absolutely not be justified by reference to a future.[59] This paranoid avoidance of any hint of the teleological surely results in a strange privileging of presence. The dangerous memory of the past subverts contemporary ideologies. The dangerous memory of the future provides an utterly open utopic impulse, proleptically represented in the Christian tradition through the resurrection, and figured as messianism in the work of Walter Benjamin. This is an eschatological hermeneutic of remembrance promulgated from a present which is never self-identical with itself. Past, present and future are then figured as incomplete, pregnant with possibility, always construed and reconstrued from particular locations and imbued with potentially seditious significance.

Destabilization

If remembrance is oriented towards specificities, destabilization irrupts from the *shiftiness* of interpretation. The one points to materialities, the other to flux. This might appear to set the two in polar relationship to each other. This is not, in fact, the case. We shall see why this is so presently. For the moment, however, it is necessary to unpack somewhat more carefully just what is involved in this proposed hermeneutic strategy.[60] It is helpful, therefore, to recap on the analysis which prompted its promulgation.

---

[58] Sharon Welch also argues this (*Communities of Resistance and Solidarity*).

[59] See Taylor, *Altarity*, 293-4.

[60] Alicia Ostriker (*Feminist Revision and the Bible*) also proposes what she calls a hermeneutics of indeterminacy, highlighting the contradictory, multiple and indeterminate nature of scriptural meaning. I mean to say something rather different; by using a verbal noun, I want to point more explicitly to an *active* and resisting strategy, which can root itself in interpretative flux but is deliberately exploiting that. Furthermore, by focusing on the site of meaning-production rather than the nature of textuality as indeterminate, I want also to stress the role that discursive locations play in readings in general and destabilizing readings in particular.

Primarily, this took its leave from critical consideration of Trible's hermeneutic of 'redemption' in *God and the Rhetoric of Sexuality*. Following through her methodology in practice led to the conclusion that her 'positive' readings were founded on unsustainable claims to be articulating the meaning of the text 'properly' (which did not actually cohere with her own flexible hermeneutic principles as stated at the outset). However, I suggested that this did not negate the value of her work, but rather indicated that it was more helpfully located on a different register. Namely, dealing with predominantly kyriarchal texts makes 'reading against the grain' the norm rather than the exception. Given this, readings such as Trible's are enormously useful precisely because they highlight the cultural values inscribed in the responses to the text evident in more typical interpretations. By reading *otherwise*, the prevailing ideological inscriptions in texts and interpretations are cast into sharp relief. What is more, the very *possibility* of reading otherwise is telling. What it tells is the non-absoluteness of any given interpretation and the always present possibility of reading differently.

This plays itself out in (of course) innumerable ways. In any given interpretative paradigm for reading the Bible (historical-critical, social-scientific, formalist, narrative, psychoanalytical, pastoral-devotional and so on), interpretations abound, even where goals and criteria are quite tightly defined and broadly accepted. Where these are also subject to differentiation and dispute, it is to be expected that interpretation will become a profoundly unstable enterprise. This provides an opportunity into which feminist interpreters can leap, deliberately exploiting the precariousness of interpretative foundations to shake free readings which answer more fully to feminist concerns.

The goals of interpretation then become paramount. What manner of interpretations serve feminist ends? Can this be determined in advance of the readings themselves, and given the pluriformity of feminism, could any defined set of goals ever be promulgated? To the last, I would answer a definitive no. Feminist discursive sites spring from specific and diverse communal and individual roots. There is a double sense, then, in which feminist interpretation as an abstraction must be endless.

Nevertheless, we can begin to hazard some possibilities. These are laid forth to illustrate the panoply of potentially fruitful feminist interpretative strategies, not as categorizations which are mutually exclusive, comprehensive, or closed. This is not intended as a taxonomy of feminist biblical interpretation, but as an unfolding of some of its dimensions.[61]

---

[61] Several such have been attempted. See, for example, Carolyn Osiek's 'The Feminist and the Bible', where she sees a possible break-down into loyalist, rejectionist, revisionist, sublimationist and liberationist approaches. Katherine Doob Sakenfield offers a simple three-fold analysis: looking to texts about women to counteract prevailing patriarchal texts about women; looking to the Bible for a general theological-liberationist perspective; looking to texts about women to intersect contemporary times and past times ('Feminist Uses of Biblical Materials'); the *Postmodern Bible* identifies hermeneutics of recuperation, suspicion, survival and postmodern critique. This is by no means a full listing, but merely an indicative one.

One mode, exemplified so well by Trible's *God and the Rhetoric of Sexuality*, is revisionist and reformist: it re-reads purportedly kyriarchal texts to show them in a more positive light, it recovers forgotten texts which seem more egalitarian in orientation.[62] This is often viewed as a strategy which ossifies the texts, fixing meaning as authoritative (God-given) and ultimately undermining the broader feminist enterprise which may be left with no resources to deal with those texts which do not lend themselves to 'redemption'.[63] However, I have argued with respect to Trible's readings that actually, these also can be incorporated into a destabilizing strategy, for the very practice and possibility of such readings disrupts dominant kyriarchal codes both in texts and interpretations.

Texts can be liberated from scholarly interpretation as exposition and become the fecund realm of bibliodrama, midrashic retellings of stories, dance, song and role-play. What is common to these various actualizations of the text is imaginative identification,[64] with a strong element of bodily perfomativity. Womanist interpretation is often an exemplar of this kind of approach; African-American women consciously draw on their slave experience, which meant black people were forbidden to read and write, and therefore developed deep roots in practices of imaginative elaboration of biblical texts.[65] Such dramatizations and retellings were frequently wound around motifs of liberation and paradigmatic figures such as Hagar and Moses. Traditions of oral hermeneutics predispose Asian feminists to this sort of strategy.[66]

Feminist interpretation can be an activity in subversion through the very asking of questions about textual ideologies and perspectives.[67] It goes far beyond simply asking questions about gendered roles and lives of women in kyriarchy (although that in itself is an important task); it resists the ideologies of the texts and interrogates them to disclose textual motivations, suppressions and concealments. It is attentive to silences as well to speech, portrayal and action; it seeks to show whose points of view are opened most obviously before us. It asks questions about power and its distribution and in whose interests a text might appear to function. Thus textual ideologies are dismantled, defused and apertures for resistance opened out.

---

[62] This was very typical of nineteenth-century feminist interpretation, such as that of Sarah Grimké or Frances Willard.

[63] This might well seem both hermeneutically and theologically inadequate, moreover. However, Mary McClintock Fulkerson reminds us of the need not to cut the strategies and resistances of those women who do not inhabit academic feminist circles out of the loop. See *Changing the Subject*.

[64] This is Schüssler Fiorenza's phrase; see *But She Said*, 26-28.

[65] See Baker-Fletcher, 'Anna Julia Cooper and Sojourner Truth: Two Nineteen-Century Black Feminist Interpreters of Scripture'; Katie Cannon, 'Womanist Interpretation and Preaching in the Black Church'.

[66] See Kwok Pui-Lan, 'Overlapping Communities and Multicultural Hermeneutics'.

[67] J. Cheryl Exum's cultural-anthropological approach characteristically exemplifies this; also Trible in *Texts of Terror*, Mieke Bal, Athalya Brenner, P. Bird, Peggy Day, Alice Bach, Esther Fuchs.

Feminists can destabilize biblical readings by setting one element into interplay with another, allowing the complexity, contradictions and incoherences of the Bible to do the honours in terms of setting the foundations trembling. This is often coupled with a theological recontextualization of the whole within a part: Ruether sets correlative prophetic principles of liberation up as her hermeneutic matrix;[68] Letty Russell sites hers within God's household of freedom.[69] Thus, from the twists, ridges and turns of biblical textual landscapes, liberating threads are carefully picked out and used to encircle the whole.

And remembrance as a hermeneutic may also be destabilizing in its brushing of history and texts against the grain. This we saw in the work both of Trible and Schüssler Fiorenza. I identified remembrance as a materialist strategy; it is opportune to point out once more that destabilization and remembrance, flux and materiality, are not mutually opposed but can coinhere. The exhibiting to visibility of *different*, subjugated materialities is an act of destabilization; destabilizing interpretations and dismantling cultural ideologies is a way of marking out naturalized, dominant or concealed inscriptions of discourse, which are always played out in material realms. Reading differently, likewise, may point to new and more emancipatory vistas, which again, discursively relate to the material.[70]

Those then are some of the ways in which destabilizing tactics and practices can offer illuminating pathways for feminist interpretation. However, the question of how such a paradigm might relate to *theology*, is not obvious. Within the Christian tradition, the Bible is after all supposed to function as scripture. Providing ways in which feminists can relate to it as feminists does not explain what theological contexts and paradigms might enable a mutual hospitality between theology and feminism rather than disjunction and dissonance. This is especially so since a significant component of approaching scripture as a feminist requires a deeply critical perspective. This, I contend, is actually a question about God: more specifically, the relationship between truth and God, since scripture is on some understandings supposed to be paradigmatically the Word of God, the truth of God made text. It is a question which, as I shall go on to argue, is anyway demanded by discourses of truth and meaning (or dissolution of truth and abandonment of meaning) because of the link which I trace between truth, reality and God. My philosophical perspectives and my hermeneutical conclusions thus converge to demand a turn to the question of truth and deity.

---

[68] See Ruether, *Sexism and God Talk*.

[69] See Russell (ed.), *Feminist Interpretation of the Bible*.

[70] For example, Trible's reading of the feminine in God could be re-located into Irigarayan philosophies of the feminine and point to a new sacralization of the female body in divine horizons. Bodies and texts are not divorced one from another. See Beal and Gunn (eds.), *Reading Bibles, Writing Bodies*. Asian feminist readings of the Syro-Phoenician woman's story can shed light on Japanese honour/shame systems. See Kwok Pui-Lan, 'Overlapping Communities and Multicultural Hermeneutics'.

Chapter 7

Truth, God and Interpretation

Hermeneutic activity proceeds from particular ontological and epistemological presuppositions. The shape of my analysis and critique throughout this book has a dialectic relationship to the principles which underpin it. Whilst peripheral to my work in the sense that they fall outside of its particular scope and goals, they are nevertheless fundamental to it in that the arguments are brewed within their parameters. Clearly a full and comprehensive articulation of the philosophical presuppositions on which this book rests is not possible within its confines. The aim of the book is necessarily limited: I seek to contribute towards feminist theologies of interpretation through suggesting a particular hermeneutic framework and set of principles. Nevertheless, the clarity and coherence of the discussion demands some consideration of its broader philosophical location. Specifically, the question of 'truth' is raised at every turn. Truth and God, truth and reality, truth and interpretation, truth and ethics: this book foregrounds interpretation but at the very least implicit in this is an understanding of each of these other sectors of truth-games. This is most especially the case given the account of interpretation which emerges in this chapter, where the intersection of interpretation with reality and ethics is indicated, and which begins to intimate a manner of relating the framework of interpretation adopted to God. This section clears the ground for the analyses and proposals which follow in relation to this conjunction of issues.

It does this is in a number of ways. Its most substantive contribution is twofold: it outlines an epistemological model that I label 'discursive realism' and which provides the perspective in operation throughout the book, and it prefigures the ontological reflections to follow by forging the link between truth and God. I move on from here to sketch out the implications of the epistemological purview adopted for textuality on the one hand and ethics on the other. Each of these subsections radiates from the central issue of how truth and interpretation interrelate, which is a subterranean motif throughout the book.

Thus, the point is pressed that implicit in any model of interpretation are concepts of meaning which depend on the relationships perceived between truth, reality, textuality and ethics, and that – as I shall shortly go on to argue – to speak of truth is necessarily to speak of God. Therefore, one way in which this section contributes to my overall project is through its contention that hermeneutics necessarily are sited within an implicit or explicit theological framework. It is not that, as a theologian, I am impelled to add a further building block labelled 'God' into my philosophical edifice, which is otherwise independent and self-standing.

Rather, to speak of meaning and truth is to articulate a worldview inevitably complicit with religious perspectives: any hermeneutic model is always already (a)theological. Hence, the urgent question raised is how epistemological positions taken up relate to theology as an enterprise which speaks in horizons constituted by God.

Postmodernism problematizes the relationship of God to metaphysics. It has become something of a truism in postmodern thought that the 'onto-theological tradition' has a symbiotic relationship with models of the Christian God. *God* is seen to be articulated within a metaphysics of presence which postulates deity as the Transcendental Signified – the ultimate ground and arbiter of Truth. Against this, I am in this book advocating a theology of interpretation in which meaning is context-bound, provisional and multiple. This understanding of meaning in general and biblical interpretation in particular is quite at odds with postulations of God as the Transcendental Signified. Expanding on an alternative model of the relationship between God and interpretation, better fitted to my hermeneutic framework, is a task undertaken towards the end of this chapter. There, I delineate a metaphysics in eschatological perspective from within which my epistemology can proceed. Here, I explain the necessity of doing so.

This section divides into three uneven parts. The majority of it is devoted to an analysis designed to elucidate the position I adopt on truth and reality and to explain why I agree with those theorists who insist that speaking of truth is also to speak, or not to speak, of God. Thereafter, brief attention is given to the manner in which the epistemological viewpoints arrogated are played out in the field of textuality, and finally, in ethics.

Truth and the Reality of God

Given its thematic basis, the shape of this section is unusual in that for the bulk of it I have chosen to dialogue very closely with one particular work: Ian Markham's *Truth and the Reality of God*. The debates into which I now enter are enormous. This section is a outline of the positions with respect to epistemology and ontology which I adopt. Because of the criss-crossing nature of our analyses, *Truth and the Reality of God* can act as a focal window into the areas I wish to sketch. Markham raises and interweaves the very issues which I am concerned to clarify in a condensed and lucid way. A thorough engagement with his arguments enables me to demarcate my own perspectives, which do differ substantially from his in several crucial respects. As will become apparent, this dialogue is the more interesting for the fact that my own analysis diverges sharply from Markham's at certain points, whilst yet in sympathy with some of his key presuppositions.

Thus, the purpose of my engagement with Markham's work over the ensuing pages arises from its exceptional applicability to the twofold goals of this section. Firstly, it enables me to develop a fuller account of why hermeneutics are inevitably theological. Secondly, it will provide the opportunity for my own understandings of truth and reality to be unpacked. Since I have suggested that particular interpretations of 'truth' and 'reality' are implicit in hermeneutic models, clearly it is desirable that I make explicit those philosophical trajectories in which my own conceptualizations are sited. Obviously, in this short space, I make no claim to developing rigorous and systematic models of either truth or reality. That would entail a far fuller interrogation of traditions in analytic and continental philosophy than is possible here.

Those, then, are the reasons for my close reading of Markham's recent work. His thesis, in a nutshell, is that belief in the possibility of truth necessarily involves a belief in God. As he states this:

> The argument of the book attempts to demonstrate that 'critical realism' depends on theism. It is developing and defending the traditional argument, found in Augustine, from truth to God. The initial chapters defend critical realism; the concluding chapters illustrate that ultimately such a defence needs theism. In the end, I believe that anybody who believes that it is possible to describe the world in better or worse ways ought (logically) to believe in God [emphasis removed].[1]

What I hope to demonstrate in conversation with Markham's work is that he has correctly pinpointed a crucial link between God and truth, whilst disagreeing with the critical realism from which his argument proceeds. I then sketch the alternative model and label it 'discursive realism', reasoning that significant portions of Markham's conclusions can hold on the basis of this, although on somewhat different premises. The simplest starting point for the negotiation of these similarities and differences is to follow through the carefully plotted argument of the book one step at a time. Thereafter some detailed critique will be provided and preferred understandings will be identified.

Truth and the Reality of God is an exercise in natural theology. It makes claims about the nature of the relationship between God, world and truth based on reason and evidence. However, it is important for proper contextualization of Markham's arguments to realize that he perceives natural theology as description. It proceeds on particular assumptions about the nature and existence of God; it does not act as justification for a religious world-perspective starting from the very different assumptions of an atheist one. The recognition of a fundamental difference in base assumptions between religious and non-religious outlooks is a key point. Underpinning religious world-perspectives is a commitment to seeing the universe as the result of purpose and love, and as the site of possibilities for creative actualization. This distinction between a world-perspective which is religious rather than secular humanist or naturalist is all-embracing, and therefore cannot be overstressed. 'God is not an appendage belief topping up or crowning all our other beliefs about reality: it is that in the absence (or presence) of which all beliefs are changed.'[2]

From these premises, Markham moves to the position that only the religious world-perspective can sustain the possibility of truth. But firstly, it is of course necessary to clarify just what is understood by 'truth'. As Markham outlines, variations on the correspondence theory of truth dominated Western metaphysics

---

[1] Markham, *Truth and the Reality of God*, 4.
[2] Ibid., 22.

from Aristotle to the Enlightenment, when thinkers such as Hume and Kant interjected telling interruptions into established modes of conceptualizing knowledge. Kantian epistemology inserted an 'unbridgeable gap' between reality and our perception of it, within a post-Cartesian frame which demanded an equation between knowledge and certainty. This precipitated adjustments to discourses about truth which recognized more fully the constructive role of humanity in the production of knowledge; criteria of coherence and consistency on the one hand, or pragmatic expedience on the other, became central to accounts of truth.[3]

Philosophical exposition of truth can, then, be seen to emerge from particular historical contexts – which in itself tells us something about the nature of truth. Markham here focuses on Alasdair MacIntyre's writings on truth and rationality. MacIntyre illustrates the extent to which rationality is constituted by tradition, and to this extent accepts the historicist critique and Wittgensteinian analyses that insist upon the contextuality of knowledge. What makes MacIntyre's position distinctive is his simultaneous rebuttal of relativism. Peter Winch, by contrast, considers that the cultural framing of knowledge makes cross-cultural comparison impossible and illegitimate. It could only take place from some supposedly tradition-transcendent external perspective – which can never be attained. Otherwise, it is simply a form of cultural imperialism, in which the standards of one tradition are imposed on another. But we can never know that our standards are right, because perspectivalism means we can never escape from own cultural locations to evaluate what the world is *really* like.

MacIntyre does not want to accept the incommensurability of different traditions, whilst yet accepting that all knowledge and rationality are 'traditioned'. 'For', he writes, 'there are not two alternatives: either embracing the metaphysical fiction of one over-all "norm for intelligibility in general" or flying to total relativism.'[4] MacIntyre thus rejects the relativist solution to the issue of contextualized knowledge. This becomes coherent when it is realized that relativists work on expectations which MacIntyre does not share: namely, that discrimination between rival traditions would only be possible if a neutral standard existed, enabling the discovery of an absolute truth. The relativist response is to disclaim the possibility of such standards and such truth-discernment and therefore to refuse to arbitrate between traditions. MacIntyre's response is to reject the expectation that arbitration could only be done if such standards and such truth-discernment were possible. Those expectations are identified as false and products of the (failed) Enlightenment project.[5] Inquiry, for MacIntyre, is tradition-constituted and tradition-constitutive in a flexible system which includes the possibility of change: as the dynamics of historical process demonstrate, traditions can develop or founder in light of changing circumstances or in engagement with different traditions. Accounts such as Winch's, on the other hand, do not accommodate transition in worldviews, which represent cultural shifts to

---

[3] Ibid., 30.

[4] A. MacIntyre in B. Wilson (ed.), *Rationality* (Oxford: Basil Blackwell, 1970), 66.

[5] Markham, *Truth and the Reality of God*, 35.

perspectives evaluated as more adequate and capable of making better sense of the world. Furthermore, there could on Winch's analysis be no basis on which cross-cultural communication and translation could take place. That communication and translation do take place, however imperfectly, points to a footing on which cross-cultural comparison is made possible.

Markham is sympathetic to this notion of traditioned rationalities, although cautious about the apparent assumption of criteria for coherence and intelligibility which would be true across all traditions.[6] He recognizes the cogency of Milbank's criticisms of MacIntyre in this respect. Milbank suggests that explaining transition in traditions as occurring on the criteria of the older one is implausible. Furthermore, the notion of shifting towards a tradition which 'explains more' is highly problematic.[7] How could such a claim be evaluated? MacIntyre's position rests on the assumptions that traditions are attempts to make sense of reality and that criteria for evaluating success at this are cross-cultural.

Markham, like MacIntyre, is interested in developing a conceptualization of enquiry as 'tradition-constituted' which combines a robust account of truth with recognition of the contextuality of knowledge. This is the point at which critical realism becomes pivotal to Markham's argument, as the condition for communication and translation being meaningful possibilities. And it is the possibility of communication and translation which opens up the prospect of cross-cultural dialogue and comparison, from locations which are nevertheless always themselves within traditions and have no claim to represent neutral, tradition-transcendent ground.

Thus Markham sees it as necessary to affirm a critical realism which takes 'reality' to indicate a stable world independent of the mind, and which involves three claims:

> World perspectives are attempts to make sense of reality as experienced.
> Reality is the ultimate control on the legitimacy of truth claims.
> Certain world perspectives are better than the alternatives.[8]

Markham accepts that knowing is located in communities and that interpretative frameworks seek 'to impose order on reality, not the other way round'.[9] However, he argues that critical realism is a prerequisite of such insights, for communities require a shared reality for communication and translation to be possible or intelligible. Language constructs '*emerge as an attempt to explain reality* [italics original]'.[10] So the tradition-constituted nature of truth, knowledge and language does not, for Markham, demand a move to anti-realism.[11]

---

[6] Ibid., 39.
[7] Ibid., 38.
[8] Ibid., 49.
[9] Ibid., 50.
[10] Ibid., 54.
[11] Anti-realism for Markham is the conclusion that 'the human mind cannot transcend its particular frame of reference and know which assertions correspond to reality'(ibid., 33). However, he also includes a working definition of realism as 'the existence of objects not

Furthermore, even whilst tradition-constituted, an underlying universal is discernible: logic.

Logical thinking, according to Markham, is not timeless or immutable. It functions within particular frameworks of assumptions: but we cannot operate without its laws. What is more, for logic to be logical, it needs to fit the world. Nevertheless, different world-perspectives will apply logic differently and reach varying conclusions. They will however be engaged in the same sort of rational activity, with the aim of producing coherent and consistent explanations of the world. Any self-contradictory world-perspective could not be true: circles are not simultaneously squares. The question then is: 'does this coherence mirror the world or is it imposed?'[12] Markham prefers the former position and identifies it as that of the critical realist, in contradistinction from that of a Kantian anti-realist. This is because Markham finds it 'incredible' that the world should be chaotic:

> The world is indeed coherent. It is a stable, explicable entity, which does not contradict itself. If the world were contradictory, then the logical processes would be misleading our mind. We would not be constructing a true picture of the world, because the coherence demanded by logic would be mind imposed. The point is simple; reality must be stable, coherent and intelligible; otherwise our logical categories on which all truth claims depend are misguided.[13]

For Markham, then, our success in communicating (even if on occasion with difficulty and only partially) is evidence for an underlying coherence in reality which is mimicked in the logical structures of our language. This coherence could be explained as arbitrary and accidental – or, according to the religious world-perspective, it could be explained as grounded in God. The first of these options is, according to Markham, antithetical to a critically realist concept of truth. This is because a coherence figured only as arbitrary opens out on to the potential for incoherence: 'If the coherence of reality is arbitrary, then it is possible that either the universe could at any moment cease being orderly or coherent, or its coherence only extends to certain parts.'[14] This inserts a fundamental doubt into all truth-claims, damaging our bases for belief and dissolving the condition for critical realism. For, 'when every assertion can be doubted then reality can no longer be the arbiter among different descriptions'.[15]

Markham argues that the resources necessary for a robust critical realism can be provided by natural theology. As has already been pointed out, natural theology is, of course, itself a traditioned rationality: it provides explanation and

---

dependent on mind'(49). The two positions may of course both be held simultaneously. For this reason, anti-realism as used by Markham is very often indistinguishable from what Michael Devitt labels 'weak' realism and attributes to Kant: i.e. things in the world exist, but we only know about them as they appear to us. The phenomenal is the only way in which the noumenal is apprehended. (30).

[12] Markham, *Truth and the Reality of God*, 63.
[13] Ibid., 64.
[14] Ibid., 80.
[15] Ibid., 80.

insight from *within* the Christian tradition. This may – or may not – be persuasive to those outside of it, but natural theology does not engage with alternative world-perspectives from a neutral, tradition-transcendent ground. This is the context for Markham's embrace of the cosmological argument, which he uses as a justification for intelligibility in the universe. Only a self-explanatory, logically necessary being can provide an explanation for the universe which is not contingent, and only non-contingent explanations can properly account for a universe which is coherent, intelligible, and therefore explicable. Since traditioned rationalities depend on the view that the universe is intelligible (being attempts to make sense of the world), they also depend on theistic perspectives. The alternative is to abandon accounts of the universe which assume its intelligibility; only then can God, alongside truth, be coherently discounted from the picture. Only an unjustifiable rationality attempts to explain a world which is conceived as fortuitous, wholly contingent, potentially incoherent and therefore ultimately inexplicable.

With grand rhetorical flourish, Markham presents us with a stark choice based on this analysis: Nietzsche or Aquinas. These figures stand as paradigmatic of the two options he has delineated. 'You cannot', he asserts, 'assume a rationality and argue that there is no foundation to that rationality. Either God and rationality go or God and rationality stay. Either Nietzsche or Aquinas. That is our choice.'[16]

Markham's analysis is significant to my own project because I share his aims. I also want to stand with Nietzsche and Aquinas to assert a fundamental link between conceptions of God and conceptions of truth; I too want both to insist upon the traditioned nature of rationality and to reject that this necessarily leads to relativism. However, I cannot agree with a number of his arguments. In the process of this critical engagement my own stances on realism and the relationship between 'truth' and God will be elucidated. My discussion of relativism must wait until a subsequent stage.[17]

My first difficulty is with his account of 'critical realism'. I shall attend initially to Markham's second claim in respect of this: that reality is the ultimate control on truth-claims. I would contend that on this issue Markham has paid insufficient attention to the ways in which 'reality' is discursively constructed, despite his epistemological acceptance of knowledge as formulated in and for communities. Markham's argument is to point out that 'external reality' not only exists, it is the precondition of our communication and impacts upon that communication and our being-in-the-world in fundamental ways. As he comments: 'Even if I – philosophically – doubt the existence of the door, I still have to open it upon departure.'[18] What is more, visitors to other countries using euphemisms for requiring the toilet facilities would expect external reality to control the outcome of their request: if such a visitor were shown to the bedroom or kitchen, they would have been wrongly understood.[19] Thus Markham substantiates his claim that 'reality is the ultimate control on the legitimacy of truth claims'.[20]

---

[16] Ibid., 115.
[17] See Chapter 8.
[18] Markham, *Truth and the Reality of God*, 49.
[19] Ibid., 55.
[20] Ibid., 56.

In some respects, that is all very well. But the Kantian rift between the phenomenal and noumenal has not really been bridged here; rather it has been circumvented. This is through the conflation in critical realism of two different philosophical critiques of the nature of truth, the idealist and the constructivist.[21] Denying the external existence of the world is one thing; suggesting that the world is unavailable to us except as interpreted is another. A constructivist account of truth can accommodate a (weak) realist worldview. I can accept the 'external' reality of the chair whilst acknowledging that my understanding of it as 'chair' – an everyday object on which one sits, differentiable from 'table', and so on – is a construction. Inasmuch as Markham accepts both critical realism and the notion of rationality as traditioned, he too finds houseroom for both perspectives. However, he is troubled that an overemphasis on constructivism will fail to make sense of the extent to which we do actually communicate across traditions and, moreover, lead down Winch's road, where the 'realities' of different cultures become incommensurable.

Markham accepts what he calls the 'anti-realist' insight that language provides the framework for interpreting the world; he agrees that knowing is community-orientated.[22] But, ironically, he sees critical realism as the precondition for this aspect of the anti-realist position:

> One needs to affirm my three related claims before one can accept that knowledge is community-orientated. Communities imply the existence of other minds. Even Rorty and Cupitt accept the reality of a world of objects in which we all live and communicate.... As the early MacIntyre noted against Winch, a denial of any sort of shared reality would make communication and translation impossible.[23]

I suggest that an ideational aporia has been introduced here, brought about by a failure to take a post-Kantian distinction between the noumenal and the

---

[21] Markham in effect makes the accusation of conflation against those 'anti-realists' he critiques, Rorty and Cupitt. He identifies a 'frustrating' tendency in their work to shift between affirmations that reality – i.e. objects and events external to the mind – does actually exist, and statements which seem to identify reality with linguistic constructions. 'Rorty it seems does believe in objects. However, the problem is that so many of his arguments point in the opposite direction;' 'Cupitt slips between insisting that the actual external world is irrelevant to the purposes of language and conceding its reality as an assumption of language' (Markham, *Truth and the Reality of God*, 48). I suggest that Markham also performs this 'double' manoeuvre, in a different way, by including a value judgement in his definition of 'critical realism'. To say that objects actually exist and exert formative influence on our constructions of the world is one thing; to say that realism means we can distinguish between better and worse descriptions of those objects is another point. Markham performs this manoeuvre deliberately to allow for the development of a more complex realism. I would argue that this begs the question of the relationship between the two and incorporates a fundamental difficulty into 'critical realism' as outlined. I develop further comments along these lines in the succeeding paragraphs.

[22] Markham, *Truth and the Reality of God*, 50.

[23] Ibid., 50.

phenomenal sufficiently seriously. The three related claims in Markham's critical realism include, firstly, that world perspectives are 'attempts to make sense of reality as experienced', and secondly, that '[r]eality is the ultimate control on the legitimacy of truth-claims'.[24] But the distinction between 'reality' and 'reality-as-experienced' can only be upheld at the conceptual level. It is reality-as-experienced which constitutes the sum of our potential knowledge of reality. And here I agree with Cupitt: 'The surface play of phenomena – words, signs, meanings, appearances – is reality. Why seek to downgrade it? The fatal illusion is to believe that we can pierce the veil and find more real and unchanging verities behind it.'[25]

So – back to my insistence upon reality as discursively constructed – it can only be reality-as-experienced which acts as a control on truth-claims. However, this does not equate to a severance between reality-as-external-world and reality-as-experience. Markham criticizes the Cupitt position as odd, for asserting that 'although the external world exists, our language constructs do not have any relation to it'.[26] To accept that position would, in effect, be to embrace solipsism and idealism by another route. It is an unnecessary component of the worldview Markham variously identifies as anti-realist or weak-realist.

To say that reality is always interpreted does not reduce 'external' reality to our own constructions of it. Indeed, one could argue that reality always exceeds our (partial) understandings of it. Reality generates proliferations of interpretations, none of which is or ever could be self-identical with the (inaccessible) object of interpretation. It is by the flip-side of the same coin that reality is never simply available to us. Recognizing a door as a door, through which one walks, is an act of interpretation. So too is knowing the function of a Western toilet when presented with one. A shared reality may be a precondition for communication, but so too is an interpreted reality. With this, I do not think Markham would disagree.

So, then, I believe Markham has correctly identified a need not to discount reality, and that denial of shared reality cannot, as he argues, account for a world in which communication and translation do occur. However, reality is interpreted all the way along the line. We can only discuss truth and knowledge in relation to reality-as-experienced and reality-as-interpreted. Part of the valence of this is the way it problematizes Markham's third 'plank' of critical realism: that certain world perspectives are better than the alternatives. Now I do not disagree with this – as a feminist, how could I? – but it is not so easy to discriminate between 'better' and 'worse' world-perspectives by saying one or the other makes 'better sense' of reality, if reality is itself an interpreted product. The manner in which 'reality' acts as a legitimator for truth-claims is problematized when by reality we mean, not a stable external world, but unstable and dynamic interpretations of the world as experienced. This intensified problematization in fact has greater explanatory power than critical realism: it does not preclude truth-claims which are relatively simply arbitrated,[27] but it provides a more nuanced framework for understanding competition and conflict in worldviews which are not so easily resolved.

---

[24] Ibid., 49.
[25] Don Cupitt, *The Long-Legged Fly* (London: SCM Press, 1987), 20.
[26] Markham, *Truth and the Reality of God*, 50.
[27] For example, Markham's test-case that 'there is a raven on the lawn'.

Markham and I concur that there is an external world; we concur that this external world is always interpreted. The crucial difference is in how we perceive the relationship between the two. The model on which Markham's analysis implicitly builds is one in which a given object in the world gives rise to multiple interpretations. But the object itself remains and can act as a reference point and control over the validity of the various interpretations. My model also rests on the assumption that there are given objects in the world. But these are never uninterpreted; they are always already caught up into webs of signifying practices. The object cannot then act as a 'pure' control; it is dissolved into the interpretations of it. Nevertheless the object remains – but only in what I have named its discursive formations.[28] These are not divorced from what the object-in-itself, but as object-in-itself it is unavailable to us. In the act of perceiving, we construct. So the object perceived is only accessible in its constructions, which nevertheless, since these are a response to the object, will generally intersect and overlap; this enables the concept of a shared reality to become viable. It is though a shared *interpreted* reality. Critical realism is here revisioned as a discursive realism. This has clear implications for other aspects of Markham's argument, which will be further analysed below.

So Markham's critical realism is, I contend, insufficiently attentive to discursivity. This is not, furthermore, the only dimension which it neglects. He designates world-perspectives as attempts to make sense of reality as experienced, and says that some make better sense of it than others. This may be fine, as far as it goes, but it just does not go far enough. Crucially, it does not address the ideological nature of 'truth' and 'reality'. Basically, are world-perspectives wholly descriptive, or are they also prescriptive? Do world-perspectives make sense of reality as it is – as experienced – or are they also attempts to make sense of reality as ideologues want it to be, or are habituated to supposing it to be? World-perspectives may suppress experiences of the world because they challenge dominant interests. From a feminist point of view, this point must be granted the fullest consideration. World-perspectives produce reality: they do not only explain it. World-perspectives are ideologies. And as Kavanagh states, ideology 'has the function of producing an *obvious* "reality" that social subjects can assume and accept, precisely as if it had not been socially produced and did not need to be "known" at all'.[29] World-perspectives, in short, are not only about truth and meaning: they are about relations of power and domination.

It is this type of analysis which has produced critical social theory, with which feminism has much in common. Critical theory[30] accepts that worldviews are historically specific, arising from particular contexts. The corollary of this is an understanding of social discourses as *inevitably* originating from and addressed to particular socio-political interests, and enmeshed within networks of material

---

[28] It is crucial to note here that 'discursive' can be deployed with a broader scope than merely 'linguistic', and that this is the context of my use of the term. 'Discourse' can refer to the sum of our reality-constructs, which include material forces of socio-economics and relations of power. See Fulkerson, *Changing the Subject*.

[29] Gunn and Fewell, *Narrative in the Hebrew Bible*, 190.

[30] I refer here to the perspectives emerging from the Frankfurt School and its successors.

practices.[31] As Jean Grimshaw states: 'Theories, ideas and ideologies are not *only* ways of making sense of the world, but may also be the means through which one group of people dominate or exercise control over another.'[32]

Marilyn Frye, in her article on the politics of reality, demonstrates the extent to which world perspectives are exclusionary practices through a discussion of lesbianism: 'Lesbians are not visible to men because lesbians are women-centred and do not focus on males' projects; so lesbians do not exist. Erasure.'[33] She expands on her theme by playfully juxtaposing a reading of 'real' as 'that which is' with a reading of 'real' as 'royal':[34]

> Real property is that which is proper to the king.
> Real estate is the estate of the king.
> Reality is that which pertains to the one in power, is that over which he has power, is his domain, his estate, is proper to him.
> The ideal king reigns over everything as far as the eye can see. His eye. What he cannot see is not royal, not real.
> He sees what is proper to him.
> To be real is to be visible to the king.
> The king is in his counting house.
> I say, 'I am a lesbian. The king does not count lesbians. Lesbians are not real. There are no lesbians.'[35]

Lesbians, then, are 'spat' out of reality. Customary understandings of sex make a nonsense of lesbian experience. And yet it would be naïve to suppose that homophobic societies would change their worldview in this respect, merely by having it demonstrated that a more inclusive understanding of sexuality makes 'better sense' of reality as experienced.[36] Homophobic societies make sense of gayness by declaring it deviant and appear to consider this a logical, coherent act. The laws of logic could perhaps, as Markham says, be considered universal;[37] but

---

[31] The influence of Foucault on materialist theories of discourse should not be underestimated.

[32] Grimshaw, Jean, *Feminist Philosophers: Women's Perspectives on Philosophical Traditions*, 99.

[33] Marilyn Frye, 'To See and be Seen: The Politics of Reality', 77.

[34] This is based on the fact that the Spanish for royal is 'real'. Frye also draws upon an arguable etymological relationship between the English word real as 'that which is' and the Latin word 'regal', royal. This last is debatable. A more probable etymology for the English 'real' traces it back to the Latin '*res*', thing. However, it is true that real tennis is another term for royal tennis, and the etymological link is anyway less important than the allusive one.

[35] Marilyn Frye, 'To See and be Seen: The Politics of Reality', 79.

[36] I do not suggest that Markham would think it that simple either. Rather, I am identifying an important dimension to discussions of world-perspectives which his analysis does not bring into focus.

[37] When Markham talks about logic as universal, he is referring to principles of sound reasoning, such as non-contradictability. He explicitly does not mean that particular acts of logical reasoning are transcontextual.

he also sees as constitutive of logic that it should fit the world. Since 'the world' is experienced so differently by different people, that may not advance us very far in arbitrating which world perspective makes 'better sense'. I do not know anyone who would assert that a circle is simultaneously square, but suspect that homophobic logic depends upon putting a lesbian into the same category as a square circle. A circle cannot be a square because it is a circle. A woman cannot be sexually attracted to women (unless there is something wrong with her, or she is somehow damaged), because (proper) women are sexually attracted to men.

Markham believes that world-perspectives are in the business of producing coherent explanations of reality-as-experience. As he states this:

> Individuals live in community. Each person grows up within the interpretative framework of the community. As persons learn to reason, so they find elements in reality that both endorse and undermine the framework. The weight given to those elements in reality will vary considerably from community to community, but the means of weaving them together will be shared, whether applied truly or falsely.... both Christian and atheist will process the material in a way that observes the fundamental requirements of logic.[38]

I do not discount Markham's insights here, but in the end, I simply find his account of world-perspectives over-focused on logic and insufficiently focused on the politics of difference and marginality. Logic is not the only tool by which we make sense of the world. Post-Freudian psychoanalysis and twentieth-century anthropological theory both demonstrate this to be the case. Worldviews are complex and may be contradictory; indeed, 'worldview' or 'world-perspective' is a fractured category. The symbols produced and reproduced in hegemonic discourses may actually point to contradiction and conflict within worldviews. A symbol may retain its dominance whilst yet imbued with multiple contradictory 'meanings'. A hegemonic world-perspective may command consent, but actually be composed of aggregations of conflictive perspectives; thus as a world-perspective it is successful not because it is homogenizing and coherent but because it is enveloping and fissured.

What is more, not only is it possible for a given discourse to be contradictory or inconsistent, people may inhabit multiple discourses which do not cohere. Markham's logical community would seek to eliminate contradiction and inconsistency. It is at least as likely that communities and individuals suppress, ignore, or just live with incoherence in their experiences of the world. One may reject, refuse to acknowledge or refuse to engage with elements in experience or worldview which might suggest one's current understanding of the world is inadequate or unsatisfactory. There may, in fact, be dissonance between world-perspectives and lived experience. Yet, even if it is consciously recognized that a worldview is failing to make sense of experience, discarding it is not an option in any simple sense. A feminist finds patriarchal discourse incongruent, but nevertheless (as is argued elsewhere), feminism is a gesture *within* patriarchy. Thus

---

[38] Markham, *Truth and the Reality of God*, 62.

it can be argued that world-perspectives are established on patterns of incoherence, rather than only on the logical structures they may claim to embody.

Deconstructive impulses collude with this recognition that texts and discourses fail to sustain the logics which they presuppose. This is why postmodernism and psychoanalysis currently enjoy such a mutually parasitic relationship. As Lacan says of the unconscious: 'That which is central in the analytic discourse is always this – to that which the signifier expresses you give a reading other than what it means.'[39] That means the focus is on transgressive and digressive elements, on silences, on aporia. For deconstructionists, systems are posited on a series of exclusions and repressions, whilst sustaining an illusion of completeness and coherence. Deconstruction puts pressure on the points where contradictions are masked, revealing the failure of the system to 'make sense'. Coherence is actually feigned in systems, through the ejection into otherness of all that threatens its precarious logic. This is the 'absolute indigestible', which may yet play a fundamental, albeit abyssal, role.[40] Systems *pretend* a logic; the socially and politically aware will thus be suspicious of the means by which 'sense' is made and attend to the margins of discourse where 'non-sense' lurks.

So I would lay less stress than Markham does on 'logic' as the means through which we make sense of the world and on the demand of logic that explanations of the world are coherent. The connection between logic and coherence is also made, for Markham, through structures of language and the facts of communication and translation. He then wants to know whether this coherence is an imposition on the world, or a reflection of the world. He, of course, takes the latter position, leaving the former to an anti-realist of Kantian persuasion – who at the least 'would say that we cannot get beyond our mentally created "coherent explanations" to find out what reality is really like. On this view reality might be chaotic.'[41] I depart from Markham in two ways here. The first is, as has been seen, that I have less faith in the coherence of our explanations of the world. The second is, I would like to suggest that a constructivist view of knowledge does not require one to suppose coherence is only imposed upon the world. The perspective I labelled 'discursive realism' shares with post-Kantian epistemology a belief that the 'real world' is, strictly, inaccessible, and suggests that it is known only in and through our constructions of it. Yet I argue that discursive realism can in fact accommodate a worldview which takes the universe to be 'coherent' subject to the provisos detailed below. This is for two reasons.

My first rests on pragmatism and 'lived experience'. As has been seen, I have argued that we do not, in fact, know what reality is 'really like', but that we construct reality in the act of apprehending it. However I can still have confidence that the 'external world' is not chaotic, because if it were, a complex, delicately

---

[39] Lacan, *Ecrits: A Selection*, 37.
[40] Derrida, *Glas*, trans. John P. Leavey, Jr., and Richard Rand (Lincoln: University of Nebraska Press, 1986), 151.
[41] Markham, *Truth and the Reality of God*, 63.

balanced biochemical organic entity such as myself could not live and could not be reflecting on the chaos or contrariwise of the cosmos.[42]

My second reason is founded upon the supposition that coherence is demanded by intelligibility. It is my contention that a discursively realist position can, like Markham, postulate that the world is intelligible, and that this is what makes the world explicable. Particularly important for me to clarify here, though, is a delimitation of just what I mean by 'explicable'. For starters, provisionality and partiality are, for me, inserted into any talk of explicability. This undermines any claim to 'explain' the world in the sense of fully account for it. But it does not evacuate all content from the notion of 'explicability'. The discursive realism I outlined depends not on the absence or non-existence of the external world or actual events but on their inaccessibility except as embedded within interpretative constructs, which nevertheless emerge under their impact.

I can, therefore, speak of the world as 'intelligible', as capable of explication, on grounds that we do (partially) (provisionally) explain it. The fundamental doubt thereby accompanying all of our explanations does not destroy the presupposition of all explanatory acts: that there is sense to be made. This is one of Markham's most important insights, which he himself recognizes as 'the crucial move': 'It is the *assumption* of coherence and intelligibility which requires justification [italics added].'[43] At this highly significant point, our analyses can converge. A discursively realist position does not, then, require rejection of the viewpoint that explanation presupposes coherence. What it does insist upon is the diachronic and culturally particular rather than synchronic and culturally universal power of any given explanation. Once more, this is entirely in keeping with Markham's embrace of rationality as traditioned. Hence, attempts to explain the world from a discursively realist perspective depend on a dual assumption which is held in common with Markham's critical realism: firstly, that the world is explicable (hence intelligible, hence coherent); and secondly, that our explanations will never be tradition-transcendent. Nor could they be either timeless or comprehensive.

So, like Markham, I do consider the universe to be non-chaotic. Like Markham, I am a theist and therefore agree that this is not arbitrary. Moreover, I am persuaded by his suggestion that the notion of intelligibility depends on coherence, and that a universe only arbitrarily coherent might cease to be so. Thus, it is reasonable for him to draw the link he does between intelligibility, explicability and theism, as an understanding of the universe which is not arbitrary, and which can therefore sustain an understanding of it as coherent. And again, it is important in all such discussions to bear in mind Markham's own point that this is not an exercise in supposedly tradition-transcendent reasoning. It is an exercise in

---

[42] It should be noted, though, that this is not an appeal to a science as an objective determinant of reality. I would want to stress the extent to which science is itself a traditioned rationality and, therefore, that all judgements of 'intelligibility' and 'coherence' are complexified. (As one who stands within the Western scientific and philosophical traditions, I shall however continue to use the language of 'coherence'.)

[43] Markham, *Truth and the Reality of God*, 77.

natural theology, and he has taken great care to state that this is an enterprise which takes place within rather than outside of traditions.

Thus at this crux of Markham's argument, I am drawn into agreement with some of his key contentions. To attempt to explain the world is to suppose there is sense to be made of it, which depends on a belief in its intelligibility, hence its coherence. A universe figured purely as arbitrary provides less basis to consider the world coherent than a non-arbitrary interpretation. Therefore discursive realism, like critical realism, can forge a link between the drive to make sense of the universe and God. To express particular ideas of 'truth', 'reality' or 'meaning' is to express a theology – negatively or positively. Interpenetrating all such concepts is a worldview which either does or does not allow for God, purpose and coherence in the universe.

This is where Nietzsche's writings remain powerful. He expresses with vigour and creativity the view that without some concept of God, the parameters enabling us to speaking meaningfully of truth or truthfully of meaning have been stripped away. As Nietzsche himself put it, with typical lyricism, the murder of God leads to utter destabilization:

> The madman jumped into their midst and pierced them with his eyes. 'Whither is God?' he cried; 'I will tell you. *We have killed him* – you and I. All of us are his murderers. But how did we do this? How could we drink up the sea? Who gave us the sponge to wipe away the entire horizon? . . . Whither are we going? . . . Are we not plunging continually? Backward, sideward, forward, in all directions? Is there still any up or down? Are we not straying as though an infinite nothing? Do we not feel the breath of empty space? Has it not become colder?'[44]

Of course, Nietzsche's work is enmeshed within ironies. In Henry's phraseology: 'He believed that absolute truth was a great delusion, but he was fired by an ethic of truthfulness;' he excoriated faith for shutting its eyes to 'truth' – and yet thought 'truth' was a fiction.[45] He evacuated meaning from concepts such as 'goodness' and 'justice' whilst presupposing such values in his denunciation of Christianity as immoral.[46] The denial of truth and value leads to an attitude of unconditional affirmation of reality. Life must be embraced in all its irrationality and passion, and the will to power given free rein.

Nietzsche or Aquinas? asks Markham. God, truth and rationality: or none of the three? Suppose we could introduce here a third option, one that does not become on Markham's terms an 'unjustified rationality' by supposing we can have truth but no God. Suppose we refuse the binary choice with which that seems to leave us: no God and no truth (Nietzsche) or God and truth (Aquinas)? What about a worldview which accepts God, rationality and a presupposition therefore of coherence and intelligibility in the universe, but refuses, or at least profoundly destabilizes, 'truth' as something which can be merely present to us? We are now at the heart of the problematic I shall go on to address.

---

[44] Nietzsche, *The Gay Science*, para. 125.
[45] Henry, *On Not Understanding God*, 240.
[46] Nietzsche, *The Anti-Christ* [*passim*].

Discursive realism, as I have already indicated, accommodates the critically realist insistence upon reality as shared. However, this is explicitly reconfigured as a shared *interpreted* reality, with reality-as-such always inaccessible. Discursive realism can also take on board critical realism's presupposition of the universe as explicable. Yet it also assumes that we cannot in fact 'explain' it except in terms provisional, partial and contingent. Some of our explanations we may have more confidence in than others, but for a discursive realist, truth as an epistemological category is undermined.[47] We can continue to speak of 'truth' in the same manner as we continue to 'explain': with no external guarantees or extra-discursive foundation.[48] Truth is not something that is simply discovered: it is something that we construct, in and through our interpretations of a world which is always already interpreted.

'Discursive realism' is, then, the model of how 'the real' is apprehended which underlies my work. The 'turn to discourse' stresses the site of meaning-production as constitutive of signification: it does not, however, reduce reality to language. It simply insists that the material is coded and cannot be accessed as pure thing-in-itself outside of domains of meaning. Social and political forces are implicated in discursive formations. Discourses are multiple, they may be hegemonic or marginal, they may intersect and converge in ways generative of conflict or contradiction. Discursive realism does not preclude commonality and communication between different traditioned rationalities – to use MacIntyre's term – since discourse as employed here figures fluid matrices of meaning rather than fixed and hermetically sealed straitjackets. Discursive realism also allows consideration of relations of power to emerge in questions of meaning. The advantages of discursive realism over critical realism are then several: it provides, I would argue, a more adequate model of how reality is apprehended and constituted; it allows for multiplicity and mobility as well as for specificity; it incorporates contradiction and conflict in world-perspectives; it is attentive to distributions and flows of power.

Truth and Textuality

Analogous to the issue of how 'the real' is constructed are questions of textuality. Indeed, the interpenetration of the debates is well encapsulated in the tendency to refer to the inescapability of interpretation as the textualization of the world. There is nothing outside the text: this is one of Derrida's most misunderstood aphorisms. There is nothing outside the text because everything is in the text: everything is interpreted. However, here I wish to use 'text' in a narrow sense, to refer to written

---

[47] This does not, it should be noted, preclude pragmatic norms emerging from experience of the world, nor reasonable beliefs. Nor does undermining truth as a category signify that there are no truths. For example, science is a discourse; its norms have changed over time and it has evolved its own sets of criteria and modes of reasoning. That it is a discourse does not mean the results of science are untrue.

[48] Again, I stress that discursivity is not reducible to linguisticality nor rejection of material realities in our constitutions of the world.

documents. The debate here typically focuses on permutations of perceived relationships between three major protagonists, author, text and reading subject. It is representative of a shift from understanding texts as referential mediators of authorial intention to controversy over the relative roles of the elements constitutive in the production of meaning from texts. The volume of literature on this is enormous, and I do not propose to survey or evaluate it.[49] It gathered pace from the 1960s onwards through to the early 1980s.[50]

Although I shall not investigate the dazzling array of theories and positions set forth, it is nevertheless important to specify the model of textuality I prefer, since this is the standpoint from which I promulgate my own critiques and constructive proposals in the realm of feminist biblical hermeneutics. As we saw, it also emerged as a significant factor in evaluating Phyllis Trible's methodologies. Therefore I sketch out in brief the relationship I perceive. It follows similar lines to the discursive realism outlined above. It takes its cue from a recognition that there is an epistemological stutter between the text-as-given-object-in-the-world, and text-as-interpreted. Into this stutter, difference and plurality of interpretation are inserted. There is never an uninterpreted text to which one can appeal for adjudication of 'right' readings. Ricoeur correctly notes that texts are 'autonomous with respect to the intention of the author'.[51] And yet, whilst the text may be open, it is not absent. The 'world behind the text', its circumstances of production, is inscribed within it. In this way, although we cannot recover 'authorial intention' we have resources for arguing on basis of textual and extra-textual evidence that this or that was the 'original meaning'. Of course, this remains a rhetorical construct of the reader/s, justified by criteria and rules internal to their own discursive locations; it does not suggest that meaning can be fixed at a site external to the interpreter.[52] At this point Stephen Moore's analysis becomes useful to elucidation of my position here.

Moore, speaking of New Testament criticism, identifies three 'hypostases' supposed to pre-exist the activity of the interpreter: 'transcendentalized textual content, assumed to be independent in principle of attempts to paraphrase it; transcendentalized *Sitz im Leben*, assumed to be independent in principle of attempts to reconstruct it; and transcendentalized authorial intention, assumed in principle to be a kind of Procrustean bed to which virtually all features of the text can one day be adapted'.[53] The problem with all such hypostasization of meaning

---

[49] Such a task would be both too lengthy and too peripheral to the purposes of this book.

[50] As Stephen Moore puts it: 'During this time the amazing reader had many aliases and roles, engaging the text or emerging from it in guises such as the Implied Reader, the Informed Reader, the Narratee, and the Model Reader. The carnival also featured the Reader in the Text and the Flesh-and-Blood Reader, the Competent Reader and the Literent, the Encoded or Inscribed Reader, the Subjective Reader, Superreader, the Newreaders, and the wilful Misreader.' *Literary Criticism*, 71.

[51] Ricoeur, *Hermeneutics and the Human Sciences* (Cambridge and New York: Cambridge University Press, 1981), 139.

[52] It should be noted again that whilst given criteria may be internal to particular discourses, this in no manner suggests exclusivity.

[53] Moore, *Literary Criticism*, 172.

is that it ignores the process of production at the site of interpretation and posits closure as the goal of right interpretation. However, the terrain changes if we work on the understanding that meaning is not discovered, it is invested. This may be in relation to differential networks which are relatively stable, but nevertheless it opens up a space which can accommodate, and sometimes may insist upon, differences and multiplicity in interpretative acts. Its most important feature is the stress on discursive communities as productive of meanings.

This does not remove the text from the process of interpretation, any more than discursive realism removes the real. However, it stresses that interpretative acts are formulated according to regulatory rules, which may not only be diversely applied but may also vary according to the site of interpretation.[54] A preacher does not usually exposit a biblical text in the same way as a biblical scholar in her professional capacity; a child does not read *Huckleberry Finn* in the same way as a postcolonial theorist. The point is obvious, but its banality does not detract from its significance, the implications of which are often passed over. If reading is conducted by rules and interests at the discursive site, then these are themselves subject to challenge and renegotiation. This is especially important to feminist hermeneutics, which may want to change not only the readings but also the rules.

Truth and Ethics

Discursive realism revalues the world. By this I mean that its insistence upon reality-as-constructed plunges all our apprehensions into meaning-laden networks of differences. This renders ours relationship to the world profoundly ethical in orientation, if by ethics is signified questions of value. This sits comfortably with feminist epistemologies, which stress the impossibility of objectivity for the knowing subject.[55] At the same time, it also sets a certain difficulty before the feminist interpreter.

Feminism as a worldview is profoundly ethical. Elizabeth Frazer defines feminism as having 'a normative orientation to the liberation of women from sexual injustice'.[56] Feminism is oppositionally related to patriarchy. However, this may be the normative vision of feminism but the worldview I have outlined can only discard the idea of normative grounding. Discursive realism might seem to

---

[54] See Fulkerson, *Changing the Subject* (117-182), for an extended discussion of the relationship between textuality and discourse with specific reference to feminist biblical interpreters. With reference to Moore's three hypostases of transcendentalized meaning, she suggests that: 'The dominant feminist approaches to Christian texts, biblical and extrabiblical, press on the edges of these assumptions with their own commitment to the situated, interested character of all knowing. They do not go far enough, however, because of their failure to press the very notion that texts have fixed meanings. Fixed meaning assumes a unitary subject; and the complexity of interest, its webs of social power, can be developed no further than as attributes of a unitary subject and the fixed text' (140).

[55] See Chapter 2.

[56] Frazer, 'Feminist Ethics', 273.

lead inevitably to relativism, for how can we arbitrate between different interpretations of the world, if the world itself, or God, or the transcendental self, can offer us no uninterpreted grounds for making ethical judgements?

This clearly will not do for feminism, which by definition refuses a relativist account of the world. At the same time, feminism must also ensure it does not sink into inconsistency at this point: namely, there are no universal, extra-discursive norms except those on which feminists draw.[57] At this point, I want to affirm the position earlier described and associated with Alasdair MacIntyre. MacIntyre refuses the polarity between universal, overarching norms and total relativism, and that only neutral standards would enable arbitration between competing accounts of the world. This begins to suggest a way through this apparent impasse. It is an issue which will be taken up again in some detail in Chapter 8: as can be seen, the ethical constitution of discourse is an issue which is returned to repeatedly.

These, then, are the philosophical underpinnings of this work. It proceeds from an epistemological perspective of discursive realism; an account of textuality which stresses the discursive location of meaning-production (without excising the text from the process); and an ethics which acknowledges the non-universality of truth-claims but nevertheless wants to reject relativism. It is located in a framework which perceives all discourse to be (a)theological and that does, therefore, require subsequent consideration of how this particular model of truth coheres with the reality of God.

God and truth: that is the end-goal of this discussion. However, to approach this question, I want to take a tour through interpretation: writing. This is not a detour, however; interpretation, as shall be seen, is fundamental to the question of God and truth. The analysis moves from Derrida, via Heidegger, to a theological metaphysics which takes its cues from eschatology.

Eschatology and Interpretation

The aim of the discussion here is, again, necessarily limited. The purpose is to sketch in the shapes for theological thinking which might underlie the epistemological and hermeneutic manoeuvres which I am advocating. I do not propose to survey or interrogate the vast array of Western philosophical texts which are implicated in this field of inquiry. Rather, I take my point of departure from particular critiques of Western metaphysics and suggest some resources for a metaphysics according to a different morphology.

---

[57] Feminists find different ways through this potential impasse. Standpoint theories locate the normative in the superiority of particular experiences as grounds for advancing judgements; radical feminists tend to locate it in female subjectivity as transcending the problematics of patriarchal worldviews. Neither of these is adequate for a feminism which posits a non-unified subjectivity, women as a fractured category, and experience as always interpreted within particular discourses. See Chapter 8.

Postmodern Critique of Metaphysics

There is a conflation in this sub-heading, of course: critiques of metaphysics preceded the contemporary preoccupation with the so-called 'postmodern'. However, I mean to identify configurations of criticisms which are post-Hegelian, surfaced strongly in Nietzsche, were a major component of Heidegger's works, and which are now diffused into significant portions of current thinking. Nietzsche announced the end of a metaphysical epoch (whilst yet inhabiting it[58]) in his rejection of foundations, grounds and origins which are not themselves projections from human ego, will and desire. Significantly, as we have already seen, for Nietzsche this was profoundly interrelated with the death of God. The metaphysics which is thus assailed is, since Heidegger, frequently dubbed a 'metaphysics of presence'.

What is a metaphysics of presence? Derrida characterizes it in this way:

> Successively, and in a regulated fashion, the center receives different forms or names. The history of metaphysics, like the history of the West, is the history of these metaphors and metonymies. Its matrix . . .is the determination of Being as *presence* in all senses of the word. It could be shown that all the names related to fundamentals, to principles, or to the center have always designated an invariable presence – *eidos, arche, telos, energeia, ousia* (essence, existence, substance, object) *aletheia*, transcendentality, consciousness, God, man and so forth.[59]

So this is an ontology, or a variety of ontologies, which have in common a privileging of immediacy and presence. This is manifest in the philosophical priority of being, essence, identity, permanence, subject, object, truth. It expresses itself in the craving for grounds and centres, foundations which can be relied on, which are always present. Metaphysical concepts of being demand, depend upon, presence and stability.

Derrida continues the critique of a metaphysics of presence, in such a way that its relation to interpretation and textuality becomes paramount. He relates his critique to logocentrism, the impulse to ground truth in an ultimate and undivided origin. Western philosophy carries and establishes logocentrism, for it operates on binary oppositions which are hierarchically organized. One term is privileged, set on the side of the logos (being, presence, mind, man, etc.); the other is subordinated, it is projected as lack, as hostile to the truth of truth (non-being, absence, body, woman, etc.). Logocentrism is thus also dependent on assumptions of presence, associated with the privileged term.

This is why the opposition between speech and writing becomes pivotal to Derrida's thought. For signs are always signs *of* something, they are a substitute for presence: speech conveys the myth of full presence; writing, by contrast, depends on absence. Metaphysical thinking is hence obliged to subordinate writing. Derrida, by contrast, focuses on it. Writing disrupts the presence it tries to

---

[58] Heidegger, *Nietzsche*, vol. 3, trans. Joan Stambaugh *et al.* (New York: Vintage, 1968), 481.
[59] Derrida, 'Structure, Sign, and Play in the Discourse of the Human Sciences', 279-80.

establish. Meaning is differential; signs only have meaning in relation to other signs. If meaning is made in relation to other signs which are absent, yet meaning-making is in relation to them, they nevertheless are present. Metaphysics of presence necessarily assume an absence which is repressed. Absence infects presence. This is so with the whole range of metaphysical oppositions which are structured hierarchically in binary pairs. The privileged signifier depends on its subordinated opposite for its meaning, which supports the system even in its apparent ejection from it.

This introduces the trace. For all words, all signs, depend on other words, other signs for their meanings. Language is a relay of differences without closure. What this means is that whatever is written, whatever is spoken, each element is constituted by the trace of other elements which are neither present, nor absent. The trace is therefore an undecidable. The undecidability it betrays is structural and exposes the play of presence and absence at the non-originary origin of meaning.

Thus writing – language itself – is inherently unstable. 'Writing', indeed, refers to this undecidable play, rather than script as distinct from speech. Writing, then, is a product of *différance*. This neologism incorporates both differing and temporal deferring; it is actively disruptive. It is the condition of both the possibility and the impossibility of communication. Similarly, iterability – the possibility of repetition – also carries with it both the possibility and impossibility of communication. Undecidability, *différance* and iterability indicate the potentiality of signs to mean – but destabilize the possibility of presence and identity of meaning in signs.

Destabilization is more fruitful than simply reversing the binary oppositions; for this does not escape metaphysical binarisms, which need rather to be *disrupted*. This is where undecidability enters into play, for it acts by displacement; it refuses the either/or. All language is differential, slippery, differed and deferred. It cannot escape from its own instabilities. The play of the trace plays always and everywhere. As absent-presence and present-absence, the trace fundamentally destabilizes the claims of words to presence.

Therefore we learn from Derrida that undecidability is both a condition and generative of a strategy. The differential networks of signification, the circulations of meaning, provide for the possibility of deconstruction: dismantling, the drawing out of fissures, oppositions and exclusions, the tracing of the disruptive marginal, and of the instabilities in meaning which characterize texts. This, as I have already argued, allows for feminist destabilizations.

So, destabilization and interpretation are intimately linked. Destabilization is not an ingredient added to interpretation but constitutive of it. It shakes a metaphysics of presence, whilst yet (necessarily) inhabiting it.[60]

---

[60] 'There is no sense in doing without the concepts of metaphysics in order to shake metaphysics. We have no language – no syntax and no lexion – which is foreign to this history; we can pronounce not a single deconstructive proposition has not already had to slip into the form, the logic and the implicit postulations of precisely what it seeks to contest' (Derrida, 'Structure, Sign, and Play in the Discourse of the Human Sciences', 280-1).

Where, then, does theology enter this picture? With, in fact, the very link between God and truth I have said I want to draw: 'the intelligible face of the sign remains turned towards the word and the face of God'.[61] *God* is associated with the very metaphysics of presence which is held to be founded on error. As Grace Jantzen puts it:

> This obviously has grave consequence for any positive theology which seeks a divine guarantee for names of God, reliant, for example, on an idea of revelation in which God's real presence is guaranteed in the words/signs of scripture or sacrament ... But Derrida also warns against an appropriation of *différance* for a project of negative theology.[62]

The interpenetration of God and the metaphysics of presence was argued before Derrida, by Heidegger. The leitmotif of Heidegger's work was not *différance*, but Being. Heidegger resuscitated 'the question of the meaning of Being', and this theme dominated his works. Heidegger's argument was that the ontological difference between Being and beings had been obscured in the history of Western metaphysics. Metaphysics, according to Heidegger, is fundamentally related to grounds and grounding:

> Metaphysics thinks of beings as such, that is, in general. Metaphysics thinks of beings as such, as a whole. Metaphysics thinks of the Being of beings both in the ground-giving unity of what is most general, what is indifferently valid everywhere, and also in the unity of the all that accounts for the ground, that is, of the All-Highest. The Being of beings is thus thought of in advance as the grounding ground. Therefore all metaphysics is at bottom, and from the ground up, what grounds, what gives account of the ground, what is called to account by the ground, and finally what calls the ground to account.[63]

Metaphysics, thus, is onto-theo-logical: it is theological, it is ontological. This is on account of the representation of the Being of beings as *causa sui*: this, says Heidegger, 'is the metaphysical concept of God'.[64] This manifests itself in various ways, for 'Being is in being as ground in diverse ways: as Λογος, as 'υποκειμενον, as substance, as subject.'[65] Metaphysics of necessity thinks in the

---

[61] Derrida, *Writing and Difference*, 13.
[62] Jantzen, *Becoming Divine*, 189. Jantzen also notes (rightly), along with thinkers such as Kevin Hart, that this is not in itself an argument for atheism. Derrida is not arguing for or against a God, but noting a metaphysical matrix which founds itself on presence, and therefore in God as ultimate ground, being and origin.
[63] Heidegger, 'The Onto-Theo-Logical Constitution of Metaphysics', 58.
[64] Ibid., 60.
[65] Ibid., 60. It is argued that this type of metaphysics extends from Plato and Parmenides to the present day. Whilst I do not propose to enter this debate, it should be noted that John Milbank, Graham Ward and Catherine Pickstock are amongst those who would complexify this picture and see a quite different framework at work in, for example, writers of the early Church up to the modern period. It is argued that a liturgical and

direction of deity 'because the matter of thinking is Being'; thus, metaphysics is theology whether it owns to it or not. Metaphysics is not theology because it is ontology, however, it is theology ('a statement about God') because 'the deity enters into philosophy'.[66]

Indeed: we have already seen that for myself also, the deity enters philosophy. This is because to speak of truth is necessarily to speak or not to speak of God. As we saw, I advanced my argument in close dialogue with Markham, who suggested that to attempt to explain the world supposes its intelligibility and coherence, which is better supported by a theistic worldview than a non-theistic one. Any articulation of truth or meaning expresses a theology, in that it either is or is not threaded through with presuppositions of God, purpose and coherence in the universe. Aquinas and Nietzsche stand for mutually reinforcing opposite poles, in which either we have God and truth, or neither of the two.

Is my work, then, to be conceived as proceeding from the assumptions of onto-theology ('bad metaphysics'[67])? This would seem to posit a decisive break between this thesis and postmodern philosophies, which are frequently conceived as attempts to *overcome* metaphysics as constituted by the onto-theo-logical tradition.[68] It would also indicate a rent at the heart of my hermeneutics, since destabilization, which flows from *différance*, iterability and undecidablity, is a major element of my suggested strategies. My response to this is twofold: firstly, I concur that metaphysics is onto-theological, but dissent from the need thereby to overcome it or move beyond it. Rather, I want to reshape it in light of postmodern critique. Secondly, the way I propose that this be done is by rethinking metaphysics through the eschatological imagination.

Clearly, this task as is beyond the scope of what it is possible to achieve in this book. Nevertheless I want to suggest certain pointers, indicators, which might open up fruitful paths for future development.

Firstly: why do I not object to the term onto-theological? This is because ontology and theology are indeed fundamentally intertwined. A rupture between God and being cannot, I would argue, be sustained within theologies of creation and redemption. This analysis I accept, as I have already indicated elsewhere. However, when we move on to discussing what exactly is wrong with this

---

doxological understanding of language and an understanding of world as gift destabilizes 'presence'. Therefore, the metaphysics of presence is seen as an invention of modernity.

[66] Heidegger, 'The Onto-Theo-Logical Constitution of Metaphysics', 55.

[67] Caputo, *Heidegger and Aquinas*, 118.

[68] Heidegger's own project is in this vein. See also Ward, *The Postmodern God*, xxvi, on the two tasks of postmodern philosophies: 'First is the overcoming of metaphysics as conceived in modernity as the correlation of Being and reasoning (the thinking through and therefore intelligibility of all that is).' Heidegger himself rejected all metaphysical reasoning, for he considered it made it impossible to think Being-as-such, since the ontological differing between Being and beings is rendered into oblivion. This is precisely because metaphysics construes Being as the ground of beings. It therefore fails to think the real matter to be thought, which Heidegger comes to term *Ereignis* (usually translated as the 'Event of Appropriation'). *Ereignis* is not Being. It is that which grants Being to thought.

interweaving of ontology and theology, the answer appears to emerge from thinking of being in categories belonging to the metaphysics of presence – that is to say, being which is fixed, static, congealed and grounding ground.

We can rethink this. It is in fact surely demanded that we do so because of the weight of contemporary philosophies and theologies which do actually conceive of being in terms which stress mobility, change, becoming and groundlessness.[69] What if, like Cupitt, we were to think, not being, but be(com)ing? We could write this be-ing, stressing the verb form. Cupitt characterizes being, be-ing, be(com)ing – which is emphatically not fixable, but always elusive – as follows:

> ... Being is its own Becoming; it continually slips into itself and slips away. It is pure contingency, the underlying unmasterable givenness or gratuitousness – or graciousness – of everything, and we should not ask either where it comes *from* or where it is going *to*.[70]

Pure contingency does not sound very like God, and this an important clue to thinking being. Being is not God. Being is a universalized abstract predicate which manifests only in concrete, bodily, temporal beings. It is a condition. The relationship of God to being is not one of small beings grounded in an infinitely larger being, but of givenness. Creation is a gift. The giver is in the gift only in traces, not as ground.[71] Only in this way can human freedom be truly thought.

But the gift is not a once-and-for-all given, it is continually renewed. Renewed, not maintained; creativity, change and temporality are aspects of what it is to be. In Christian theology, the gifts of Christ and Spirit are indicative of the continuously upflowing giving of God. Yet these are themselves not simply present, once-and-for-all-given, and fixed: they are promissory, proleptic, pointing forward to a more intense transformation and renewal in redemption.

This is where the eschatological imagination enters the discussion. A crucial part of Christian writing of time-space is its eschatological orientation. Eschatology points towards, not a singular and identifiable *telos* in time/space, but to the shattering open of finite writings of time/space. Eschatology is marked by a dialectic of presence/absence and now/not yet. Thus the eschatological proceeds with a dialectic of both spatialization and temporalization and embodies the promise of radical transformation of both.

However, since I am working in dialogue with postmodern thinking, my alighting on eschatology as hermeneutical key may seem somewhat strange. Eschatology is often taken as the fullest representative of onto-theological thinking. It brings the Christian cycle through from definitive origin to definitive end. It could be seen to mark closure of the most particularist kind. Hegel's

---

[69] Deleuze; Guittari; Merleau-Ponty; Bataille, Marion; Levinas; Kristeva: all of these major philosophers are suggesting philosophies which, at the very least, do not fit quite so easily into the 'package' of modernity. Mark C. Taylor, Cupitt, Winquist, Wyschogrod, Ward are amongst those rethinking theology in (differently) transgressive ways.

[70] Cupitt, *The Religion of Being*, 28.

[71] See Marion, for example, on the importance of gift to theologies in the postmodern.

absolutist system might be seen as a realized eschatology: 'In the fullness of time, the unsettling emptiness of temporal representation becomes the reasoning fullness of eternal presentation. This atemporal present/presence marks the arrival of the Parousia.'[72] However, I argue to the contrary: that eschatological discourse marks not the dream of onto-theological presencing, but its radical disruption.

Taylor identifies eschatology as atemporal. As such, it becomes both the hoped for escape from the flux of temporal representations and dialectically opposed to the temporal – just as in Hegel's *Aufhebung*, the Infinite is dialectically opposed to the Finite which it eventually sublates. But what if we do not read eschatology from the point of view of Hegelian dialectic but in the key of Derrida's *pas-là*?[73] This is a presence/absence which is neither presence nor absence nor the sublation of either. In the Christian mythos, eschatology is not atemporal but nor is it comprehended within the temporality of history. As not yet now or here, yet not then or there, the eschatological horizon cannot be comprehended within Hegel's system. Eschatology is not only unrealized; from our perspectives, it is, like tomorrow: unrealizable. Eschatology is now/here but also nowhere; both now and not yet; both here and not here. Thus the eschatological is unassimilable into discourse. Eschatology is a theology of the trace, a trace which has already passed and has still yet to come.

Being in eschatological perspective is by definition unfinished, open. It is not grounded in presence or certainties, but givenness, and oriented towards a proleptically discernible but not known or knowable future which is not fixable or identifiable in logocentric terms. Eschatology disrupts a metaphysics of presence because God is not, in eschatological horizons, either present as such or absent as such. God gives God-self in traces: textuality.

Textuality, truth, and God: if the Word of God is in any sense addressed to the world, it can only do this by being immanent within the world. As such the Word of the God is apprehended within the structures of the world. It is embodied. It is textualized. The Word made (literally) flesh is, of course, at the heart of classical Christology; the Word made (literally) text is the crux of orthodox understandings of Christian scripture. Word as flesh, Word as text: this immanence of the Word of the God can be deemed its textualization. There can then be no direct correspondence between the truth of God and the Word of God. Howsoever the truth of God is known to us, if at all, it is not through a self-presencing. The textualized Word of God does not denote a majestic presencing of guaranteed truth. It does not reveal 'the truth', but its ambiguity and partiality. The Word of God in these horizons is far removed from the Word of God as authoritative Word of the Father.

So truth is textualized; and if the truth of God is likewise textualized, it becomes subject to the differentiality of interpretation; truth in eschatological horizons is not present but undecidable. This does not, however, cut us loose into aimless wandering over relativistic plains. This would seem to be the danger, if the

---

[72] Taylor, *Altarity*, 293.

[73] See ibid., 294, 255-303. This indicates the being-there of the not, which, being there, is not, is not there. (293). This is a Derridaen disruption of the Hegelian system. It is akin to the Freudian *fort-da*.

implication is that textuality sets Truth adrift. This is to lose sight, however, of the eschatological as symbol of hope. The eschatological is paradigmatic of hopes for transformation and the consummation of the passion for a just world. It is a call not to passive resignation but to transformative action. An eschatological metaphysics is one which is not grounded, but it is oriented: it is oriented towards horizons of hope.

Chapter 8

The *Ekklesia*

Feminist Biblical Hermeneutics and the *Ekklesia*

Eschatology has emerged as the leitmotif of the hermeneutic framework I propose. From analysis of Schüssler Fiorenza and Trible, I took remembrance and destabilization (related to Derridian *différance*) as primary principles for interpretation; these were located within a feminist emancipatory framework inspired by utopic impulses and a theology of hope. The eschatological imagination, I argued, captures this movement between remembrance and hope in a context where meaning is differed and deferred. Thus *différance*, remembrance and hope can be identified as the three primary moments of an eschatological hermeneutic. Eschatology also provided the resources for the metaphysical frame in which I sited this hermeneutic: a frame set against that of the so-called ontotheological tradition, radically disruptive of a metaphysics of presence, and in which it is possible to discern the traces of God.

At the centre of this eschatological hermeneutic I shall follow Schüssler Fiorenza, and place the *ekklesia*. This is demanded by the epistemological principles I have accepted; if interpretation is discursively produced, then the question of the discursive location of interpretation is axial to hermeneutic reflection. It is not a secondary consideration but integral to it. The *ekklesia* represents the discursive community for Christian feminist interpretation. What manner of community do I perceive this to be? That is the first question to which I shall address myself.

What is the *Ekklesia*?

The nature and function of the *ekklesia gynaikon* in Schüssler Fiorenza's work was extensively examined in Chapter 3, where we saw that she used it to signify a feminist rhetorical space, both partially realized and ideal, which would incorporate the voices of the oppressed and the marginalized emanating from an interfaith and secular context. Crucially, the *ekklesia* was postulated as operating on a counter-kyriarchal logic.

In contrast to Schüssler Fiorenza, I will not use the terminology of *ekklesia gynaikon* at all, but will refer instead to the *ekklesia* alone, understood to be the *ekklesia* of wo/men. 'Wo/men', I use in the same sense as Schüssler Fiorenza does on occasion – as a gender-inclusive term, which highlights the visibility of women and the normativity in this context of a feminist, counter-kyriarchal worldview. 'Wo/men' signifies more than the sum of gendered humanity: it denotes women and men oppressed and marginalized within kyriarchy; and, further, as I understand it, the *ekklesia* of wo/men represents also those who align themselves oppositionally to kyriarchal worldviews, practices and institutions.[1] A rather more significant difference between my use of the term and Schüssler Fiorenza's, however, is that I will restrict my use of the term '*ekklesia*' to refer to the *Christian* feminist movements. This is because of the reasons outlined in Chapter 3. In the end, I think it unacceptable to project on to a secular and interfaith community a semantic category self-identical with the naming of a specifically Christian community. This is partially ideologically motivated, then. It is additionally in the interests of clarity, since for the '*ekklesia*' to refer simultaneously to a Christian and a non-Christian feminist community cannot enhance transparency in communication. This means I require a term with which to signify the broader feminist imagined community, which is analogous to the *ekklesia* but not Christian in constitution. I shall adopt here the label of '*métissage*'.

'*Métissage*' is a notion discussed by the Bible and Culture Collective. It is the 'braiding together of cultural forms'.[2] Lionnet uses it to denote a sheltering site, in which differences can be nurtured.[3] Thus, I can usefully deploy this to refer to a 'knotted bridge' of feminist community. It signifies hybridity, and so can convey a sense in which this is a community of communities, with many diverse elements brought together but not reduced to one thing or the other. It is a crossbreed community, multiparented, composed of differences which are nevertheless gathered together into a shared but differentiated space. The *métissage* occupies in my work the same space as the non-Christian *ekklesia* does in Schüssler Fiorenza's, and the *ekklesia* is understood as a Christian 'knot' within the collectivity.

Again following Schüssler Fiorenza, the *métissage* is a justice-seeking rhetorical space; it is not an organization or an institution; it is an imagined community of communities. It designates a positioning and a commitment towards justice. It may find local and ad hoc expression in 'base communities' (such as the women-church movements), or, increasingly in cyber-communities. Although the *métissage* as a community of wo/men may include men, it may also have its women-only components as a pragmatic response to kyriarchal co-optation of women and the need to 'hear each other into speech'. It will, of necessity, be underdetermined: to lay out groundrules in advance would exclude. Reflection on

---

[1] This removes an ambiguity in Schüssler Fiorenza's analysis: it is not always clear whether the *ekklesia* includes the oppressed simply by virtue of their oppression, or whether a specifically anti-kyriarchal perspective effects entry into the *ekklesia*. As I mean this, to be located oppositionally to kyriarchy certainly does not require one to be a 'card-carrying feminist' or to be able to fully articulate the sources and modes of experienced oppression; it indicates a standpoint of *resistance*, which may be expressed in practices and articulations not embraced under ideological feminism.

[2] Its conceptual origins are with Edouard Glissant.

[3] See The Bible and Culture Collective, *The Postmodern Bible*, 243.

feminist values and praxis is an activity for the *métissage* itself to undertake. It expresses solidarity between feminism, womanism, the *mujerista* movement, and other varieties of groupings countering kyriarchy and gender-oppression; but it is a solidarity which is loosely woven together and made up of differences. It provides for an overlapping of 'communities of resistance and solidarity',[4] in a space oriented towards polyphony, dialogue and inquiry.

It is counter-kyriarchal, but kyriarchy is understood as a 'dissipative system' which cannot sustain the fixed categories it presupposes. I owe this concept to Christine Battersby's *The Phenomenal Woman*; here she employs the concept of a 'dissipative system' in her reconstruction of subjectivity according to a feminist metaphysics. She takes it from contemporary physics, which has moved from static models of forms and linear theories of change to dynamic topologies in which form and matter are not fundamentally distinct and in which systems are open and liable to transformation. 'The new topologies see form as no more than an apparent and temporary stability in the patterns of potentiality or flow . . . Forms – apparent stabilities – are brought about only because dissipative systems tend to remain in equilibrium or at a state of rest up to a certain threshold of destabilization.'[5] The advantages of applying this topological paradigm to kyriarchy are many. It makes coherent sense of both stability and change. It is a model on which leaks into and out of the system can occur; it allows for the inertia of kyriarchy whilst not blocking off the possibilities for deformation, critique and transformation which the dynamic equilibrium of a dissipative system model can account for. It also offers a measure of hope in that a critical threshold for destabilization does exist.

Thus, understood in this way, kyriarchy mutates. Its mutations are not bound to repeat it but can simultaneously be products of it, within it, and oppositional to it. Such is the *métissage*. It is then a resident alien, a concept discussed in Chapter 3, yet this is an inadequate model for it takes as read its own otherness and perpetual marginality. Again the eschatological imagination can help: it introduces a temporal dimension which opens up the possibility of transformation and change and allows for a positive appropriation of the relationship of inside/outside. 'Inside' may be transfigured such that the dissonance of being simultaneously inside and outside disperses, whilst yet not merely reducing 'outside' to 'inside'. To prefigure a discussion yet to come, the *métissage* is 'memory of the future'; it is called to critique the present structures within which it is embedded, empowered by remembrance of the past which patterns its own identity. Again, my leitmotif appears: the *métissage* is a community of communities which can fruitfully employ the categories of *différance*, remembrance and hope in its own self-understanding.

The discussion which follows, however, focuses on the *ekklesia* rather than the *métissage* into which it is knotted. This reflects the Christian theological context of this thesis. It is the *ekklesia* which is at the centre of the feminist biblical hermeneutics I propose. The reflections in Chapter 3 provide the springboard for the coming discussion. Sifting Schüssler Fiorenza's work on the *ekklesia gynaikon*

---

[4] See Sharon Welch, *Communities of Resistance and Solidarity; A Feminist Ethic of Risk*.
[5] Battersby, *The Phenomenal Woman*, 51.

allowed for the identification of certain elements in need of further elaboration or clarification. Namely, I concluded that it would be either necessary or fruitful to explore somewhat more fully the relationship of the *ekklesia* to three distinct areas: the Christian Church, gender-identity and ethics.

The *Ekklesia* and the Church

As indicated, it is productive to explore further the relationship of the *ekklesia* to the Christian Church. Schüssler Fiorenza does not develop this aspect of her work beyond an insistence that the Christian *ekklesia* is neither assimilated to the Church nor reducible to it. As we saw in Chapter 3, on her understanding the *ekklesia* opens up a space for different theologies, worship and liturgical practices geared to particular needs and anti-kyriarchal perspectives, whilst yet not conceiving of this space as located in an 'exodus' community. It remains lodged within the kyriarchal Church although in certain respects counter to it. The *ekklesia* is then both in the Church but not of it. This, in effect, is the overlapping of two 'imagined communities': the feminist *ekklesia* and a universalized kyriarchal Church. I will now consider these two imagined communities in relationship to a third: the Eucharistic community. This will provide the focal point for my discussion of how the *ekklesia* and the Christian Church relate one to another. Why this should offer a particularly appropriate route through this question will become apparent as, through the heuristic lens of the Eucharist, I map the relationship of the *ekklesia* to the Church.

We may begin by noting the very close parallels between the eschatological hermeneutic I propose and the Eucharistic imagination. The eschatological hermeneutic, it may be recalled, rests on three primary principles: *différance*, remembrance and hope. The overlaps between this eschatological hermeneutic and a Eucharistic model are significant: this is an important point and one which advances and deepens the theological valence of the hermeneutic frame. The points of contact can be sketched out with respect to two major themes: time and community.

The connection between the Eucharist and eschatology is oft-noted. Eucharistic time is eschatological time.[6] It is also, and fittingly with respect to my hermeneutic model, time in which acts of remembrance of the past and hopeful anticipation of the future are central. Its horizons are not the present, set over against a non-present and irretrievable past and a non-present and unknowable

---

[6] For an extensive elaboration of this, see Geoffrey Wainwright, *Eucharist and Eschatology* (London: Epworth Press, 1971). See also Gerard Loughlin: 'The eucharistic gift includes the fundamental terms of the temporality of the gift. According to the order of the gift, the eucharistic present is temporalized not from the here and now, but from the past, the future and finally the present. From the past it is temporalized as memorial; from the future as eschatological announcement, and from the present as 'dailyness and viaticum'. This is not the metaphysical concept of time, which understands the whole from the preseent; rather it is a gifted concept of time, which understands the present from the whole' ('Transubstantiation: Eucharist as Pure Gift', 134).

future. It is the anamnestic re-enactment of the historical body of Christ within the context of a redemptive fulfilment which has both yet to come and already been given. This is a disruption of a secular conception of time as centred on the present. The Eucharistic present emanates from both past and future, which converge within it; moreover, its completion is announced from both past and future, as the eschatological event inaugurated by Christ in the past unfolds from the future. In Zizioulas' words, the '*anamnesis* of Christ is realized not as a mere re-enactment of a past event but as an *anamnesis of the future*, as an eschatological event'.[7] Remembrance, hope and an eschatological temporal perspective are thus profoundly diffused into the Eucharistic imagination, paralleling the eschatological hermeneutic of *différance*, remembrance and hope which I have outlined.

Understanding time in Eucharistic terms theologically enriches an eschatological conception. This is because of the Christological and pneumatological particularization.[8] The Eucharist is embedded within the body of Christ, which it commemorates and represents, and which the Church both already is and aims to build. Redemptive promise and actualization take concrete form. In the person of Christ, there is no dualism between history and eschatological fulfilment. In Christological, pneumatological and Eucharistic context, history can be seen as a real bearer of the ultimate.[9] This problematizes a neo-Platonic ontological dualism and a post-Kantian 'cut' between the epistemologically apprehensible and the transcendent. In Christ, the transcendent is incarnated into history; in the Spirit, divinity is outpoured into history; and in both, the eschatological consummation of history is achieved. Time becomes not only eschatologically figured, but also Christologically and pneumatologically. This transforms understandings of history and its relationship to God. This is performatively recalled in the Eucharist.

Clearly, there is no space here to develop the theological significance of the Eucharist in its relationship to configurations of time and transcendence, the Trinity and the world; this would be beyond the parameters of the argument. At this stage I simply want to signal some of the theological doors which are opened more obviously by a focus on the Eucharist rather than on eschatology alone. The Eucharistic frame of reference incorporates both a theological stress on remembrance, and the eschatological perspective on time, but offers also a clearer Trinitarian context. This could provide a way into a theology of time which likewise takes remembrance and eschatology as its keynotes, but by beginning epiclectically from the body of Christ funds a specifically Trinitarian framing of Church, world and redemption.

It is the relationship of the Eucharist to the body of Christ which takes us into the next thematic resonance: community. This has multiple expressive power.

---

[7] Zizioulas, *Being and Communion*, 254.

[8] The Christological context of the Eucharist is readily apparent, howsoever it is theologized as body and blood of Christ and in terms of anamnesis, sacrifice and presence. Its pneumatological dimensions should not though be passed over. Epiclesis as the invocation of the Holy Spirit has an ancient association with Eucharistic consecration and unity which persists in various expressions in contemporary liturgies.

[9] See Zizioulas, *Being and Communion*, 186.

The Eucharist, as a liturgical enactment of the body of Christ, is profoundly connected to the very notion of Church, as body of Christ. The Eucharist unites the Church, or, put conversely, the Church unites in the Eucharist. The Eucharistic assembly is a sacramental gathering in Christ in which again, the eschatological dimension is at the forefront: the body of Christ is both what the Church is and what it is meant to be, and this is anticipated in the Eucharist. Hence the Eucharist, as community, is not only assembly, but also movement.[10] The Eucharist, then, can sum up the eschatological community of the body of Christ in its partial historical manifestation and its unrealized fullness.

The Eucharistic community transcends linear divisions of time because of its eschatological nature; it also offers a theological transcendence of social divisions. The Eucharist can provide resources for social justice through its undercutting of hierarchical stratifications, again in a way potentially disruptive of splits between the spiritual and the worldly, the mystical and the political. Cavanaugh explains why this should be the case:

> . . . the eschatological imagination of the Eucharist overcomes the secular imagination of separate spiritual and temporal planes . . . in the Eucharist the Kingdom irrupts into time and 'confuses' the spiritual and the temporal. The Eucharist thus realizes a body which is neither purely 'mystical' nor simply analogous to the modern state: the true body of Christ.[11]

Therefore the Eucharist can embody an ideal of social equity, in which all are called to the table of Christ, within parameters which blur boundaries between the political and the mystical and can thus resource a theology of social action.[12] A Eucharistic theology of this type, stressing the corporate nature of the body of Christ and an eschatologically impelled ethic of social justice, clearly resonates with the feminist model of *ekklesia* as it has been outlined. The Eucharistic community is a partial historical incarnation of an ideal yet to come but which it

---

[10] See ibid., 61: 'The eucharist is not only an assembly in one place, that is, a historical realization and manifestation of the eschatological existence of man; it is at the same time also *movement*, a progress towards this realization. Assembly and movement are the two fundamental characteristics of the eucharist . . .' Whilst agreeing with this eschatological concept of the eucharist as community, I would not phrase this in terms of 'progress': this implies a linear sense of *Heilgeschichte* which, as I argued in Chapter 7, in fact is not only unnecessary to an eschatological vision of time but actually oppositional to it.

[11] Cavanaugh, *Torture and Eucharist*, 206. See also Wainwright, *Eucharist and Eschatology*, 149.

[12] Tissa Balasuriya, for example, provides an account of the Eucharist which makes it central to liberatory theology, seeing the Eucharistic table as a prefiguration of an ultimate liberation which demands social action (*The Eucharist and Human Liberation*). It is important to bear in mind, with him, that the connection between the Eucharist and social justice is only rarely historically discernible: 'the history of the Eucharist is one of very close association with oppression. After Christianity became the religion of the Roman Empire, the celebration of the Eucharist was absorbed by the social establishment as a special expression of its triumph. It gave divine legitimation to power' (58).

nevertheless represents. Again, this strikes chords with the vision of *ekklesia*, as partial bearer of hoped-for future realization.

So if, as I have argued, the Christian *ekklesia* can fruitfully operate with a hermeneutic resourced by eschatology, it might seem that the Eucharist could offer yet richer reserves as a primary theological matrix. Eschatology and remembrance are profoundly important to the Eucharistic imagination, and the Eucharist additionally can offer a Trinitarian foundation which an eschatological vision alone does not foreground. What is more, the Eucharist is deeply theologically related to community: to the body of Christ, again in eschatological horizons – and as suggested, it can also act as a locus for socio-political ethical impetuses. However, despite these undeniable assets, I do not wish to place the Eucharist at the hermeneutical centre of the *ekklesia*. This is for two reasons.

My first reason is ecclesiological. As apparent, I have followed Schüssler Fiorenza in placing the *ekklesia* at the centre of my hermeneutical reflections, and the *ekklesia*, as Church of wo/men, is a Eucharistic community. To say otherwise would be to disempower theologically and spiritually the *ekklesia*. However, both Schüssler Fiorenza and I rejected an understanding of *ekklesia* as 'true' exodus-Church, in polar relation to the kyriarchal Church. The *ekklesia* then, inasmuch as it is lodged within the kyriarchal Church, cannot claim to be the real Eucharistic community in contradistinction from it; what is more, this would not only result in a logical incoherence but would actually undermine the very notion of the Eucharistic community. I take seriously here the Eucharist as 'sacrament of unity' and the Eucharistic community as an expression of the universal and catholic Church – although, as Wiles ironically notes, '[t]he so-called sacrament of unity has been a notorious cause of Christian division'.[13]

This ecclesiological discussion is complicated by the fact that we are threading our way through various partial and historical manifestations of unrealized ideals. In ideal terms, the imagined community of the Eucharist is co-terminous with the imagined community of a universal catholic Church;[14] from a

---

[13] Wiles, 'Eucharist Theology – The Value of Diversity', 115.

[14] The divergent position of the Salvation Army and the Society of Friends must be noted here. In Quaker theology, the sacramental dimension of the Eucharist is foreign; nevertheless, corporativity and communion are still important. This can be discerned in the Quaker statement to the 1927 Faith and Order Conference at Lausanne: 'And we believe that a corporate practice of the presence of God, a corporate knowledge of Christ in our midst, a common experience of the work of the living Spirit, constitute the supremely real sacrament of a Holy Communion' (cited by the Canadian Yearly Meeting of the Religious Society of Friends in their response to the Lima Document of 1982, in Thurian [ed.], *Churches Respond to BEM*, Vol III, 300). The same response also comments that Friends can recognize, along with a Salvation Army representative who had recently addressed this Canadian group, that 'there are certain sacramental observances, which, though not practised by us, are a means of grace to the believer who desires to share in the spiritual reality of which the sacrament is a symbol' (301), and also, as affirmed in the 1916 London Yearly Meeting statement, that '[t]rue unity may be found under apparent differences' (302). What this points toward is a necessary blurring of boundaries as to the nature of Church; it would be possible for a Eucharistic church to conceive of Christian groups which did not practice the ritual of the Eucharist as

feminist point of view, this postulated ideal Church would be non-kyriarchal and therefore there would be no necessity for a Christian *ekklesia* distinguishable in the manner outlined from the Church as such. In real terms, the global Church is predominantly kyriarchal and fractured into numerous bodies claiming autonomy from each other and not in communion with each other.[15] The *ekklesia* is not equivalent to an ecclesiastical body of this type; it is transdenominational and non-institutional, and as formulated here, it is not and makes no claim to be an exclusive Eucharistic community. Whilst this in no way implies that the *ekklesia* should refrain from understanding itself as a Eucharistic community at all, I argue that it is only logically and theologically coherent to do so in respect of its relationship to the Church and not in its contrariness to it. The *ekklesia* of wo/men is, I would in fact insist, truly Church and truly Eucharistic community, but it is Eucharistic community because it is Church and not because it is Church of wo/men. As such for the *ekklesia* as Church of wo/men to congregate around the Eucharist as the primary structuring motif might misleadingly imply an ecclesiological separation from the Church which has already been rejected. In short then, the *ekklesia* may well understand itself as Eucharistic community, but this is because the *ekklesia* as church of wo/men can genuinely claim to be Church and not because it is the feminist community of the *ekklesia*. To stress the Eucharist as a hermeneutic springboard leads theologically to the assimilation of the *ekklesia* within the Church, because the Eucharist is expressive of the whole corporate body of Christ; not only its feminist members and critics.[16]

The second reason why I choose not to centralize Eucharistic motifs in the hermeneutics of the *ekklesia* is on account of the latter's dual membership; it is incorporated not only into the Christian communities but also into the broader feminist *métissage*. This point is subtle, for it should be stated very explicitly at the outset that I do not register this objection because there is any difficulty with a specific religio-cultural perspective feeding into the *métissage*. As has been stressed, the feminist *métissage* is not a space in which cultural specificity and

---

nevertheless part of the imagined Eucharistic community, understood as the entire body of Christ in communion. This is a question of Christian identity which is outside the scope of this book.

[15] Wainwright in *Eucharist and Eschatology* suggests that there is a distinction between the Eucharist as expressive of an existing unity and as creative sign for a fuller unity yet to come, and that the circumstances of Christian disunity actually require a greater emphasis on the 'creative sign' dimension (142). Similarly, he considers that the Eucharist can figure unity better when understood as the Lord's Supper rather than the Church's Supper (141). See also 115-117.

[16] Nicholas Lash makes this point well, arguing that the Church 'does not admit of division into parts and whole. When a group of Christians assemble to celebrate the eucharist, they are the body of Christ sharing in the body of Christ: they are the church, not a 'part' of the church' (*His Presence in the World*, 185). Understood in this way, the Eucharistic community of the *ekklesia* can claim the fullness of Church inasmuch as it is corporately the body of Christ. However, as Eucharistic community, it is the continuity and identity with Church which is stressed, not the oppositionality to it.

differences are ideally obliterated: quite the reverse. In the context I deploy it, an eschatological hermeneutic is, in any event, likewise rooted in the particularity of Christian cultural and religious formulations. Nevertheless, despite this, I want to argue that the relationship of the *ekklesia* to the *métissage* means that the Eucharist is not the most appropriate founding symbol and structuring motif for the *ekklesia*.

The overriding reason for not making the Eucharist central to the *ekklesia* in this respect is precisely because of the corporate significance of the Eucharist. The corporate feminist *métissage* is not the body of Christ. The *ekklesia* is, but in its relationship to the Church and not in its relationship to the *métissage*. This certainly does not preclude the *ekklesia* from participating in the *métissage*, but, since the *ekklesia* is a feminist construct, it fosters a reluctance to identify its primary self-understanding as community in terms that emphasize its Christian rather than feminist roots. I stress, it is the founding constitution of the *ekklesia* as *community* which is at issue here, and this is why I perceive a distinction between recommending a Christian-based eschatological hermeneutic over against advocating an Eucharistic understanding of the *ekklesia* as a corporate body. The *ekklesia* is the *ekklesia*, and not simply reducible to the Church, because it is a feminist group – and this should be reflected in its self-constitution. An eschatological hermeneutic such as I have suggested here is, of course, articulated with reference to Christian matrices and narratives,[17] but it is contingently related to the *ekklesia*. It is one possible hermeneutic framework and set of principles which I have argued can profitably be adopted by the *ekklesia*. It is not definitive of the *ekklesia*, whilst an Eucharistic modelling of the *ekklesia* as community would be.

All this is very far from asserting that the Christian *ekklesia* should not understand itself as an Eucharistic community; it is, contrariwise, to draw back from making the Eucharist the central gathering point for the hermeneutic framework of the *ekklesia* as feminist space. This is for the two dangers stated: that the ideal catholicity of the Eucharist would undermine the distinctiveness of the *ekklesia* as church of wo/men by necessarily stressing the *ekklesia* as Church; and that the location of the *ekklesia* within the feminist *métissage* would be undermined by stressing the *ekklesia* as a community constituted by the body of Christ rather than as a feminist and counter-kyriarchal community.

However, the parallels between Eucharistic articulations of time and community, and the *ekklesia* when figured in relation to an eschatological hermeneutic such as I have described, are a positive feature. It emphasizes that the

---

[17] It is worth pointing out that an eschatological hermeneutic is here framed in Christian terms, but it could also be transposed into secular or non-Christian key. As hermeneutic, eschatology is a Christian articulation of a messianic or ethical-utopic impulse which could actually be figured in other ways – or, which can be theologically saturated with Christian metaphysical beliefs. Hence, whilst an eschatological hermeneutic is a specifically Christian articulation of a religio-temporal perspective and ethical imperative, this could be given expression in secular or other-religious terms. The eschatological model I suggest for the Christian *ekklesia* is then rooted in particular cultural and religious formulations, but I would argue that it is in fact sufficiently permeable and plastic to be reshaped outside of Christian horizons.

ekklesia is wo/men-*as-church*. It opens up creative theological spaces for the *ekklesia*, and points to the Eucharist as a resource for the *ekklesia* in its mission to transform the kyriarchal Church. Focusing on the Eucharist has allowed for a mapping of the connection of the *ekklesia* to the Church as Christian community. This has enabled an articulation of the relationship of the *ekklesia* to the Church as one of a proleptic Eucharistic identity and a discursive differentiation which would, in eschatological horizons, be redeemed into unity.

The *Ekklesia* and Gender-Identity

In Chapter 3, we saw that Schüssler Fiorenza is determined to move beyond the sex-gender framework which she believes is inherently dualistic, reinforces kyriarchal models of identity, and fails to take account of both the multiple nature of subjectivity and the multiplicative nature of oppression. The *ekklesia* as church of wo/men is, then, positioned by Schüssler Fiorenza in the logic of democracy rather than in the logic of identity. Thus far, I am in full agreement with Schüssler Fiorenza; there is indeed a need to rethink identity and subjectivity in ways that do not reproduce kyriarchal economies and, in Schüssler Fiorenza's language, a logic of democracy is appropriately counterpoised to a logic of identity as a 'home' for the justice-seeking *ekklesia*. Nevertheless, the point was made earlier that Schüssler Fiorenza does not in the end provide an adequate account of the category of 'women' nor of sexual difference within the logic of democracy. Addressing this problematic will constitute the bulk of what follows. Within the *ekklesia*, proceeding from counter-kyriarchal logic, how might gendered identity be coherently conceived outside of the sex-gender framework?

Before moving on to this issue, I shall make one prior semantic point: whilst I concur with Schüssler Fiorenza's reasoning with respect to the logic of democracy or equality, I consider this terminology to be flawed. The political flavour of the term 'democracy' is on the one hand a positive thing in Schüssler Fiorenza's terms of reference, for it highlights the public and political character of the *ekklesia*. However, against this, historical socio-political investments in democracy are inextricably bound up with kyriarchal structures and worldviews, as Schüssler Fiorenza's own analysis actually demonstrates. It is therefore a deeply ambivalent concept to set against a kyriarchal logic of identity. Similarly, in feminist circles the language of equality can resonate with liberal socio-political programmes which, it is argued, end up by equating equality with sameness within perduring kyriarchal structures. I shall, hence, employ the language of equity rather than either equality or democracy. This is intended both to retain a socio-political force and to avoid a liberalistic reduction to sameness connoted by the language of equality.

So, within the logic of equity, let us consider how we might think the category of 'women'. Firstly, it is important to establish the parameters for working within such a frame. What are the crucial defining features which might distinguish a logic of equity from a logic of identity? The most significant of these is indubitably a hospitality towards differences. I use the plural advisedly. If we speak of difference in the singular, it can raise the question: difference from what? This can actually end up by reifying existing patterns of Norm/Other which privilege the white, the male, the middle-class, the heterosexual, and lock discussion back into a Hegelian reduction of difference to identity. Differences, plural, are not so reducible. Differences are excessive, and cannot be contained. Similarly, I would draw attention to the fact that I speak of the category 'women' not 'woman'. The latter lends itself to an essentializing account of femaleness in a way which the former can potentially resist.

Differences, plurality, multiplicity: these are features which lay out a landscape of much greater texture than can or does identity politics.[18] This is a thick account of the world. We can add fluidity to this set. If the logic of equity does not proceed from reduction to essentializing categories, nor does it posit categories as fixed and stable. Against sameness and fixity is set multiplicity and fluidity. The logic of equity is, then, one which invites flux rather than strives to contain it, order it, control it. The logic of equity, in this respect, offers a thoroughly shifting and unstable framework for theorizing. This is not so, however, in all respects. The point was made in Chapter 3 that stress on differences can actually leave a political agenda bereft, for one step forward from this is into an ethical abyss which sees a collapse from acknowledgement of differences into socio-political *in*difference. This may perhaps be a different logic from that of identity but it could scarcely be one congruent with a feminist perspective. If differences and flux are the terrain in which the logic of equity is positioned, emancipation is the direction towards which it points. The *ekklesia* is thoroughly ethical in constitution. As such the *ekklesia* repeats the double manoeuvre already described in Chapter 3, where the hermeneutic of destabilization was contextualized within a hermeneutic of remembrance and hope which encapsulated the ethical location of feminist interpretation. Likewise the logic of equity in which the *ekklesia* constitutes itself is *both* multiple, shifting and fluid *and* ethically oriented. Some considerations as to how these two aspects might cohere are offered in the next section.

But as regards the immediate task at hand; we have now established the principles which characterize a logic of equity and within which my account of sexual difference must be set forth. It is helpful at this point to reprise the problematic. The salient factors are, firstly, an acknowledgement that the sex-gender framework must be abandoned, for it works on the logic of identity which has been rejected. Coupled to this is a recognition that subjectivity is both multiply mapped and fluid, according to a number of co-ordinates such as race, gender, economics and sexuality. Furthermore, these categories are themselves mobile and heterogeneous social constructs, and discursive rather than simply 'natural' points of reference. This is all in accordance with Schüssler Fiorenza's account. However,

---

[18] I use 'identity politics' here to signify socio-political frameworks ordered according to particular identity categories, whether understood as constructed or pre-discursive. The connection between identity politics in this sense and the logic of identity should be plain. This is a necessary clarification, because the phrase is variously utilized: Linda Alcoff uses it in a quite different sense, to denote the construction of identity by political action ('Cultural Feminism vs. Post-Structuralist Feminism', 432).

the story so far can narrate differences, but it offers no basis for a movement such as feminism to congregate around. It undercuts the positing of any unitary group which can advance common cause in solidarity for emancipatory purposes. To echo Tania Modleski, how do we have feminism without women?[19] Schüssler Fiorenza's answer to this was a pragmatic acknowledgement that we cannot in fact do away with the category 'women' entirely without erasing the specific oppressive situations which feminism seeks to critique and overturn. She therefore suggested that the way to retain 'women' outside of a sex-gender framework was to conceive of the category in socio-political terms. The destabilization of 'women' as it operates in kyriarchal logic was signalled by the neologism 'wo/men'.

I identified the preliminary difficulty with this strategy in Chapter 3 – namely that, by conceiving of 'wo/men' in socio-political terms alone, it actually fails to think sexual difference outside of the logic of identity. The critical aporia in the socio-political category wo/men, I argued, is laid bare by Schüssler Fiorenza's own definition of it. This, as we have seen, was a response to the question of how can we talk about 'women', and therefore legitimate a feminist enterprise, without sinking back into gender-dualistic worldviews. Yet, defining 'wo/men', Schüssler Fiorenza said that she means it to include not only all women, but also oppressed and marginalized men.[20] Therefore, wo/men as a socio-political category does not actually signify the female sex, but the oppressed and the marginalized. So, it seems that despite her protestations to the contrary, Schüssler Fiorenza's feminism is indeed a 'feminism without women', and one in which sexual difference is repressed as a category.

I take a diametrically different line on this point. Schüssler Fiorenza uses the socio-political category wo/men to allow for the differences between women (which she considers a sex-based definition of 'women' obliterates), whilst not erasing women as an oppressed group. However, this project fails. It fails for two reasons. The first I have already outlined: the category wo/men is not, in Schüssler Fiorenza's terms, an 'exclusive universalised gender term'.[21] Therefore it is difficult to see in what sense the category 'women' is in principle retained, although Schüssler Fiorenza does in practice continue to use the language of 'female', 'male' and 'woman', 'man'. This merely underscores the continued primacy of sexual difference by theoretically refusing it as a basis for theorizing but nevertheless being obliged still to use it in the interests of coherence. The

---

[19] Tania Modleski, *Feminism Without Women: Culture and Feminism in a 'Postfeminist' Age* (New York: Routledge, 1991). The opposing view is taken by thinkers such as Denise Riley, who deny that 'women' exist at all except as social practices (*'Am I That Name?' Feminism and the Category of 'women' in History* (Minneapolis: University of Minnesota Press, 1988). Riley postulates that feminism can still be coherently thought, as the site at which the battle over the unstable category 'women' is fought. For excellent discussion of the identity of 'women' see also Linda Alcoff, 'Cultural Feminism vs. Post-structuralism'; pertinent to the current discussion is her question 'What can we demand in the name of women if 'women' do not exist and demands in their name simply reinforce the myth that they do?' (420).

[20] *Jesus – Miriam's Child, Sophia's Prophet*, 191 n. 1.

[21] Ibid., 191 n. 1.

second reason why it fails is that it betrays its own purposes, in respect of letting differences between women destabilize naturalized notions of 'woman'. This is because significant differences between women are, in fact, socio-political. Therefore a socio-political model of the category 'wo/men' least of all can provide space for differences to take their proper place and not be subordinated to an overarching metanarrative. The traditional understanding of 'women' rests on socio-political narratives of femininity. This feminist understanding of 'women' rests on socio-political narratives of oppression. Schüssler Fiorenza is absolutely right in her argument that oppression is multiplicative, and a socio-political category based on oppression fundamentally fails to capture the differences between oppressions. What is more, the concepts and categories of 'women' and 'men' would in all likelihood persist even if the sexes could not be distinguished by their socio-political locations with respect to distributions of power.

So; how then do I propose to retain the category 'women' *outside* of an essentializing or universalizing sex-gender framework? Ironically, the answer is to return to sexed bodies. I hasten to add that whenever I speak of sex, or sexed bodies, I explicitly do not refer to a neutral biological 'slate' on to which cultural codes are 'written'. As indicated earlier in the argument, a discursively realist account can accommodate both an insistence on materialism and a recognition that everything is always already interpreted – but, again as previously argued, this does not negate the real or render it non-constitutive in discursive formations. So, sexed bodiliness remains as a discursive construct which is biologically marked. The key point here is that retaining the category 'women' based on bodily features is not of itself essentialist: it all depends on how you construct it. I shall return to this question of essentialism and sex-categories below. Here, I want to push the argument on in a related direction. Namely, that *only* by beginning from a biologically marked understanding of women is the obliteration of differences between women avoided.

This works, precisely because we are not working in an essentialist framework. If we do not suppose that 'biology is destiny' or that being a woman necessarily entails this or that particular socio-political situation or personality structure or sexuality,[22] then being a woman is to live from a category which is neither universal nor essential. Being a woman is a biologically constituted

---

[22] It is the issue of sexuality which prompts feminists such as Monique Wittig to deny the category 'women' except as a political and economic class; she considers that lesbians are living, practical proof of its bankruptcy. However, she is operating with a different understanding of it which defines 'women' as subjects necessarily economically, politically and ideologically determined in the logic of kyriarchy; by relocating the category 'women' in the logic of equity as I here attempt, it becomes a radically underdetermined category within which heterogeneity flourishes. Basically, Wittig's analysis demonstrates my earlier point: it is a socio-political understanding of 'women' as category which, in fact, hamstrings attempts simultaneously to conceive of women's differences and of a subject, who is a woman. She moves beyond this dilemma by denying the category of sexed identity; I move beyond it by retaining the category of sex but relocating in a different and anti-kyriarchal framework. See Wittig, 'One is not Born a Woman', in *The Straight Mind* (Hemel Hempstead: Harvester Wheatsheaf, 1992), 9-20.

condition – remembering, once more, that I do not perceive biology as falling outside of the realm of discourse. But it is a condition which in current socio-political structures (kyriarchy) is scored by a certain contingent commonality: the rendering as Other to man, played out in myriad ways in the realms of language, production, reproduction, metaphysics and so on. However, this is only a *certain* commonality, since it has already been suggested that subjectivity is mapped not in gender-dualistic terms but by a whole set of co-ordinates which are themselves culturally shifting and various.[23] If identity is modelled as fluid and multiply shaped, then retaining 'women' and 'men' as categories does not imply habitation of a framework structured along a fracture line of sex/gender, but a framework which presupposes differences, overlaps and mobility in the discursive constitutions of selves and world.[24] At the same time, it enables solidarity for political action by allowing configurations of common interest and positionality within prevailing socio-political conditions to be identified. Thus, 'women' is not a socio-political category, but feminism is a coalition based on opposition to particular contingent and variant configurations of socio-politics and ideologies which overdetermine women and work to their detriment.

The conflation of essentialist accounts of sexedness with retention of sexuate categories comes from a failure to distinguish between an Aristotelian doctrine of real essence and a post-Lockean nominalism.[25] Locke rejected the notion that the essence of a thing inhered in itself but argued that ideas of particular properties could justify the attachment of general categorial names. Seeking to introduce a more explicit framework for cultural variability into this debate, Christine Battersby adds Kant's voice to the discussion: 'Kant denied that abstract ideas are obtained simply in a bottom-up way, by simply generalizing from

---

[23] Furthermore, I take the view that the subject is self-constituting as well as constituted.

[24] This is a crucial point. Identity as a 'woman' or a 'man' is, I am arguing, only reducible to a sex-gender framework when it is dualistically conceived as closed and oppositional categories. Elizabeth Grosz shows how a dualistic understanding inevitably reduces 'woman' in kyriarchal society to a negative: 'Dichotomous structures take the form of A and not-A relations, in which one term is positively identified and the other is defined only as the negative of the first . . . the term [not-A] is purely negatively defined, and has no contours of its own; its limiting boundaries are those which define the positive term' (Grosz, *Sexual Subversions*, xvi). I cite this to differentiate my own retention of the categories of man/woman from an A/not-A framework. Rather, what I am suggesting is more analogous to an infinite series of identities which are not oppositionally and dualistically related but interrelate, overlap, and intertwine and are subject to change, but which could be nominally organized into various heterogeneous categories according to some of the features by which they are marked. Biological marking into men/women is one such axis.

[25] Diana Fuss offers a classic account of the complexity of what is actually at stake when 'essentialism' is invoked, and draws a distinction between ontological and linguistic forms of essentialism which can be represented in terms of real (Aristotelian) as distinct from nominal (Lockean) expressions. As she notes, however, the former is nominal and the latter remains essentializing (Fuss, *Essentially Speaking: Feminism, Nature and Difference*). The discussion here seeks to go beyond this impasse.

particulars. Instead, he posited an intermediate level of *rules* that mediate between the categories of the mind and experience itself.'[26] Such a perspective enables her to see all descriptions as regulative and discursive, which means that membership of a class is not timeless, neutral or indicative of uniformity. With respect to the sexual identification of women, '[w]hatever acts as the dominant regulatory norm in different cultures and historical periods would count as the 'schematic essence' of the human female'.[27] A nominalist understanding of sexed categories can accommodate cultural change and does not need to presuppose the existence of fixed or timeless properties which ontologically naturalize categorial distinctions, nor that within these pragmatic groupings enormous diversity may not be found. The question as to whether such categorial distinctions are essentialist depends, I would argue, on how categorizing is itself conceived. On my analysis, it is, as I have stated, a pragmatic act. As long as the current biological constitution of humanity prevails, sexed differentiation will be an aspect of being human, but employing categories based on sexuateness is only essentialist if it is then constructed in closed, stable and uniform ways.

This provides a jumping-off point for theorizing the relationship of gendered identity to the *ekklesia*. If 'women' and 'men' are permeable and heterogeneous categories, the task is not to formulate a 'woman's subjectivity'. This would lapse back into essentialism. Rather, in this dynamic landscape of non-identical identity, what is needed is a space marked out for human becoming which does not repeat the mind/body dualism and in which the subjectivity of both women and men can become.[28] A desire to integrate bodiliness into accounts of human being is, indeed, another reason why it is important that we do not relinquish sexuateness as an organizing principle. In the richness of bodiliness, constructed in all its various ways, sexuateness is an important variable. It is not essentialist to theorize from the sexed body because, as argued, it is unnecessary to suppose that a particular identity follows from a particular bodiliness, but rather space is left for a particular bodiliness to shape identity in particular ways. The model I propose also rejects the idea that there are two socio-symbolic structures (one male, one female) and that the problem is that the female one has been

---

[26] Battersby, *The Phenomenal Woman*, 30.

[27] Ibid., 31.

[28] This sidesteps the problematic of identity/difference as defined by Joan C. Tronto: 'the powerless have only two options available to them to try to change the distribution of power. The two options are: to claim that they should be admitted to the centre of power because they are the same as those already there, or because they are different from those already there, but have something valuable to offer to those already there' (*Moral Boundaries and Political Change*, 15). The position I am outlining is a refusal of the terms of that debate (as in fact Tronto goes on to do, in a different way); it does indeed suggest that subjectivities are the 'same' but they are the 'same' in sharing an envelope of differences, multiplicity and fluidity. It is not the case that those 'outside' must articulate either their sameness to or difference from those 'inside', but that the inside/outside line is recognized as a construct along many particular axes of oppression which require challenge such that those both 'inside' and 'outside' specific discursive structures can become *differently* in relation to each other.

repressed. This again is an essentialist analysis. The problem, rather, needs framing differently. The crisis in 'women's subjectivity' has arisen because of the dominance of a phallogocentric symbolic order, which positions both men and women in particular ways. This privileges the male, but it is not a necessarily male mode of subjectivity any more than the ejection of women into silence and lack is a necessarily female mode of subjectivity. What is needed is an alternative symbolic order which would position both men and women differently and within the logic of equity.

I have, then, rejected conceptions of gendered identity based on sameness – signalled, indeed, by my preference for speaking of identity as gendered rather than of gender-identity. At the same time I have already indicated that, given the kyriarchal ordering of current conditions, it is expedient to recognize commonalities in the position of women within this system as a basis for political action. This could be deemed a form of 'strategic essentialism', for it appears to accept the kyriarchal projection of women into a culturally consistent grouping – however, in fact, it operates in a different key: it recognizes commonalities in the causes of women which are not reducible one to another but which nevertheless offer a basis for a shared but differentiated ground for speaking. This model mirrors that of the *métissage*, as a knotwork of differences which are nevertheless loosely woven together. This 'knotting together' is an important move because it disrupts and dislodges the dominant order by letting one of its repressed others 'speak', which might allow space for an equitable order to emerge. That, of course, is the ultimate goal of the *ekklesia*.

The *Ekklesia* and Ethics

It should be clear that the *ekklesia* is a profoundly ethical construct. Indeed, a commitment to equity and to justice within a counter-kyriarchal logic are the defining characteristics of the *ekklesia* as laid out here. However, a commitment to respecting differences, within a metaphysical worldview which denies sure foundations from which to speak, poses certain questions of the ethical constitution of the *ekklesia*. Namely, the *ekklesia* is certainly not relativist; how, then, do we theorize this such that it is consistent with a rejection of epistemological warrants grounded outside of the discursive site?

One response would take its cues from Habermas. Certainly, this would seem to be a logical move: Habermas, in his formulation of discourse ethics, utilizes the notion of an ideal speech-community which surely resonates with an understanding of the *métissage* as an ideal rhetorical site from which to speak. Habermas famously adheres to the metanarratives of modernity as an unfinished project; observing the fragmented conditions of late modernity, his answer is not to turn to postmodernist gestures, but to reinvigorate the post-Enlightenment emancipatory impulses. The principle on which Habermas sees ethics proceeding is communicative action. This supposes that the goal of rational dialogue is to seek agreement; and the regulative centre for ethics is therefore an ideal speech situation; truth and justice become discursively oriented but not relativist. Critical philosophy should be guided by emancipatory interest, with the objective of exposing the socio-economic private interests and forces which distort communication.[29] Norms and values can then be established intersubjectively in a compulsion-free speech situation by rational consensus, in which the only force is that of the better argument, and in which no argument should be excluded. This is the ideal speech situation. It depends on a distinction between distorted and undistorted communication and the premise that norms and values can in fact be decided by rational consensus.

Habermas recognizes the contextuality of communication and reflection but developed the theory of universal pragmatics to justify the possibility of genuine intersubjective communication. This aims to demonstrate that meaningful communication presupposes certain conditions held in common: linguistic comprehensibility, propositional truth, intentional veracity and appropriateness. Discourse is the meta-communicative level at which criteria for truth and value are decided. Whilst all meaningful communicative action depends on the four validity-claims above, the rational decidability of truth and norms is presupposed at the level of discourse. The belief that norms and values can be rationally discussed is, for Habermas, justified within a framework of communicative ethics, in which only those interests which are universalizable and generalizable survive.

Clearly, the discursive theorization of truth and justice in Habermas' work also, like the idea of an ideal speech situation, points to a certain common ground between his framework and my own. Yet despite these obvious affinities, Habermas may not in the end be so useful a resource as one might initially suppose. Feminist philosopher Seyla Benhabib notes three distinct difficulties with Habermas' proposals.[30] The first springs from the goal of his ideal speech situation, which is to deliberate rationally on generalizable interests: these, indeed, could *only* be articulated in the ideal speech situation, for only in such a context could interests be agreed as generalizable.[31] Yet, given that we inevitably speak from particular contexts, how could we actually formulate and judge such claims? Benhabib considers that there is a gulf in the positing of an ideal speech situation between 'the ideal and the actual, the normative and the empirical' which cannot be bridged. Furthermore, even if ideal speech conditions could be established, that does not in fact guarantee that rational intersubjective communication will take place, only that participants would have equitable access to the advancement of claims. This, then, is her second criticism: if the ideal speech situation depends on

---

[29] Habermas argues that all knowledge is constituted by interest, identifying three broad categories of human inquiry. The first is empirical-analytical and reflects a technical interest which objectifies the object of study in order to produce general laws of prediction with respect to it and to manipulate it. This is an instrumental reason. The second is historical-hermeneutical and springs from a practical interest in understanding human communication and action. The third is critical sciences and philosophies, which demonstrate an emancipatory interest as exemplified by ideological critique or psychoanalysis. See *Knowledge and Human Interests*.

[30] Benhabib, 'The Methodological Illusions of Modern Political Theory: The Case of Rawls and Habermas', *Neue hefte fur philosophie* 21 (Spring), 1982, 47-74.

[31] Habermas, *Legitimation Crisis*, 111-17.

the rationality of arguments and evaluation, what is rational must be decided *a priori*. And thirdly, from whence would come the universal standards necessary to determine the validity of given communicative acts which are the basis for the discursive positing of generalisable norms? By homing in on the generalizable rather than the particular, there is another *a priori* distinction between legitimate and illegitimate interest claims, between distorted and undistorted communication, which imports the ideal of impartial decision-making into a contextually based forum proceeding from the assumption that reason is, by nature, interested.

In effect, the argument is that Habermas' discourse ethics runs aground on its failure to let go of the ideal of universalism. Beginning from a recognition that there is no guaranteed ground for making judgements, he nevertheless seeks to establish objectively valid and universalizable norms on the basis of communicative reason. This leads him to the positing of the ideal speech situation, as the only forum in which such principles could be impartially established. Yet the conditions for the ideal speech situation founder fatally on empirical inequitablities in discursive practices, and on what basis could one critique the non-ideal speech situation if the basis for universalisable critique is an ideal speech situation?

Therefore, the ethical constitution of the *métissage* as outlined here shares Habermas' commitment to an ideal rhetorical speech situation and to the discursive formation of truth and justice, but takes leave of his communicative ethics in several crucial respects. The most important of these is an abandonment of the ideal speech situation as the ground of ethical procedure, and its relocation as, rather, the goal. This means that we must look elsewhere for the ethical grounds of the *métissage*, and it also means that the nature of the ideal speech situation changes in key respects which follow from a foregrounding of the fact that it is unrealized. We shall see how this articulates in the discussion below.

Firstly, though, it is important to establish a distinction between stating that norms are historical and contingent and stating that norms are arbitrary. The two do not equate. The charge of relativism is often brought against worldviews proceeding from postmodern rejection of absolutes and universal foundations. This is an error which conflates the recognition that truth and values are formulated in specific contexts and from specific interests, rather than from the hypothetical 'Archimedean point', with a belief that all values and truth-claims are thereby of equal worth. Ethical viewpoints may be ultimately ungrounded, but that does not make them groundless. Merely the grounds are themselves contingent. This leads to the protestation that it then becomes impossible to justify one set of values and practices rather than another. On the contrary, it does not become impossible: it becomes a matter of profound importance, which is, however, a site of contestation. This introduces nothing new into the practice of ethical discourse, which is historically anything but monolithic.

It is necessary, I would argue, to ground feminist ethics in contingency because of the potential epistemological crisis which arises from the destabilization and historicization of the subject. Under the impact of anti-foundationalist philosophies, appeals cannot simply be made to unmediated truths located externally to subjects. However the 'subject' is itself a shaky foundation for theorizing. Selves understood to be contextually anchored cannot occupy the transcendent subject site of Kantian ethical theory. Selves which are fluid and non-unified sites of conflict cannot act as a foundation for self-transparent ethical theorizing. Selves which do not form part of stable and unified categories such as 'woman' cannot ground ethics in appeals to privileged corporate standpoints such as 'women's experience'. The instabilities inherent in individual and communal constitution render identity politics of any sort a problematic starting point for ethics. We need, therefore, to set forth the non-arbitrary but contingent bases from which the ethics of the *ekklesia* can proceed.

Linda Hogan has offered some helpful principles for a feminist ethic which takes seriously the instability of 'woman' as subject and category. Praxis remains a central feature, understood as a noetic characteristic,[32] as does 'women's experience'. However, she also observes that methodological consistency requires that 'one would be reluctant to make any claims apart from the radical historicity and diversity of women's experience and praxis. The social and historical character of feminist ethics' primary resources makes the language of certitude impossible to retain.'[33] Hence, there is a danger of impotence in the ethical realm which she seeks to overcome. The crucial move is to resist both universalism and relativism. This is achieved in her articulation of provisional prolegomena to the development of a feminist ethical theory.

The limitation of ethical appeal to pragmatic rather than ontological foundations plays a central role in her account. Such pragmatic grounds in a feminist ethic would be based on the positionality of women in networks of shifting power relations.[34] This enables a critical ethical voice to be raised which is rooted in women's locations within and outside of ideologies and institutions, validated by the nature of commitment and values inspired.[35] The risk of a subjectivism which would not allow for arbitration between perspectives and experiences is combated by the centralization of community. This reflects a commitment to dialogue as epistemological context. It might seem that relativism has here simply been displaced from the personal to the social; Hogan concedes that at one level this is 'inevitable', but points out that the community, as centre of

---

[32] Hogan relies here on the work of Matthew Lamb and Charles Davis for an articulation of the relationship between praxis and theory. The interdependence between the two is stressed: 'Critical theory is the conscious component of revolutionary praxis, a theoretical consciousness inseparable from the concrete, historical effort to overcome the contradictions in existing society' (Davis, 'Theology and Praxis', *Cross Currents* 23.2 (1973), 154-68, cited Hogan, 'Resources for a Feminist Ethic', 84). For Lamb's work, see *Solidarity With Victims: Towards a Theology of Social Transformation* (New York: Crossroad, 1982). The importance of praxis has not been enlarged upon in this thesis, but it is methodologically central to feminist and other liberatory theologies. See Hogan's *From Women's Experience to Feminist Theology*.

[33] Hogan, 'Resources for a Feminist Ethic', 89.

[34] 'Positionality' is a concept elaborated in Linda Alcoff's important article on cultural feminism, poststructuralism and epistemology: 'Culture Feminism versus Post-Structuralism: The Identity Crisis in Feminist Theory'.

[35] Hogan, 'Resources for a Feminist Ethic', 92.

'enquiry, debate and dialogue' is not the individual 'writ large'.[36] A bulwark against relativism is introduced by Carol Christ's notion of 'embodied thinking',[37] which unsettles a polarization between 'truth' and 'contextuality': 'We should think of our "truth claims" as the product of embodied thinking not as eternally or universally valid thought.'[38] This resources the advocacy of one worldview rather than another with reference to experience, praxis and embodied being; whilst all universal truth claims are culturally relative, not all truth-claims are thereby deemed equal. Injustice is validly denounced because of particular experiences of injustice. This may suggest that no transcontextual critique could be offered, and that we could have nothing to say to injustices perpetrated on others and not ourselves. That possibility is warded off by insisting, with Sharon Welch, that to express our resistance to injustice in its multiple formations what we need is a concept of universal *accountability*; this begins from the particular, but is attentive to the particular experiences of others and the impact of our own practices upon them.[39]

Hogan's sketch leaves us with four preliminary principles for an adequate feminist ethics: pragmatic foundations, the centrality of community, embodied thinking and accountability. In my articulation, the *métissage* clearly occupies the central site of community, as a community of feminist communities. This is the feminist rhetorical space of debate and disagreement. We can now begin to perceive some of the ways in which the *métissage*, as centre of feminist ethics, differs from the ideal speech situation as central to Habermas' discourse ethics. Accountability means that the *métissage* is not only concerned with interests which are generalizable, but with the particularities of others' experiences and articulations of the world. Indeed, if thinking is embodied, then it is the particular and not the general which excites orientation towards the other in the ethical imagination. 'Rational argument' is displaced from a position of primacy, to be replaced by the articulations of 'communities of resistance and solidarity' which are rooted in experiences of oppression. This does not, of course, exclude or marginalize 'rational' ethical debate; rather, it broadens the kind of discourse which the *métissage* hosts. The *métissage* proceeds from the assumption that the speech situation is not ideal. If the speech situation were ideal, then conditions of equity would already have been established. The *métissage* is an ethically oriented speech space lodged in profoundly inequitable socio-political discursive orderings. It seeks to establish an ideal speech situation in its commitment to polyphonic and open enquiry and dialogue, but it does not aim monolithically to solicit agreement and consensus. Such would be, as Benhabib terms it, a 'transcendental illusion' requiring the elimination of plurality and human differentiation into a 'self-identical collectivity'.[40] It is also a frankly *a priori* justice-seeking community of

---

[36] Hogan 'Resources for a Feminist Ethic', 94.
[37] Carol Christ, 'Embodied Thinking: Reflections on a Feminist Theological Method'.
[38] Christ, 'Embodied Thinking', 15, cited in Hogan, 96.
[39] Sharon Welch, *Communities of Resistance and Solidarity*, 81. The influence of this significant work is apparent in many liberation feminists' accounts of community and solidarity.
[40] Benhabib, 'The Methodological Illusions of Modern Political Theory: The Case of Rawls and Habermas', *Neue hefte fur philosophie* 21 (Spring), 1982, 47-74, 71.

communities, constituted by a feminist emancipatory interest, pragmatically grounded in particular embodied experiences, praxis and thinking.

The refusal of normative, ontological foundations in ethical thinking with relation to theology projects us once more to the realm of the metaphysical and picks up again the question opened out in Chapter 7. Namely, I earlier traced Markham's position in respect to the relationship between truth, reality and God in some detail, and in the execution of this developed the discursive realism which has underlain this study. The provocative question on which that analysis ended was whether or not we could identify a third way beyond the stark choice Markham offered us: Nietzsche or Aquinas? God and truth or neither of the two? I then outlined a third way within an eschatological imagination. This – counter to the hypostasized metaphysics of presence – does not point to God as 'present' or 'haveable' but as appearing through disappearing. Theological thinking takes its cues from *traces* of the divine. Similarly, transposed into the ethical realm, we may talk of an orientation towards God rather than a grounding in God.

Such an orientation walks the epistemological abyss: God may draw us on and inspire us with a desire to act according to 'the good', but 'the good' is not there for us to discover: we must create it for ourselves. It is an unfolding from and towards the future.

Chapter 9

Conclusions

For feminists working within Christian traditions, it is necessary to articulate models for biblical hermeneutics which are not only feminist but also can be related to theological frameworks. This task is problematized by the thoroughgoing nature of feminist critique, which both philosophically and theologically is required to rescript its own landscapes. This means that feminist questions necessarily spill out in innumerable directions, all of which interrelate.

The task of this book was to put forward constructive proposals for a paradigm of feminist and theological interpretation. Contextually located as I am, such an endeavour was inevitably sited also within contemporary philosophies. Specifically, the most significant philosophical impact on this thesis was from postmodern and post-structuralist perspectives, which furnished yet another point of intersection from this inquiry proceeded.

To achieve this goal, I engaged in dialogue with two important feminist biblical interpreters, namely Elisabeth Schüssler Fiorenza and Phyllis Trible. Since each works within different paradigms, this enabled significantly different questions and explorations to take place with respect to each. Nevertheless, it was also interesting that certain points of important convergence emerged: most particularly with respect to hermeneutics of remembrance as a rhetorical practice.

At the meta-level, although Schüssler Fiorenza and Trible operate with very distinctive methodologies, it was nevertheless possible to articulate a hermeneutic frame which embraced both. The primary principles of interpretation advocated were those of remembrance and destabilization. That these strategies actually coinhere was stressed, although as a strategy remembrance emphasizes the materialist dimension of feminist interpretation and destabilization its deconstructive modes. Both are potentially strategies of resistance. These two moments in the broad-brush feminist hermeneutic I advocate allow for both recovery of specificities and the dislodging of any given interpretation. The emancipatory siting of a feminist hermeneutic was signalled by my placement of both of these strategies into a dialectic with hope. Moving between oppression, resistance and hope, I suggested, can provide the resources for political action.

This hermeneutic of remembrance, destabilization and hope, I argued, could constitute an eschatological hermeneutic. This enables theological doors to be opened and allows feminist endeavours and interpretations to be located in Christian as well as feminist trajectories. This was highlighted yet further by my suggestion that the most appropriate siting for this eschatological hermeneutic was within a metaphysics which took its cues from an eschatological imagination. Such a strategy, I argued, allowed for the radical disruption of a metaphysics of presence. This was necessary for two reasons. The first was because this argument proceeded from the assumption that any explorations in realms of truth and meaning necessarily were implicated in (a)theology; this made it crucial that I at least indicate how my hermeneutic might relate to my theological ontology. Given postmodern critique of the metaphysics of presence as onto-theological, this task was particularly pressing. The second reason arose simply from the actual hermeneutics I ultimately advocated. Set in creative play with Derridian *différance*, there was plainly a tension between such destabilizing hermeneutic strategies and foundational philosophical and theological frameworks in which the ontological reality of God is affirmed.

However, it is also a key contention of this book that interpretation is produced at discursive locations. As such it was important that some consideration be given to the site of meaning-production. I developed here the concept of the *ekklesia* which featured prominently in Schüssler Fiorenza's work. This featured as a rhetorical site for feminist deliberation, both partially realized and ideal, which would operate on the logic of equity as distinct from identity (associated with kyriarchal economies). The *ekklesia* was then suggested as the discursive centre for Christian feminist interpretation. However, it must be stressed that this was conceived as a knotwork of differences, rather than as one unity. The microcosm of the *ekklesia* as a Christian feminist community was mirrored by the suggestion of a macro-scale feminist community of communities, hospitable to differences and committed to dialogue and which I called the *métissage*. This signalled a hybridity-in-solidarity.

Hence, the *ekklesia* is the discursive location for the feminist hermeneutics I propose. Interpretation could then proceed according to an eschatological hermeneutic, within a metaphysics constituted by the eschatological imagination. And all of this, I argued, was profoundly connected to an ethical orientation and praxis.

Selected Bibliography

Alcoff, Linda, 'Cultural Feminism vs. Post-structuralism: the Identity Crisis in Feminist Theory', *Signs*, 13.3 (1988), pp. 405-36

Anderson, Hugh, *Jesus and Christian Origins* (New York: Oxford University Press, 1964)

Archbishops' Commision on Church Doctrine, *Thinking about the Eucharist* (London: SCM, 1972)

Archer, Léonie J., 'Bound by Blood: Circumcision and Menstrual Taboo in Post-exilic Judaism', *After Eve*, ed. Soskice, Janet Martin (London: Marshall Pickering, 1990), pp. 38-61

Armstrong, Karen, 'The Acts of Paul and Thecla', *Feminist Theology: A Reader*, ed. Loades, A. (London: SPCK, 1990), pp. 83-88

Bach, Alice (ed.), *The Pleasure of Her Text* (Philadelphia, PA: Trinity Press International, 1990)

Baker-Fletcher, Karen, 'Anna Julia Cooper and Sojourner Truth: Two Nineteen-Century Black Feminist Interpreters of Scripture', *Searching the Scriptures*, Vol. 1, ed. Schüssler Fiorenza, Elisabeth (New York: Crossroad, 1993), pp. 41-51

Bal, Mieke, *Lethal Love* (Bloomington: Indiana University Press, 1987)

Balasuriya, Tissa, *The Eucharist and Human Liberation* (London: SCM, 1977)

Barker, F., Hulme, P. and Iversen, M. (eds.), *Uses of History: Marxism, Postmodernism and the Renaissance* (Manchester: Manchester University Press, 1991)

Barker, Francis, 'Which Dead? Hamlet and the Ends of History', *Uses of History: Marxism, Postmodernism and the Renaissance*, eds. Barker, F., Hulme, P. and Iversen, M. (Manchester: Manchester University Press, 1991), pp. 47-75

Barr, James, *Old and New in Interpretation: a Study of the Two Testaments* (London: SCM, 1966)

Barton, John, 'Historical-critical Approaches', *The Cambridge Companion to Biblical Interpretation*, ed. Barton, John (Cambridge: Cambridge University Press, 1998), pp. 9-20

Barton, John (ed.), *The Cambridge Companion to Biblical Interpretation* (Cambridge: Cambridge University Press, 1998)

Battersby, Christine, *The Phenomenal Woman* (Oxford: Polity Press, 1998)

Bauckham, Richard, 'Moltmann's Eschatology of the Cross', *Scottish Journal of Theology*, 30.4 (1977), pp. 301-311

Bauckham, Richard, 'Moltmann's Theology of Hope Revisited', *Scottish Journal of Theology*, 42.2 (1989), pp. 199-214

Beal, Timothy K. and Gunn, David M. (eds.), *Reading Bibles, Writing Bodies: Identity and the Book* (London: Routledge, 1997)

Becher, Jeanne (ed.), *Women, Religion and Sexuality* (Geneva: WCC Publications, 1990)

Belenky, Mary *et al.*, *Women's Ways of Knowing* (New York: Basic Books, 1986)

Belsey, Catherine, 'Making Histories Then and Now: Shakespeare from Richard II to Henry V', *Uses of History: Marxism, Postmodernism and the Renaissance*, eds. Barker, F., Hulme, P. and Iversen, M. (Manchester: Manchester University Press, 1991), pp. 24-46

Benhabib, Seyla, 'Feminism and the Question of Postmodernism', *The Polity Reader in Gender Studies*, ed. Polity Press (Cambridge: Polity Press, 1994), pp. 76-92

Benjamin, Walter, *Illuminations*, trans. Zohn, Harry, ed. Arendt, Hannah (Glasgow: Fontana, 3rd imp. 1979) (1973)

Berdyaev, Nicolas, *The Beginning and the End* (London: Geoffrey Bles, 1952)

Berger, Peter L., 'Different Gospels: The Social Sources of Apostasy', *Different Gospels*, ed. Walker, Andrew (Revised Edn, London: SPCK, 1993) (1988), pp. 105-119

Bible and Culture Collective, *The Postmodern Bible* (New Haven and London: Yale University Press, 1995)

Bishop, Jonathan, *Some Bodies: the Eucharist and its Implications* (Macon, Georgia: Mercer University Press, 1993)

Bottomley, Frank, *Attitudes to the Body in Western Christendom* (London: Lepus Books, 1979)

Braidotti, Rosi, *Patterns of Dissonance* (Cambridge: Polity Press, 1991)

Brenner, Athalya and Fontaine, Carole (eds.), *A Feminist Companion to Reading the Bible: approaches, methods and strategies* (Sheffield: Sheffield Academic Press, 1997)

Briggs, Sheila, 'The Deceit of the Sublime: an Investigation into the Origins of Ideological Criticism of the Bible in Early Nineteenth Century German Biblical Studies', *Semeia*, 59 (1992), pp. 1-23

Brooke, George J. (ed.), *Women in the Biblical Tradition* (Lewiston/Queenstown/Lampeter: Edwin Mellen Press, 1992)

Brown, David and Loades, Ann (eds.), *Christ: The Sacramental Word* (London: SPCK, 1996)

Bührig, Martha, *Women Invisible: A Personal Odyssey in Christian Feminism* tr. Walpole, J. M. (Stuttgart: Kreuz Verlag, 1987) (Tunbridge Wells: Burns & Oates, 1993)

Burke, Peter, 'Overture: The New History, its Past and its Future', *New Perspectives on Historical Writing*, ed. Burke, Peter (Cambridge, Polity Press, 1991), pp. 1-23

Burke, Peter (ed.), *New Perspectives on Historical Writing* (Cambridge: Polity Press, 1991)

Burrows, Mark S. and Rorem, Paul (eds.), *Biblical Hermeneutics in Historical Perspective* (Grand Rapids, Mich.: W.B. Eerdmans, 1991)

Butler, Judith, *Gender Trouble: Feminism and the Subversion of Identity* (London: Routledge, 1990)
Bynum, Caroline Walker, *Fragmentation and Redemption* (New York, NY: Zone Books, 1991), pp. 181-238
Cady, Linell E, 'Theories of Religion in Feminist Theologies', *American Journal of Theology and Philosophy*, 13 (3) (1992), pp. 182-193
Cannon, Katie G., 'Womanist Interpretation and Preaching in the Black Church', *Searching the Scriptures*, Vol. 1, ed. Schüssler Fiorenza, Elisabeth (New York: Crossroad, 1993), pp. 326-337
Capper, Brian, 'Public Bodies, Private Women', *Theology and the Body: Gender, Text and Ideology*, eds. Hannaford and Jobling (Leominster: Gracewing, 1999)
Caputo, John D., *Heidegger and Aquinas: An Essay on Overcoming Metaphysics* (New York: Fordham University Press, 1982)
Carmody, Denise Lardner, *Feminism and Christianity: A Two-way Reflection* (Nashville: Abingdon, 1982)
Carroll, Bernice (ed.), *Liberating Women's History* (Urbana: University of Illinois Press, 1976)
Castelli, Elizabeth A., 'Les Belles Infidèles/Fidelity or Feminism?: The Meanings of Biblical Translation', *Journal of Feminist Studies in Religion*, Spring (1990), pp. 25-39
Cavanaugh, William T., *Torture and Eucharist* (Oxford: Blackwell, 1998)
Chopp, Rebecca S., *The Power to Speak* (New York, NY: Crossroad, 1989)
Christ, Carol P., 'Embodied Thinking: Reflections on Feminist Theological Method', *Journal of Feminist Studies in Religion*, Spring (1989), pp. 7-15
Clines, David J., *What Does Eve Do To Help?* (Sheffield: JSOT Press, 1990)
Clines, David J., Gunn, David, M. and Hauser, Alan J. (eds.), *Art and Meaning: Rhetoric in Biblical Literature* (Sheffield: Sheffield Academic Press, 1982)
Code, Lorraine, *What Can She Know?* (New York and London: Cornell University Press, 1991)
Connor, Steven, *Postmodernist Culture* (Oxford: Blackwell, 1989)
Cooey, P., Farmer, Sharon A. and Ellen, M. R. (eds.), *Embodied Love: Sensuality and Relationship as Feminist Values* (San Francisco: Harper & Row, 1987)
Crawford, J. and Kinnamon, M. (eds.), *In God's Image: Reflections on Identity, Human Wholeness and the Authority of Scripture* (Geneva: WCC Publications, 1983)
Crosby, Christina, *The Ends of History: Victorians and 'the Woman Question'* (London: Routledge, 1991)
Cupitt, Don, *Taking Leave of God* (London: SCM, 1980)
Daggers, Jenny, 'Luce Irigaray and "Divine Women"', *Feminist Theology*, 14 (1997), pp. 35-50
Daly, Mary, *Gyn/ecology* (London: Women's Press, 1979)
Davaney, Sheila Greeve, 'Problems with Feminist Theory: Historicity and the Search for Sure Foundations', *Embodied Love: Sensuality and Relationship as Feminist Values*, eds. Paula Cooey, Sharon A. Farmer and Mary Ellen Ross (San Francisco: Harper & Row, 1987)

Davis, Natalie Zemon, 'What is Women's History?', *What is History Today..?* ed. Gardiner, Juliet (London: Macmillan Education, 1988), pp. 85-87

Dennis, Trevor, *Sarah Laughed: Women's Voices in the Old Testament* (London: SPCK, 1994)

Derrida, Jacques, *Of Grammatology* (Baltimore: John Hopkins University Press, 1976)

Derrida, Jacque, 'Structure, Sign, and Play in the Discourse of the Human Sciences', *Writing and Difference* (London: Routledge, 1978), pp. 278-293

Derrida, Jacques, *Writing and Difference* (London: Routledge, 1978)

Derrida, Jacques, *Margins of Philosophy* (Chicago: University of Chicago Press, 1982)

Docherty, Thomas (ed.), *Postmodernism: A Reader* (Hemel Hempstead: Harvester Wheatsheaf, 1993)

Douglas, Mary, *Purity and Danger* (London: Routledge & Kegan Paul, 1966)

Dowell, Susan and Hurcombe, Linda, *Dispossessed Daughters of Eve* (London: SCM Press, 1987)

Dragga, Sam, 'Genesis 2-3: A Story of Liberation', *Journal for the Study of the Old Testament*, 55 (1992), pp. 3-13

Elwes, Teresa (ed.), *Women's Voices* (London: Marshall Pickering, 1992)

Exum, J. Cheryl, *Fragmented Women: Feminist (Sub)versions of Biblical Narratives* (Sheffield: Sheffield Academic Press, 1993)

Fander, Monika, 'Historical-Critical Methods', *Searching the Scriptures*, Vol. 1, ed. Schüssler Fiorenza (New York: Crossroad, 1993), pp. 205-224

Fatum, Lone, 'Women, Symbolic Universe and Structures of Silence. Challenges and Possibilities in Androcentric Texts', *Studia Theologica*, 43 (1989), pp. 61-80

Featherstone, M., Hepworth, M. and Turner, B.S. (eds.), *The Body* (London: Sage Publications, 1991)

Felperin, Howard, "'Cultural Poetics' versus 'Cultural Materialism': The Two New Historicisms in Renaissance Studies', *Uses of History: Marxism, Postmodernism and the Renaissance*, eds. Barker, F., Hulme, P. and Iversen, M. (Manchester: Manchester University Press, 1991), pp. 76-100

Ferguson, Duncan, *Biblical Hermeneutics* (London: SCM, 1986)

Flax, Jane, *Thinking Fragments* (Berkeley and Oxford: University of California Press, 1990)

Frazer, Elizabeth, 'Feminist Ethics', *The Oxford Companion to Philosophy*, ed. Ted Honderich (Oxford: Oxford University Press, 1995)

Frei, Hans W., *The Eclipse of Biblical Narrative* (New Haven: Yale University Press, 1974)

Frye, Marilyn, 'To See and be Seen: The Politics of Reality', *Women, Knowledge and Reality*, eds. Ann Garry and Marilyn Pearsall (London: Routledge, 1992), pp. 77-92

Fuchs, Esther, 'Structure and Patriarchal Functions in the Biblical Betrothal-Type Scene', *Journal of Feminist Studies in Religion*, 3 (1987), pp. 7-13

Fuchs, Esther, 'Marginalization, Ambiguity, Silencing: The Story of Jepththah's Daughter', *Journal of Feminist Studies in Religion*, Spring (1989), pp. 35-45

Fulkerson, Mary McClintock, 'Contesting Feminist Canons: Discourse and the Problem of Sexist Texts', *Journal of Feminist Studies in Religion*, Fall (1991), pp. 53-73

Fulkerson, Mary McClintock, *Changing the Subject: Women's Discourses and Feminist Theology* (Minneapolis: Fortress Press, 1994)

Furlong, Monica, *A Dangerous Delight: Women and Power in the Church* (London: SPCK, 1991)

Fuss, Diana, *Essentially Speaking: Feminism, Nature and Difference* (New York: Routledge, 1989)

Gardiner, Juliet (ed.), *What is History Today..?* (London: Macmillan Education, 1988)

Gardner, Anne, 'Genesis 2.4b-25: A Mythological Paradigm of Sexual Equality or of the Religious History of Pre-exilic Israel?', *Scottish Journal of Theology*, 43.1 (1990), pp. 1-18

Gaster, Theodor H., *Myth, Legend and Custom in the Old Testament* (Gloucester, Mass.: Peter Smith, 1981) (1969)

Gatens, Moira, *Feminism and Philosophy* (Cambridge: Polity Press, 1991)

Gatens, Moira, 'The Dangers of a Woman-Centred Philosophy', *The Polity Reader in Gender Studies*, ed. Polity Press (Cambridge: Polity Press, 1994), pp. 93-107

George, Peter, 'Remembering the Dead: Kierkegaard and Dostoevsky', *Modern Believing*, 35/2 (1994), pp. 24-31

Gilligan, Carol, *In a Different Voice* (Cambridge, MA: Harvard University Press, 1982)

Gordon, Linda, 'What's New in Women's History?', *Feminist Studies/Critical Studies*, ed. de Lauretis, T. (Indiana: Indiana University Press, 1986), pp. 20-30

Gordon, Linda, 'What is Women's History?', *What is History Today..?* ed. Gardiner, Juliet (London: Macmillan Education, 1988), pp. 91-94

Gottwald, Norman K., 'Social Class and Ideology in Isaiah 40-55: An Eagletonian Reading', *Semeia*, 59 (1992), pp. 43-57

Graham, Elaine, 'From Space to Woman-Space', *Feminist Theology*, 9 (1995), pp. 11-34

Graham, Elaine, *Making the Difference* (London: Mowbray, 1995)

Grant, Robert, *A Short History of Biblical Interpretation* (London: SCM Press, 1984)

Graves, Robert and Patai, Raphael, *Hebrew Myths*, 2nd edn. (London: Cassell, 1965)

Green, Elizabeth E., 'Women's Words: Sexual Difference and Biblical Hermeneutics', *Feminist Theology*, 4 (1993), pp. 64-78

Greenburg, B, 'Female Sexuality and Bodily Functions in the Jewish Tradition', *Women, Religion and Sexuality*, ed. Becher, J. (Geneva: WCC Publications, 1990), pp. 1-44

Grey, Mary, 'Claiming Power-in-Relation: Exploring the Ethics of Connection', *Journal of Feminist Studies in Religion*, Spring (1991), pp. 7-18

Grey, Mary, 'The Dark Knowing of Morgan Le Fay: Women, Evil and Theodicy', *Women's Voices*, ed. Elwes, Teresa (London: Marshall Pickering, 1992), pp. 111-130

Grimshaw, Jean, *Feminist Philosphers: Women's Perspectives on Philosophical Traditions* (London: Harvester Wheatsheaf, 1986)

Grosz, Elizabeth, *Sexual Subversions* (Sydney: Allen & Unwin, 1989)

Gunn, David M. and Fewell, Danna Nolan, *Narrative in the Hebrew Bible* (Oxford: Oxford University Press, 1993)

Habermas, Jürgen, *Knowledge and Human Interests* (Boston: Beacon, 1971)

Habermas, Jürgen, *Legitimation Crisis* (Boston: Beacon, 1975)

Hackett, Jo Ann, 'Can a Sexist Model Liberate Us? Ancient Near Eastern "Fertility" Goddesses', *Journal of Feminist Studies in Religion*, 3 (1987), pp. 65-76

Hampson, Daphne, *Theology and Feminism* (Oxford: Blackwell, 1990)

Hampson, Daphne, 'On Being All of a Piece/At Peace', *Women's Voices*, ed. Elwes, Teresa (London: Marshall Pickering, 1992), pp. 131-145

Hampson, Daphne, *After Christianity* (London: SCM, 1996)

Hannaford, Robert and Jobling, J'annine (eds.), *Theology and the Body: Gender, Text and Ideology* (Leominster: Gracewing, 1999)

Haraway, Donna, *Simians, Cyborgs and Women* (London: Free Association Press, 1991)

Harding, Sandra, *The Science Question in Feminism* (Ithaca: Cornell University Press, 1986)

Hart, Keven, *The Trespass of the Sign* (Cambridge: Cambridge University Press, 1989)

Hassan, R, 'An Islamic Perspective', *Women, Religion and Sexuality*, ed. Becher, J. (Geneva: WCC Publications, 1990), pp. 93-128

Hayter, Mary, *The New Eve in Christ: The Use and Abuse of the Bible in the Debate about Women in the Church* (London: SPCK, 1987)

Heidegger, Martin, 'The Onto-theo-logical Constitution of Metaphysics', trans. Joan Stambaugh, *Identity and Difference* (London: Harper & Row, 1969), pp. 42-74

Heidegger, Martin, 'The Principle of Identity', trans. Joan Stambaugh, *Identity and Difference* (London: Harper & Row, 1969) pp. 23-41

Hennessey, Rosemary, *Materialist Feminism and the Politics of Discourse* (New York/London: Routledge, 1993)

Hennessey, Rosemary, 'Women's Lives/Feminist Knowledge: Feminist Standpoint as Ideology Critique', *Hypatia*, 8, Winter (1993), pp. 14-31

Henry, Martin, *On Not Understanding God* (Dublin: Columbia Press, 1997)

Hewitt, Marsha, 'The Politics of Empowerment: Ethical Paradigms in a Feminist Critique of Critical Social Theory', *The Annual of the Society of Christian Ethics* (November 1991), pp. 173-192

Hewitt, Marsha, 'The Redemptive Power of Memory: Walter Benjamin and Elisabeth Schüssler Fiorenza', *Journal of Feminist Studies in Religion*, Spring (1994), pp. 73-89

Hewitt, Marsha, *Critical Theory of Religion: a Feminist Analysis* (Minneapolis, MN: Augsberg Fortress, 1995)

Heyward, Carter, 'An Unfinished Symphony of Liberation: The Radicalization of Christian Feminism Among White U.S. Women: A Review Essay', *Journal of Feminist Studies in Religion*, Spring (1985), pp. 99-118

Himmelfarb, Gertrude, *The New History and the Old* (London: Belknap Press, 1987)

Hogan, Linda, 'Resources for a Feminist Ethic: Women's Experience and Praxis', *Feminist Theology*, 3 (1993), pp. 82-99

Hogan, Linda, *From Women's Experience to Feminist Theologies* (Sheffield: Sheffield Academic Press, 1995)

hooks, bell, *Feminist Theory: From Margin to Centre* (Boston: South End Press, 1984)

Howard, Jean E, 'Towards a Postmodern, Politically Committed, Historical Practice', *Uses of History: Marxism, Postmodernism and the Renaissance*, eds. Barker, F., Hulme, P. and Iversen, M. (Manchester: Manchester University Press, 1991), pp. 101-122

Hufton, Olwen, 'What is Women's History?', *What is History Today..?* ed. Gardiner, Juliet (London: Macmillan Education, 1988), pp. 82-85

Humphreys, Sally, 'What is Women's History?', *What is History Today..?* ed. Gardiner, Juliet (London: Macmillan Education, 1988), pp. 87-89

Hurley, James B., *Man and Woman in Biblical Perspective* (Leicester: Inter-Varsity Press, 1981)

Hutaff, Peggy, 'Response', *Journal of Feminist Studies in Religion*, Spring (1990), pp. 69-74

Irigaray, 'Equal to Whom?', trans. Robert L. Mazzola, *Differences*, 1/2 (1989), pp. 59-76

Irigaray, Luce, *An Ethics of Sexual Difference* (London: Athlone University Press, 1993)

Iser, Wolfgang, *The Act of Reading: a theory of aesthetic response* (London: Routledge and Kegan Paul, 1978)

Isherwood, L. and McEwan, D., *Introducing Feminist Theology* (Sheffield: Sheffield Academic Press, 1993)

Jantzen, Grace M., *Becoming Divine: Towards a Feminist Philosophy of Religion* (Manchester: Manchester University Press, 1998)

Jardine, Lisa, '"No offence i' th' world': Hamlet and unlawful marriage', *Uses of History: Marxism, Postmodernism and the Renaissance*, eds. Barker, F., Hulme, P. and Iversen, M. (Manchester: Manchester University Press, 1991), pp. 123-139

Jobling, David, *The Sense of Biblical Narrative 2* (Sheffield: JSOT Press, 1986)

Jobling, David, 'A Jamesonian Reading of Psalm 72', *Semeia*, 59 (1992), pp. 95-127

Johnson, Elizabeth A., *Friends of God and Prophets: A Feminist Theological Reading of the Communion of Saints* (London: SCM, 1998)
Joy, Morny, 'Equality or Divinity: A False Dichotomy?', *Journal of Feminist Studies in Religion*, Spring (1990), pp. 9-24
Joyce, Patrick, 'History and Post-Modernism I', *Past and Present*, 133 (November 1991), pp. 204-209
Kelly, Catriona, 'History and Post-Modernism II', *Past and Present*, 133 (November 1991), pp. 209-213
Kelly, Joan, *Women, History and Theory* (Chicago: University of Chicago Press, 1984)
Kelsey, David, *The Uses of Scripture in Recent Theology* (Philadelphia: Fortress Press, 1975)
Kemp, Sandra and Bono, Paola (eds.), *The Lonely Mirror: Italian Perspectives on Feminist Theory* (London/New York: Routledge, 1993)
Kennedy, James, 'Peasants in Revolt: Political Allegory in Genesis 2-3', *Journal for the Study of the Old Testament*, 47 (1990), pp. 3-14
Kimel, Alvin F., Jr. (ed.), *Speaking the Christian God: The Holy Trinity and the Challenge of Feminism* (Leominster: Gracewing, 1992)
King, Ursula, 'Women and Christianity – A Horizon of Hope', *Women's Voices*, ed. Elwes, Teresa (London: Marshall Pickering, 1992), pp. 147-158
Krieger, Leonard, *Ranke: the Meaning of History* (London: University of Chicago Press, 1977)
Lacan, Jacques, *Ecrits: A Selection*, trans. Alan Sheridan (London: Routledge, 1977)
Laffey, Alice L., *Wives, Harlots and Concubines: the Old Testament in Feminist Perspective* (London: SPCK, 1990)
Lambert, Jean C, 'An 'F Factor'?: The New Testament in Some, White Feminist, Christian Theological Construction', *Journal of Feminist Studies in Religion*, Fall (1985), pp. 93-113
Landry, Donna and MacLean, Gerald, *Materialist Feminisms* (Oxford: Blackwell, 1993)
Lanser, Susan, '(Feminist) Criticism in the Garden: Inferring Genesis 2-3', *Semeia*, 41 (1988), pp. 67-84
Lash, Nicholas, *His Presence in the World* (London: Sheed and Ward, 1968)
Lawless, Elaine J., 'Rescripting Their Lives and Narratives: Spiritual Life Stories of Pentecostal Women Preachers', *Journal of Feminist Studies in Religion*, Spring (1991), pp. 53-72
Leonard, Stephen, *Critical Theory in Political Practice* (Princeton: Oxford: Princeton University Press, 1990)
Lloyd, Genevieve, *The Man of Reason: 'Male' and 'Female' in Western Philosophy* (Minneapolis: University of Minnesota Press, 1984)
Loades, Ann (ed.), *Feminist Theology: A Reader* (London: SPCK, 1990)
Long, Asphodel P., 'Book Review', *Feminist Theology*, 7 (1994), pp. 135-139
Lorraine, Tamsin, *Gender, Identity and the Production of Meaning* (Boulder: Westview Press, 1990)

Loughlin, Gerard, 'At the End of the World: Postmodernism and Theology', *Different Gospels*, ed. Walker, Andrew (Revised Edn, London: SPCK, 1993) (1988), pp. 204-221

Loughlin, Gerard, 'Transubstantiation: Eucharist as Pure Gift', *Christ: The Sacramental Word*, eds. Brown, David and Loades, Ann (London: SPCK, 1996), pp. 123-141

Markham, Ian, *Truth and the Reality of God* (Edinburgh: T & T Clark, 1998)

Mayeski, Marie Anne, *Women: Models of Liberation* (London: Fount Paperbacks, 1990)

McFadyen, Alistair I., *The Call to Personhood* (Cambridge: CUP, 1990)

McFague, Sallie, *Metaphorical Theology* (London: SCM Press, 1983)

McFague, Sallie, *The Body of God* (London: SCM Press, 1993)

Metz, Johann Baptist, *Faith in History and Society*, trans. David Smith (London: Burns & Oates, 1980)

Mies, Maria, 'What is Patriarchy? What Are the Root Causes?', *Speaking for Ourselves*, ed. Robins, Wendy S. and Kanyoro, Musimbi R. A. (Geneva: WCC Publications, 1990), pp. 25-33

Milbank, John, *Theology and Social Theory* (Oxford: Blackwell, 1990)

Milbank, John, *The Word Made Strange: Theology, Language, Culture* (Oxford: Blackwell, 1997)

Milne, Pamela, 'The Patriarchal Stamp of Scripture: The Implications of Structuralist Analyses for Feminist Hermeneutics', *Journal of Feminist Studies in Religion*, Spring (1989), pp. 17-34

Mitchell, Margaret M., *Paul and the Rhetoric of Reconciliation* (Tübingen: Mohr, 1991)

Modleski, Tania, *Feminism Without Women: Culture and Criticism in a 'Postfeminist' Age* (New York: Routledge, 1991)

Moi, Toril, *Sexual/Textual Politics* (London: Methuen, 1985)

Mol, Hans, *Identity and the Sacred* (Oxford: Basil Blackwell, 1976)

Moltmann, Jürgen, *Theology of Hope* (London: SCM, 1967)

Moltmann-Wendel, Elisabeth, *A Land Flowing with Milk and Honey*, trans. Bowden, John (London: SCM Press, 1986)

Moore, *Literary Criticism of the Gospels* (New Haven; London: Yale University Press, 1989)

Morgan, R. with Barton, J., *Biblical Interpretation* (Oxford: Oxford University Press, 1988)

Morgan, Sue, 'Race and the Appeal to Experience in Feminist Theology: the challenge of the womanist perspective', *Modern Believing*, 36/2 (1995), pp. 18-26

Novick, P., *That Noble Dream: The 'Objectivity Question' and the American Historical Profession* (Cambridge: Cambridge University Press, 1988)

O'Collins, Gerald, 'The Principle and Theology of Hope', *Scottish Journal of Theology*, 21.2 (1968), pp. 129-144

Olson, Roger, 'Trinity and Eschatology: the Historical Being of God in Jürgen Moltmann and Wolfhart Pannenberg', *Scottish Journal of Theology*, 36.2 (1983), pp. 213-228

Osiek, Carolyn, 'The Feminist and the Bible', *Feminist Perspectives on Biblical Scholarship* (ed.) Collins, Adela Yarbro (Atlanta: Scholars Press, 1985), pp. 93-105

Ostriker, Alicia, *Feminist Revision and the Bible* (Cambridge: Blackwell, 1993)

Parsons, Susan F., *Feminism and Christian Ethics* (Cambridge: Cambridge University Press, 1996)

Parsons, Susan F., 'The Dilemma of Difference', *Feminist Theology*, 14 (1997), pp. 51-72

Pears, Angela, *Towards an understanding of feminist method in theology: women's experience and authority*, Ph. D. (Nottingham), January 1993

Pears, Angela, 'Women's Experience and Authority in Feminist Theology', *Feminist Theology*, 9 (1995), pp. 108-119

Pears, Angela, 'Women's Experience and Authority in the Work of Elisabeth Schüssler Fiorenza', *Modern Believing*, 36/3 (1995), pp. 16-21

Pearson, Brook W. R., 'Method, Metaphor and Mammaries: The Ideology of New Testament Feminist Criticism', *Religion and Sexuality*, eds. Michael A. Hayes, Wendy J. Porter and David Tombs (Sheffield: Sheffield Academic Press, 1998), pp. 226-39

Penchansky, David, 'Up for Grabs: A Tentative Proposal for Doing Ideological Criticism', *Semeia*, 59 (1992), pp. 35-41

Perrot, Michelle (ed.), *Writing Women's History* (Oxford: Blackwell, 1992)

Peukert, Helmut, *Science, Action and Fundamental Theology*, trans. James Bohman (Cambridge, Mass.: MIT Press, 1984)

Pickstock, Catherine, 'Necrophilia: The Middle of Modernity. A Study of Death, Signs and the Eucharist', *Modern Theology*, 12.4, October (1996), pp. 405-433

Pickstock, Catherine, *After Writing* (Oxford: Blackwell, 1998)

Polity Press (ed.), *The Polity Reader in Gender Studies* (Cambridge: Polity Press, 1994)

Radcliffe, T., 'Paul and Sexual Identity: 1 Corinthians 11. 2-16', *After Eve*, ed. Soskice, Janet Martin (London: Marshall Pickering, 1990), pp. 62-72

Ramsey, George W., 'Is Name-Giving an Act of Domination in Genesis 2.23 and Elsewhere?', *Catholic Biblical Quarterly*, 50.1 (1988), pp. 24-35

Rashkow, Illona, *The Phallacy of Genesis* (Louisville, Ky.: Westminster/J. Knox, 1993)

Reader, John, 'Theology, Culture and Post-Modernity: in response to Graham, Walton and Newbigin', *MC*, 34/5, pp. 58-63

Reed, Esther, 'Whither Postmodernism and Feminist Theology?', *Feminist Theology*, 6 (1994), pp. 15-29

Rich, Adrienne, *The Dream of a Common Language* (New York: Norton, 1978)

Ricoeur, Paul, *Interpretation Theory: discourse and the surplus of meaning* (Fort Worth: Texas Christian University Press, 1976)

Riley, Denise, *'Am I That Name?': Feminism and the Category of Women in History* (Minneapolis: University of Minnesota Press, 1988)

Robins, Wendy S. and Kanyoro, Musimbi, R. A. (eds.), *Speaking for Ourselves* (Geneva: WCC Publications, 1990)

Rossi, Mary Ann, 'Priesthood, Precedent and Prejudice: On Recovering the Women Priests of Early Christianity', *Journal of Feminist Studies in Religion*, Spring (1991), pp. 73-94

Ruether, Rosemary Radford, *Women-Church: Theology and Practice* (San Francisco: Harper & Row, 1985)

Ruether, Rosemary Radford, 'Catholicism, Women, Body and Sexuality: A Response', *Women, Religion and Sexuality*, ed. Becher, J. (Geneva: WCC Publications, 1990), pp. 221-232

Ruether, Rosemary Radford, *Sexism and God-Talk* (London: SCM Press, 1992)

Rutledge, David, *Reading Marginally* (Leiden: E.J. Brill, 1996)

Sakenfield, Katherine Doob, 'Feminist Uses of Biblical Material', *Feminist Interpretation of the Bible*, ed. Russell, Letty (Oxford: Blackwell, 1985)

Sarah, Elizabeth, 'The Biblical Account of the First Woman: A Jewish Feminist Perspective', *Women's Voices*, ed. Elwes, Teresa (London: Marshall Pickering, 1992), pp. 45-56

Sauter, Gerhard, 'The Concept and Task of Eschatology – Theological and Philosophical Reflections', *Scottish Journal of Theology*, 41.4 (1988), pp. 499-515

Say, Elizabeth A., *Evidence on her Own Behalf* (Savage, Maryland: Rowman & Littlefield Publishers, Inc., 1990)

Schneiders, Sandra, *Beyond Patching: Faith and Feminism in the Catholic Church* (Mahwah, N.J.: Paulist Press, 1991)

Schüssler Fiorenza, Elisabeth, 'Feminist Theology and New Testament Interpretation', *Journal for the Study of the Old Testament*, 22 (1982), pp. 32-46

Schüssler Fiorenza, Elisabeth, *In Memory of Her: A Feminist Theological Reconstruction of Christian Origins* (London: SCM Press, 1983)

Schüssler Fiorenza, Elisabeth, 'Roundtable Discussion: On Feminist Methodology', *Journal of Feminist Studies in Religion*, Fall (1985), pp. 73-76

Schüssler Fiorenza, Elisabeth, *Bread Not Stone* (Boston: Beacon Press, 1986)

Schüssler Fiorenza, Elisabeth, 'The Ethics of Biblical Interpretation: Decentering Biblical Scholarship', *Journal of Biblical Literature*, 107/1 (1988), pp. 3-17

Schüssler Fiorenza, Elisabeth, 'Text and Reality – Reality as Text: The Problem of a Feminist Historical and Social Reconstruction Based on Texts', *Studia Theologica*, 43 (1989), pp. 19-34

Schüssler Fiorenza, Elisabeth, *But She Said: Feminist Practices of Biblical Interpretation* (Boston, MA: Beacon Press, 1992)

Schüssler Fiorenza, Elisabeth, *Discipleship of Equals: A Critical Feminist Ekklesia-logy of Liberation* (London: SCM Press, 1993)

Schüssler Fiorenza, Elisabeth, *Revelation: Vision of a Just World* (Edinburgh: T&T Clark, 1993)

Schüssler Fiorenza, Elisabeth (ed.), *Searching the Scriptures*, Vols. 1 and 2 (London: SCM Press, 1994-5)

Schüssler Fiorenza, Elisabeth, *Jesus: Miriam's Child, Sophia's Prophet: Critical Issues in Feminist Christology* (London: SCM, 1995)

Schüssler Fiorenza, Elisabeth, *The Power of Naming* (London: SCM, 1996)
Schüssler Fiorenza, Elisabeth, *Sharing Her Word: Feminist Biblical Interpretation in Context* (Edinburgh: T&T Clark, 1998)
Schüssler Fiorenza, Elisabeth, *Rhetoric and Ethic: the Politics of Biblical Studies* (Fortress, 1999)
Schüssler Fiorenza, Francis, 'The Influence of Feminist Theory on My Theological Work', *Journal of Feminist Studies in Religion*, Spring (1991), pp. 95-105
Scott, Joan, 'Women's History', *New Perspectives on Historical Writing*, ed. Burke, Peter (Cambridge, Polity Press, 1991), pp. 42-66
Sharpe, Jim, 'History from Below', *New Perspectives on Historical Writing*, ed. Burke, Peter (Cambridge, Polity Press, 1991), pp. 24-41
Skevington, S. and Baker, D. (eds.), *The Social Identity of Women* (London: Sage Publications, 1989)
Soskice, Janet Martin (ed.), *After Eve* (London: Marshall Pickering, 1990)
Soskice, Janet Martin, 'Can a Feminist Call God 'Father'?', *Women's Voices*, ed. Elwes, Teresa (London: Marshall Pickering, 1992), pp. 15-29
Soskice, Janet Martin, 'Women's Problems', *Different Gospels*, ed. Walker, Andrew (Revised Edn, London: SPCK, 1993) (1988), pp. 194-203
Spelman, Elizabeth, *Inessential Woman: Problems of Exclusion in Feminist Thought* (Boston, Mass.: Boston Press, 1988)
Spiegel, Gabrielle M., 'History and Post-Modernism IV', *Past and Present*, 135 (1992), pp. 194-208
Stacey, David, *Interpreting the Bible* (London: Sheldon Press, 1976)
Stacey, David, *Groundwork of Biblical Studies* (London: Epworth Press, 1979)
Stone, Lawrence, 'History and Postmodernism', *Past and Present*, 131 (1991), pp. 217-18
Stone, Lawrence, 'History and Post-Modernism III', *Past and Present*, 135 (1992), pp. 189-194
Stuhlmacher, Peter, *Historical Criticism and Theological Interpretation of Scripture*, trans. Roy A. Harrisville (London: S.P.C.K., 1979)
Theissen, Gerd, *The Social Setting of Pauline Christianity*, ed. and trans. John H. Schütz (Edinburgh: T & T Clark, 1982)
Thiselton, Anthony C., *New Horizons in Hermeneutics* (London: HarperCollins, 1992)
Thistlethwaite, Susan, *Sex, Race, and God* (London: Geoffrey Chapman, 1990)
Thurian, Max (ed.), *Churches respond to BEM* (Geneva: World Council of Churches, 1987)
Tiedemann, Rolf, 'Historical Materialism or Political Messianism? An Interpretation of the Theses 'On the Concept of History'', *The Philosphical Forum*, XV:1-2, Fall-Winter (1983/84), pp. 71-104
Tilley, Terrence W. (ed.), *Postmodern Theologies* (Maryknoll, N.Y.: Orbis Books, 1995)
Tolbert, Mary Ann, 'Protestant Feminists and the Bible: On the Horns of a Dilemma', *The Pleasure of Her Text*, ed. Bach, Alice (Philadelphia, PA: Trinity Press International, 1990), pp. 4-23
Tong, Rosemary, *Feminist Thought* (London: Routledge, 1992) (1989)

Trible, Phyllis, 'Feminist Hermeneutics and Biblical Studies', *Feminist Theology: A Reader*, ed. Loades, A. (London: SPCK, 1990), pp. 23-29

Trible, Phyllis, *God and the Rhetoric of Sexuality* (London: SCM Press, 1992)

Trible, Phyllis, *Texts of Terror* (London: SCM Press, 1992)

Trible, Phyllis, *Rhetorical Criticism: Context, Method and the Book of Jonah* (Minneapolis: Fortress, 1994)

Tronto, Joan C., *Moral Boundaries and Political Change* (New York and London: Routledge, 1993)

Ussher, J.M., *The Psychology of the Female Body* (London: Routledge, 1989)

Wainwright, Geoffrey, *Eucharist and Eschatology* (London: Epworth Press, 1971)

Walder, Dennis (ed.), *Literature in the Modern World: Critical Essays and Documents* (Oxford: Oxford University Press in association with the Open University, 1990)

Walker, Andrew (ed.), *Different Gospels* (Revised Edn, London: SPCK, 1993) (1988)

Walker, Andrew, 'Knowing God Personally: Reflections on the Feminist Concept of Patriarchy', *Different Gospels*, ed. Walker, Andrew (Revised Edn, London: SPCK, 1993) (1988), pp. 173-193

Ward, Graham (ed.), *The Postmodern God: a theological reader* (Oxford: Blackwell, 1997)

Watson, Francis, *Text, Church and World* (Edinburgh: T & T Clark, 1994)

Watson, Francis, *Text and Truth* (Edinburgh: T&T Clark, 1997)

Weaver, Mary Jo, 'Who is the Goddess and Where Does She Get Us?', *Journal of Feminist Studies in Religion*, Spring (1989), pp. 49-64

Welch, Sharon, *Communities of Resistance and Solidarity* (Maryknoll: Orbis Books, 1985)

Welch, Sharon, *A Feminist Ethic of Risk* (Minneapolis: Fortress Press, 1990)

Wiles, Maurice, 'Eucharist Theology – The Value of Diversity', *Thinking about the Eucharist*, Archbishops' Commision on Church Doctrine (London: SCM, 1972), pp. 115-122

Williams, Arthur H., 'The Trinity and Time', *Scottish Journal of Theology*, 39.1 (1986), pp. 65-81

Williams, Arthur H., 'Theology in an Eschatological Matrix', *Scottish Journal of Theology*, 42.3 (1989), pp. 289-302

Williams, Jane, 'The Doctrine of the Trinity: A Way Forward for Feminists?', *Women's Voices*, ed. Elwes, Teresa (London: Marshall Pickering, 1992), pp. 31-43

Wire, Antoinette Clark, *The Corinthian Women Prophets: A Reconstruction through Paul's Rhetoric* (Minneapolis, MN: Fortress Press, 1990)

Wittig, Monique, 'One is not Born a Woman', *The Straight Mind* (Hemel Hempstead: Harvester Wheatsheaf, 1992), pp. 9-20

Woodhead, Linda, 'Feminism and Christian Ethics', *Women's Voices*, ed. Elwes, Teresa (London: Marshall Pickering, 1992), pp. 57-82

Wright, N. T., 'Taking the Text with Her Pleasure', *Theology*, July/August (1993), pp. 303-310

Zizioulas, John D., *Being as Communion* (London: Dartmann, Longman and Todd, 1985)

Index

Alcoff, Linda 152 n. 18, 153 n. 19, 160 n. 34
Anderson, Hugh 28
Anselm, St. 69
Aristotle 40

Bal, Mieke 84 n. 113, 85, 86
Balasuriya, T. 147 n. 12
Barker, F. 19 n. 57
Barr, James 20, 21 nn. 66, 68, 28, 63 n. 19, 65 n. 9
Barton, John 6 n. 2, 21 n. 67, 22 nn. 70, 71, 26, 30 n. 112
Battersby, Christine 144, 155-6
Beard, Mary 9 n. 17
Beauvoir, Simone de 9 n. 17, 108
Belsey, Catherine 18, 19
Benhabib, Seyla 158-9, 161
Benjamin, Walter 99, 101-112 *passim*
Bible and Culture Collective 6 n. 2, 143
Brueggeman, Walter 87, 88
Bultmann, Rudolf 22, 27, 29 n. 111

Canon of Scripture 55-6
Carroll, Bernice 101
Cavanaugh, William T. 147
Christ, Carol 161
Cixous, H. 35 n. 12, 109 n. 44
Clines, David 79
Concubine, the Levite's 88, 96, 101
Cupitt, Don 123, 124, 139

Derrida, Jacques 16, 128 n. 40, 131, 135-7, 140
Différance 99, 136-8
Dijk-Hemmes, F. van 91
Downing, Gerald 28
Dragga, Sam 79-80, 83

Ebert, Teresa 37-8
ekklesia 32-59 *passim*, 142-162 *passim*
Eucharist 145-151
Exum, J. Cheryl 86 n. 122, 114 n. 67

Fander, Monika 24

feminist historiography 20, 22-31
Fewell, D. N. 93, 125
Frazer, Elizabeth 133
Frye, Marilyn 126
Fulkerson, Mary M. 114 n. 63, 125 n. 28, 133 n. 54
Fuss, Diana 155 n. 25

Gardiner, Juliet 16
Gardner, Anne 80
Gordon, Linda 9 n. 17
Grant, Robert 22, 29 n. 111
Grimshaw, Jean 126
Grosz, Elizabeth 155 n. 24
Gunn, D. M. 93, 125

Habermas, Jürgen 109-10, 157-9, 161
Hagar 88, 95
Hampson, Daphne 21, 52 nn. 79, 83, 69 n. 47, 105
Heidegger, Martin 135, 137-8
Hennessey, Rosemary 19 n. 60, 28, 35 n. 16, 44 n. 53, 46, 99 n. 1
Henry, Martin 130
hermeneutics of remembrance 11, 98, 101, 108-112, 115
hermeneutics of suspicion 10, 11, 13, 15, 23, 86
Hewitt, Marsha 101, 102, 105, 110, 111
Hogan, Linda 57 n. 94, 160-1
Howard, Jean E. 18 nn. 54, 55

Irigaray, Luce 35 n. 12, 47-8
Iser, Wolfgang 66 n. 33

Jantzen, Grace 137
Jephthah's daughter 96-7
Jobling, David 78, 79, 80, 83

Kelly, Joan 6 n. 4
Kennedy, James 78, 83 n. 111
Kipnis, Laura 35
Krieger, Leonard 26

Lacan, Jacques 12, 128

Lanser, Susan 78, 80, 81-2
Lash, Nicholas 149 n. 16
Lerner, Gerda 14
Lloyd, Genevieve 42 n. 44
Lorde, Audre 1 n. 2
Lorraine, Tamsin E. 36-7
Loughlin, Gerald 145 n. 6

MacIntyre, Alasdair 51, 119, 120, 134
Markham, Ian 117-130 *passim*, 138
Marx/ism 13 n. 35, 18, 57 n. 94, 108, 109
métissage 143-4, 149-150, 157, 161
Metz, Johann Baptist 101, 111-2
Milbank, Alastair 110, 120
Modleski, Tanya 46 n. 55, 153
Moi, Toril 109
Mommsen, W. J. 26, 29-30
Moore, Stephen 132
Morgan, Robert 21 n. 67, 22, 30 n. 112
Müller, Karl Heinz 24, 30

New Historicism, the 13 n. 35, 16, 17 n. 50, 18, 19
Nietzsche, F. 104, 130, 135
Nineham, Dennis 28
Novick, P. 13

objectivity 13-5, 23-31
Ostriker, Alicia 112 n. 60

Pearson, Brook W. R. 12 n. 32
Perrot, Michelle 8 n. 15
Peukert, H. 109, 110

Ramsey, George 80
Ranke/Rankean 7 n. 5, 24-6, 28, 29, 30, 105-6
Rashkow, Illona 84 n. 112
Rich, Adrienne 1, 100
Ricoeur, Paul 62 n. 13, 65 n. 28, 66, 132
Russell, Letty 115
Rutledge, David 81, 84 n. 114

Sarah, Elizabeth 79
Schüssler Fiorenza, Elisabeth 5-59 *passim*, 69, 87, 101-2, 105-12 *passim*, 153
  Bread not Stone 8 n. 11, 20, 22, 23-4, 25-6, 27, 30, 45, 57

  But She Said 11, 13 n. 34, 16-7, 32, 34-43 *passim*, 49, 52, 53, 54, 57, 58, 114 n. 64
  Discipleship of Equals 32 n. 1, 33 40, 44
  In Memory of Her 6, 8, 9, 10, 11, 14, 15, 16, 30, 32, 33, 44, 45, 47, 49, 53, 57, 105, 107, 109
  Jesus: Miriam's Child, Sophia's Prophet 44, 45, 46, 55, 57, 153
  Remembering the Past 8 n. 10, 14, 106
  Searching the Scriptures 56
  Sharing Her Word 13 n. 34, 42 n. 48, 43, 45, 46, 49 n. 73, 54, 55, 59
  The Power of Naming 40, 41, 50
Schweitzer, Albert 26-7
Scott, Joan 7
Scripture passages:
  Gen. 2-3 71-3, 82-6
  Gen. 2:18-24 73, 75-80
  2 Sam. 13:1-22 90-4
Smith, Carol 98
Smith, Dorothy 33 n. 6
Spiegel, Gabrielle 14, 16 n. 44
Stacey, David 27, 28
Stone, Lawrence 16 n. 44

Tamar 90-4
Texts of Terror 60, 66, 87-98
Theisssen, Gerd 9
Thiselton, Anthony 11, 12 n. 32
Tiedemann, Rolf 102 nn. 6-9, 103, 104, 106
Trible, Phyllis 60-98 *passim*, 100-1, 113
  God and the Rhetoric of Sexuality 60-86, 90, 113, 114

Tronto, Joan 156 n. 28

Wainwright, Geoffrey 145 n. 6, 147 n. 11, 149 n. 15
Ward, Graham 138 n. 68
Watson, Francis 6 n. 2, 31 n. 116
Welch, Sharon 161
Wiles, Maurice 148
Wittig, Monique 154 n. 22

Zizioulas, John 146, 147